One Blue Child

Anthropology of Policy

Cris Shore and Susan Wright, editors

One Blue Child

Asthma, Responsibility, and the Politics of Global Health

Susanna Trnka

Stanford University Press
Stanford, California

Stanford University Press

Stanford, California

Printed in the United States of America on acid-free, archival-quality paper

Library of Congress Cataloging-in-Publication Data

Names: Trnka, Susanna, author.

Title: One blue child : asthma, responsibility, and the politics of global health / Susanna Trnka.

Other titles: Anthropology of policy (Stanford, Calif.)

Description: Stanford, California : Stanford University Press, 2017. | Series: Anthropology of policy | Includes bibliographical references and index.

Identifiers: LCCN 2016053569 (print) | LCCN 2016054563 (ebook) | ISBN 9781503601130 (cloth : alk. paper) | ISBN 9781503602458 (pbk. : alk. paper) | ISBN 9781503602465 (e-book)

Subjects: LCSH: Asthma in children—Government policy—New Zealand. | Asthma in children—Government policy—Czech Republic. | Asthma in children—Treatment—New Zealand. | Asthma in children—Treatment—Czech Republic. | Medical policy—New Zealand. | Medical policy—Czech Republic. | Responsibility—New Zealand. | Responsibility—Czech Republic.

Classification: LCC RJ436.A8 T76 2017 (print) | LCC RJ436.A8 (ebook) | DDC 362.196/2380094371—dc23

LC record available at https://lccn.loc.gov/2016053569

Cover photo by Pavel Sonnek. Reprinted courtesy of *Deník*/Pavel Sonnek.

Typeset by Thompson Type in 10.25/15 Brill

To my father, Jiří Trnka, and my daughter, Revena

Contents

Preface

THE impetus for this book was a research trip gone wrong. In 2006 I arrived in Prague, planning to spend a few months conducting research on Czechs' memories of state socialism. I was accompanied by my two young daughters. Within hours of our arrival, I was sitting in the back of an ambulance watching my nine-year-old being hooked up to a nebulizer in the midst of her first-ever asthma attack. Soon after we had stepped into our rented apartment, she had succumbed to a coughing fit that left her lips literally turning blue, effectively becoming one of the Czech Republic's "blue children," as they were later called by a public health specialist I interviewed. By luck there was a pediatrician living in the same building who tried to get my daughter's breathing under control. I watched in horror as, after administering Ventolin (an emergency reliever bronchodilator, one of the most popular on the market) and prednisone (a strong, oral corticosteroid), the doctor shouted into her cellphone that the ambulance driver better hurry up or we would have a death on our hands. "Your daughter was one of the few asthma cases I thought might pass away on me," she later explained.

Once she was released from hospital, my daughter was put under the supervision of a local respiratory specialist who immediately proceeded to conduct a spirometry test (a basic lung function test) and a wide range of allergy skin prick tests. Over the next three weeks, various pharmaceutical concoctions, followed by repeat spirometry tests, were tried out until she was deemed stable enough to travel home. In the meantime, I received strict instructions on how to administer her care, including the necessity of spending as much time as possible outside of the city. "You must take her condition very seriously," the respiratory specialist admonished me, "and ensure she continues to have regular checkups and spirometry, and only specialist care."

"How could I not?" I wondered.

But almost overnight, we transitioned from a situation of high drama where we were repeatedly told we were dealing with a serious, deadly disease that needed careful and constant attention to a context where asthma—while still disruptive and potentially lethal—was considered a much more mundane part of everyday life. When we arrived back home in New Zealand, we visited our family physician, who took a look at the medication we had received, wrote us some refill prescriptions, and told us to carry on with what we were doing. When I asked when the next spirometry test would next take place, he laughed and explained how rarely spirometry is conducted in New Zealand. He then asked to view one of my daughter's spirometry printouts as he had never seen one before. For the next few years, we regularly phoned his office to get repeats on her prescriptions, never being asked to come in for a checkup. The one time we insisted on an annual asthma review, we were summarily informed it was a waste of the doctor's time to check her when nothing was actually wrong with her breathing. It didn't take long to realize that in New Zealand my daughter, and by extension her father and I, were expected to oversee her care, seeking medical assistance only if her medication wasn't working properly.

As a medical anthropologist, I was well acquainted with the idea that similar health conditions may be responded to very differently in diverse cultural and sociopolitical contexts, but the more I looked into it, the less "different" the Czech medical system seemed to be from New Zealand's. Both countries share the same standards of technologically driven biomedical care, with a combination of predominantly public (that is, state-funded) services and private care. There is remarkable similarity in the availability of pharmaceuticals and technologies (such as spirometry and exhaled nitric oxide tests) but, as this book documents, distinct differences in how they are put to use.

Even more significantly, both countries are signatories to the same set of worldwide asthma guidelines established by the Global Initiative for Asthma (GINA). Following GINA, they have adopted policies for asthma care that focus on self-management and highlight the role of the patient in overseeing his or her own care. Indeed, in both countries, political and economic reforms have promoted the benefits of increased self-responsibility not only in the domain of health care, but as part of the broader reshaping of citizen–state relations.

But in trying to understand the meanings and effects of global and national policies promoting self-management and, more broadly, individual responsibility, the puzzle only deepened as I found myself facing even more contradictions in how the "same" disease was seen and treated in two different contexts. Although the Czech Republic has growing rates of childhood asthma, it is hardly a world leader in this area, and yet asthma is a topic that generates widespread public concern, bringing activists out onto the streets and firing up debate in Parliament. In contrast, New Zealand tops worldwide rates of childhood asthma, but one is hard-pressed to find much public debate, much less public mobilization, over how the nation should respond to a condition affecting nearly 25 percent of its children.

This book endeavors to shed light on these dynamics by looking beyond the rhetoric of policies promoting neoliberal reforms to consider the multiple, and sometimes conflicting, realities of how such policies are enacted in practice. I have chosen two divergent case studies to spotlight these differences, but, in many respects, the New Zealand example represents dynamics that are occurring across Western liberal democracies, particularly English-speaking nations, and readers in the United States, Great Britain, and Australia will spot close similarities with the health-care systems in their own countries. Likewise, although there are culturally specific inflections to it, the Czech ethnography could have been conducted in other parts of Central and Eastern Europe. The purpose of this study is thus not to compare childhood asthma in New Zealand and the Czech Republic per se but to consider two different versions of how neoliberal health reforms and policies promoting individual responsibility are being enacted. Engaging in such an explicitly cross-cultural examination enables us to see how culture, social organization, and political-economic histories intersect with policy and reform agendas, resulting in distinctive forms of familial, medical, scientific, and state practice. It also reveals the wide range of what is *possible* in terms of how people think about health, the body, and personhood. And, in very practical terms, it expands our understandings of the variety of therapeutic remedies and processes that are useful in mitigating respiratory distress—all of which is essential if we hope to put a halt to the increasing number of children in the world who are in danger of turning "blue" from asthma.

Acknowledgments

FIRST and foremost, I would like to thank my children, Revena, Anika, and Lukáš, for their generosity and patience as this project unfolded, and my husband, John, who has not only rigorously debated most of the issues in this book with me, but read and commented on the whole manuscript, *twice*. Many thanks are also due to my sister, Irena, who spent countless hours discussing Czech culture and family dynamics with me, and to my parents: my father for sharing with me his childhood memories of Ostrava and my mother for advising on some of the trickier translations, helping facilitate my research plans, and generally providing such enthusiasm and support for this and all of my research endeavors.

My stays in Prague were made both more productive and much more pleasant by my friends and family. Kateřina Křížková, who is not a cousin but should be, and her husband Víťa provided love and care, as well as vital advice, that made this project possible. My aunt, Olga Kučerová, was always on the lookout for new research leads, pointing me in directions I would otherwise not think to go. My cousin Zdeněk Prokš and his wife Kamila proved to be excellently informative and delightful hosts: *velice Vám děkuji za Vaši pomoc a štědrost*. I was also extremely fortunate to have the advice, help, and good company of my aunt Dr. Kamila Janovská, uncle Václav Janovský, and my cousins: Jana Vyskočilová and her husband Ivo, Kamil Pejchal and his wife Kateřina, Václav Janovský and his wife Monika, Petr Janovský, and the late Pavel Janovský. To Blanka Bulová, her husband Jan, and their children Blanka, Jan and Jakub—*Vaše rodina mě uvítala s otevřenou náručí. Velice Vám děkuji.*

Many Czech colleagues helped shepherd my understanding of history, social change, and the intricacies of the health-care system: thank you to Profesorka Věra Mayerová and her husband Dr. Emrich Mayer, Dr. Ema Hrešanová, Dr. Tereza Stöckelová, and Edit Szénássy. Alena Heitlinger and Haldis Haukanes deserve special thanks for their friendship and all of their insights into Czech culture. Amy Speier generously shared her experiences of Czech spas and Marek Tesar kept the conversations on all things Czech and Slovak continuing back in Auckland.

Colleagues in Auckland, Wellington, Dunedin, Sydney, and Melbourne very kindly gave detailed commentary on various parts of this manuscript. Many thanks to Julie Park, Catherine Trundle, Samuel Taylor-Alexander, and Julie Spray, who read the book in draft form. Ruth Fitzgerald, Lisa Wynn, Chrystal Jaye, and Tarryn Phillips gave feedback on individual chapters. I would particularly like to thank Catherine, Lisa, Julie, and Ruth for their enlivening conversations, support, and wit, which make being a medical anthropologist in the Antipodes so pleasurable. Special thanks are also due to Christine Dureau, for being my compatriot on writing retreats and general intellectual foil, and Cris Shore, for all his support, encouragement, and unbounded enthusiasm over the years.

I was really lucky to have seven research assistants who helped me conduct the New Zealand research. Laura McLaughlan spent two summers conducting interviews and then coauthored the first round of results. Julie Spray started off being interviewed for the project and then became an interviewer for it, before launching her own doctoral study on New Zealand children's perspectives on asthma and other health issues. Mythily Meher, Pauline Herbst, and Samuel Taylor-Alexander were vital to getting the interviews completed. Alexandra Potter and Lakna Jayasinghe assisted with transcription and deluged me with newspaper articles and other resources.

I would also like to thank Sue Wright and Cris Shore for their copious feedback and encouragement and Michelle Lipinski at Stanford University Press for steering the book through to production. Mona-Lynn Corteau proved an invaluable copy editor at the end of the writing process. This research was supported by multiple grants from the University of Auckland Faculty of Arts and the Department of Anthropology, as well as a grant-in-aid from the Asthma and Respiratory Foundation NZ: my thanks to both of these institutions for their generous support.

One Blue Child

Introduction

Taking Responsibility for Asthma

New Kinds of People, New Kinds of Health

OVER the past thirty years, there has been a phenomenal worldwide increase in rates of childhood asthma, so much so that asthma has become the most common chronic disease among children today. In the United States, currently nearly one in ten children has asthma. In the countries most severely affected—the United Kingdom, New Zealand, and Australia—the rate is even higher, with an estimated one in four or five children suffering from this condition. Since 1995, the Global Initiative for Asthma (GINA) has attempted to address the escalating epidemic by promoting worldwide policies for asthma care. Among its recommendations on diagnosis and treatment, GINA's current guidelines strongly advocate for self-management, encouraging patients to engage in "co-partnership" with physicians, take on increased personal responsibility, and become managers of their own, largely pharmaceutically focused care.[1]

Despite, however, the global reach of GINA's policy guidelines, there remains great divergence in how governments and individuals have responded to the escalating crisis. Some medical systems focus predominantly on encouraging patient compliance with pharmaceutical use, whereas others promote much more intensive medical oversight, epitomized by residential "health spa" cures, reminiscent of the tuberculosis sanitariums of the late nineteenth and early twentieth centuries. Nonpharmaceutical remedies such as breathing retraining programs (most popularly, Buteyko), water or bath therapy (balneotherapy), and climate therapy are alternatively reviled and enshrined as part of government-supported strategies for alleviating respiratory distress. The power of patients to take part in decision making over their care varies radically, with some patients feeling dehumanized through their encounters with heavyhanded medical experts whereas others are effectively in charge of their own treatment to the point of feeling abandoned by medical services. In parts of the United States, India, China, and Central and Eastern Europe, debate also rages over whether air pollution might be a major cause of the growing epidemic, and, if so, what the various responsibilities are of states, companies, and individual citizens for cleaning up the environment.

This book is about the different ways we have come to understand responsibility for health and health care. It traces how global health policies, such as the GINA guidelines as well as an array of nationally focused policies promoting self-managed care, are being used to inculcate more personalized, patient-focused approaches to health and illness. It examines how the rise of discourses and practices promoting personal responsibility for health is reshaping our relationships to ourselves and our bodies, to our families and our doctors, and to companies and the government. It also examines concerted resistance to these policies, considering how medical professionals attempt to shore up their expertise at the same time as activists endeavor to redirect responsibility for children's health onto the state and galvanize support for collective solutions.

Telling the story of how two very different nations—New Zealand and the Czech Republic—struggle to come to terms with the growing number of children in danger of "going blue" from lack of oxygen during an asthma attack, *One Blue Child* examines the wide range of policies and practices that constitute asthma care, focusing on the experiences of scientists working to halt the epidemic, parents struggling to care for sick children, activists raising the possibilities of solutions beyond pharmaceuticals, and physicians, nurses, respiratory physiotherapists, and alternative health-care providers aiming to both empower patients and make them well. Although both nations embrace advanced liberal health-care policies and actively promote patients taking increased personal responsibility for their own care, in actual fact they offer up very different perspectives on where responsibility for mitigating the epidemic lies. Looking broadly across asthma care in these two nations thus both enables us to see the variety of ways that responsibility for children's health is currently constituted and brings into view a wide range of possibilities of what else "responsibility" *could* one day be made to encompass.

In the Czech Republic, scientists and physicians such as Dr. Jarmila Veselá,[2] a public health specialist, view childhood asthma as fundamentally a political problem. When we first met in her Prague office, she brought a decidedly personal tone to our discussion of government policies on childhood asthma, describing the difficult years she spent living in Northern Bohemia, an area known for its environmental devastation. Now in her late fifties, she recounted that, when her children were young, "Sometimes I thought they might actually choke from all the air pollution. Some days it was so bad we shut all the windows, and the whole family spent the next few days in bed. So I know the fear that many mothers feel, and I feel very bad for them when their child has an asthma attack. *But why can't they say to themselves, 'It doesn't need to be this way?'"*

For Dr. Veselá, asthma is a problem whose solution lies not in medicine but in governance. The current neoliberal government's emphasis on economic growth has, she believes, outweighed the previous socialist regime's focus on collective approaches to health. As a consequence, "The industrialists tell themselves, 'I employ 7,000 people,' so having one blue child in the neighborhood doesn't matter." In the face of promises of economic expansion, who could possibly care if there is "one blue child" struggling to breathe, Dr. Veselá wonders, other than his or her mother? Under capitalism, she laments, everyone has learned to think only of themselves. Rampant economic restructuring has led to a much more individualized focus among the citizenry. Indeed, many of the postsocialist Czech state's reforms were specifically targeted at inculcating a greater sense of individual responsibility, especially in the area of health. "So what's the answer to stopping asthma?" Dr. Veselá rhetorically asked, and then replied, "Don't live next to a smoke stack!" But although such individualized solutions might help one child or one family, they clearly will not solve the problem.

In a similar vein, although Dr. Veselá embraces the idea of fostering patients' involvement and control over their own health care, to implement something akin to the self management programs for asthma that are popular in the West would ultimately only compound the crisis. Although Czech patients frequently grumble that their opinions are never elicited—much less listened to—in medical encounters, doctors and patients alike take issue with suggestions of stripping back medical oversight in order to promote increased patient self-responsibility. Instead of the figure of the "patient-expert" in charge of his or her own asthma care idealized by self-management policies in the West, most Czechs firmly posit medical *expertise* within the domain of the medical profession.

Dr. Veselá, however, raises another problem inherent in self-management policies, namely the medicalization of what she takes to be at heart an economic, environmental, and social issue. She reserves some of her harshest criticism for her fellow physicians, in particular for "the good, kind pediatrician who stuffs corticosteroids into the children and gives them their little inhalers and, when it is really bad, sends them off to the health spas so everything gets better." The pediatrician "isn't the solution," she declared, "for what we need is a change in society."

The only valid solution to childhood asthma, Dr. Veselá suggests, is for *everyone* to be mindful of the needs of the collective and work together in demanding the nation's right to a clean environment. Such a solution requires a change in thinking by not only the owners of industry who pollute the air and the government that refuses to adequately regulate them but also by the citizenry who must rise out of their complacency. What is needed, she argues, is a new kind of society, made up of new kinds of people who are responsible enough to proactively engage with civic life, working together to demand that the government take action over children's asthma.

Across the globe in New Zealand, childhood asthma constitutes a different but closely related problematic, largely focused on the question of what to do when personal responsibility falls short of resulting in good care. With its unfortunate status of having more children suffer from asthma than almost anywhere else in the world, New Zealand is a leader in scientific and medical advances in asthma care. It is the home of the International Study of Asthma and Allergies in Childhood (ISAAC), which for over twenty years (from 1991 to 2012) was the world's largest epidemiological study of childhood allergies and asthma, covering more than 100 countries and approximately 2 million children. In 1986, New Zealand, in collaboration with Australia, generated the world's first set of asthma guidelines. New Zealand is also a country that knows the costs when asthma care goes wrong, having been at the center of a scandal surrounding fenoterol, an asthma drug that was responsible for tripling the country's asthma mortality rates in the late 1970s.

As a result, New Zealand has been a pioneer in developing self-management programs designed to increase individuals' self-care through the use of asthma "action plans" that specify how to self-adjust pharmaceutical dosages and when to seek medical care. These programs are now enshrined in asthma guidelines around the world, including the widely adopted international standards published by GINA. In some countries, such as the Czech Republic, these standards are incorporated into national policies and encouraged by medical organizations but are, in fact, only sporadically implemented. In others, such as the United States, the UK, Australia, and New Zealand, they form the basis of care.

The philosophy underpinning moves toward increased self-management is often referred to as "patient-centered care." As many New Zealand physicians told me, the purpose of patient-centered care is to put the patient "in the driver's seat" for managing his or her own health. One respiratory physician explained how it worked in his practice: "Ultimately it's the patient who takes responsibility for their own health, so the role of the health-care practitioner is to help the person navigate through [the system] and provide information and education so that person can be as autonomous as possible."

Tapping into a rhetoric of self-sufficiency and autonomy that is prevalent across New Zealand, these perspectives carry much cultural cachet. They enable patients to engage in their own care at the most fundamental level and purport to create open dialogue and partnership between patients and those who provide their medical services. They also, however, mask limitations in public services and the devaluation of medical expertise and professional responsibility. In some instances, this results in accountability effectively being diverted away from those best trained to provide care (health-care workers) and onto those most in need of being taken care of (the sick). Doctors disparage patients who do not stick to their daily preventative doses of medication. Patients, in turn, frequently cobble together their own drug regimes, often ending up in the emergency room when things go wrong. Children as young as ten struggle with the responsibility of self-managing their asthma and with the symptoms that arise when self-management falls short of keeping them healthy. With the focus so firmly on the individual, collective action and moves toward collective solutions are mostly ignored, despite the efforts of many leading New Zealand respiratory physicians and scientists to advocate for government policies implementing broadscale change.

The stories in this book take place (mostly) in two locations—New Zealand and the Czech Republic—but are reflective of policies, practices, and reform movements that are reshaping health and health care globally. Both countries avidly engage in forms of biomedicine that are informed by the latest pharmaceuticals, internationally recognized "gold standards" of care, and high-level technologies, taking part in what Erin Koch describes as "the contemporary humanitarian global health enterprise [that] draws on and establishes moral imperatives and technical standards for 'proper care'" (2013a: 10). Notwithstanding the many differences between them, the struggles of citizens in both countries speak to the same overriding concerns over what kinds of measures must be taken to ensure the health and well-being of citizens in an international climate of ever-increasing commercialization of medical care. Taken together, they raise crucial questions: How much responsibility should patients have in determining their own health care? How is medical expertise being reshaped in light of increasing patient autonomy? What are the roles of states and private companies in providing care? What other kinds of citizenship rights—from access to alternative therapies to growing up in a healthy environment—do governments need to safeguard to enable the health and well-being of their citizens? And how might these issues best be addressed in the context of increasingly globalized health care?

These questions emerge out of very pragmatic and immediate struggles over ensuring effective medical care that take place as parents attempt to keep their children breathing, doctors endeavor to provide their patients with adequate services within ever-shifting regimes of health-care funding, scientists search for ways of quelling a growing health epidemic, and government officials and policy experts reconcile slashing budgets with the pressing need for more comprehensive solutions. These struggles are over determining not only the limits of medical technologies and health-care budgets but also—and perhaps more importantly—the limits of collective political will. This book is about these struggles. It is also the story of the very personal and intimate realignments that take place as people come to cope with ongoing respiratory distress. It is an account of how parents of children with asthma learn to relate to their bodies, minds, and environments in new ways, reinterpreting their own or their children's bodies for signs of distress, reflecting on their relationships to the pharmaceuticals they ingest, and looking for solutions that place them in the midst of the healing powers of nature or shield them from its potentially devastating consequences.

One Blue Child takes a broad approach to care, traversing multiple sites to reveal the intricacies of how children and adults with asthma are constituted as social, political, and medical objects and agents. The New Zealand side of the story focuses on familial strategies of self-care, examining how policies promoting self-management came into place and the effects of self-management on patient subjectivities, family relations, and the collaborative production of medical care between doctors, nurses, and patients. It considers how self-management policies have restructured patient–doctor relations, opening up a space of increased confusion and fear as well as familial experimentation with strategies to curb respiratory distress. It also considers moves toward more collective solutions for asthma as well as the experiential realities of asthma that lie beyond current diagnostic framings. The Czech case study sheds light on patients' and families' struggles to gain greater control over their health while keeping medical professionals responsible for ensuring their well-being, the entrenching of medical expertise in resistance to health policies' emphases on promoting self-responsibility, and the utility of more holistic methods of asthma care that alleviate both mental and physical distress. It furthermore foregrounds how intense contestations over environmental pollution can fracture and remold relations among citizens, companies, and the state. By comparing these two nations' responses to childhood asthma, this book builds a cumulative case for why, if we truly want to understand what it is to be a patient in the twenty-first century, we must look beyond the cultivation of self-managing subjects to consider the inherent interrelationality of healing.

The Rise of Personal Responsibility

In an increasing number of contexts, reform movements focused on promoting neoliberal values of personal responsibility are reshaping twenty-first-century personhood. Often part of moves to devolve a range of social services from the state onto individuals under the banner of increasing individual "choice," advanced liberal reforms both enable and require people to take on greater personal autonomy, self-responsibility, and self-reliance (Rose 2006).

Although the actualities of advanced liberal policies vary from context to context (Hilgers 2012), the terms *advanced liberalism* and *neoliberalism* have been widely used (often interchangeably) to refer to a set of ideals that link together deregulation and privatization, a shrinking state mandate, an increased emphasis on personal choice and freedom, and a faith in markets to govern social life (Biebricher 2011). Peter Miller and Nikolas Rose have described the promotion of the ideals of neoliberalism, including the encouragement of new kinds of subjectivities and state–citizen relations, as stemming from broad sociopolitical transformations first initiated in the 1970s. As Miller and Rose document, the change that took place entailed the deployment of new technologies of governing from the center through powerful means of governing at a distance: these appear to enhance the autonomy of zones, persons, entities, but enwrapped them in new forms of regulation—audits, budgets, standards, risk management, targets . . . It entailed a new conception of the subjects to be governed: that these would be autonomous and responsible individuals, freely choosing how to behave and act. We saw the emergence of novel strategies of activation and responsibilization . . . We saw the birth of a new ethic of the . . . responsible, autonomous individual obliged to be free. (2008: 18)

Often referred to as *responsibilization,* "the new ethic" focuses on promoting self-responsible, self-managing, and self-empowered individuals. There is, moreover, a decidedly moral undertone to responsibilization as individuals and collectives are under pressure to conduct ethical evaluations of themselves and their actions and enable themselves to be similarly evaluated by others. As Cris Shore and Susan Wright describe, processes promoting responsibilization encourage individuals to "embody a new rationality and morality," resulting in "the creation of new kinds of subjectivity: self-managing individuals who render themselves auditable" (2000: 57).

Nowhere perhaps is the constitution of responsibilized subjects more evident than in the area of health, as governments and private enterprise reorganize the provision of medical care, encouraging people to engage in an ever-growing array of activities and responsibilities to improve or maintain their own mental and physical well-being. Patient groups help formulate research agendas, people look up their own illnesses on the Internet, and an increasing number of individuals attempt to maximize their well-being through self-care (Dumit 2006; Epstein 1995; Rabeharisoa, Moreira, and Akrich 2014).

Some of these shifts in authority and control are hailed as success stories, with patients feeling more empowered, resilient, and engaged as a result of their endeavors. Others, however, reveal the underside of underfunded health care, loss of medical authority, and the vacuum of knowledge and practical experience within which patients have to make life-changing decisions about their own and their family's medical care. Very little is said of the fact that not everyone is capable, much less desiring, of turning into a responsible, self-reliant subject. In some cases, patients neither want nor accept such responsibilities, making overt as well as more subtle demands to shift responsibility back onto health professionals—requesting, in effect, to be *cared for* when they are ill.

Although many of us would like to have our opinions on what happens to us and our bodies respected, the entirely autonomous, self-reliant subject put forward by the rhetoric of neoliberal policy is a chimera in both senses of the word: a hoped-for illusion and a monster of fantastical proportions. Most of us remain reliant on our doctors and other health professionals to inform and guide us when we are ill, though our relationships with these professionals are radically changing, as are their own understandings of their expertise and authority. Many of us take part in relationships and families that provide us with care and nurturance and, in turn, care for and take care of children, husbands and wives, parents, siblings, or friends. We expect the state to provide at least the bare minimum of infrastructure for the services necessary to ensure health and well-being—though what might constitute that bare minimum seems to be continuously shifting.

In fact, we are all implicated in a variety of forms of responsibility, obligation, and duty, some of which emphasize being accountable for ourselves, whereas others underscore our inherent interrelationality with others, with the places and spaces we live in, and with larger social forms including neighborhoods, schools, workplaces, community groups, private companies, and states. Sometimes these other modes of responsibility align with neoliberal ideals and can be the very things that enable us to realize ourselves as individuals. At other times they pull us in opposite directions.

Across many advanced liberal societies, such autonomy is, however, increasingly held up as a very powerful *ideal* that motivates not only the policies of the governments we live under but also our own behaviors, opening up and closing down particular ways of thinking and acting and encouraging us to engage in projects of self-fulfillment in new and radical ways. At times, these can be powerful and uplifting activities that change our senses of self and give us the tools to reshape our lives and our health. At others, we encounter the limits of "choice" and "freedom" through radically disempowering moments that leave us stripped of not only agency but also the very possibilities of getting well.

This book examines how neoliberal policy reforms are being taken up, resisted, and reshaped in ways that change how we relate to ourselves, our bodies, and our health. Focusing on childhood asthma, I consider how new health-care policies, in particular the promotion of self-responsibility and patient expertise in light of the restructuring of state and private health services, are resulting in different kinds of medical and scientific practices, new forms of patient experience, and novel contestations among states, citizens, and private companies over rights and responsibilities to care for the sick. Here again, we have the promotion of "new kinds of people"—that is, the subjects of advanced liberalism—but quite different ones from those envisioned by Dr. Veselá. These new kinds of people, however, also take part in some much older forms of relationality, acting as mothers and fathers and children; becoming patients or doctors, nurses, or scientists; and being citizens vested with rights and responsibilities vis-à-vis the state. Each of these roles is similarly being revised in light of new political and economic agendas, but each of them also harks back to much older ideas and practices through which other kinds of responsibility, obligation, care, and sociality are constituted. The result is a series of tensions as reformist agendas open up new opportunities and foreclose others, and other kinds of social ties and duties, knowledges, and experiences demand a reframing of health and illness outside of the scope of cultivating self-knowing and self-managing subjects.

In considering these issues, this book makes three arguments. First, if we look more closely at the kinds of self-responsibility, empowerment, and patient expertise promised by neoliberal rhetorics, we recognize that they are realizable only within the context of interrelationality. Autonomy and self-realization can occur only in a framework that includes support and nurturance from others. Although this fact does not negate the possibility of becoming a self-responsible subject, it necessarily puts limits on what we mean by self-responsibility by recognizing how personal autonomy and knowledge are underpinned and supported by social relations of care and structures of obligation that are inherent within families, communities, institutions, and state–citizen relations.

Second, it has become fashionable in Western scholarship to dismiss neoliberal rhetorics of autonomy as empty promises that paper over the many detriments of widespread economic restructuring. Although I do not discount the many useful critiques of advanced liberal policy that emerge from this line of analysis, I want to suggest that there is considerable scope for considering how the ideals of increasing patient knowledge, personal empowerment, and autonomy can also be enabling, opening up possibilities for more democratic forms of patient experience and medical practice. Tracing local and global histories of asthma care reveals how the roots of neoliberal policies, in particular those encouraging self-management programs that put the onus of responsibility for monitoring and responding to symptoms on patients themselves, lie not only in the economic restructuring of health services but also in activist movements promoting patient empowerment. Whatever the problems with these programs—and, as this book shows, there are indeed many—they were born out of moves toward, and, I argue, remain, a possible site for radical political change that fosters patient rights and patient voices, enabling those who are ill to have a much more profoundly powerful role in determining their futures than was previously possible. The disjuncture, however, between the rhetoric of self-management and the need for trained professional medical oversight gives rise to serious questions over what exactly "self-management" should consist of.

Third, despite how the focus on self-management alongside the dominance of pharmaceuticals and evidence-based medicine is increasingly streamlining international approaches to asthma care, ethnographic evidence suggests that families, doctors, and scientists alike engage in other kinds of understandings of what coping with asthma actually entails. Examining a health-care system that embraces taking long outdoor walks ("climate therapy") and spa baths (balneotherapy) alongside one that focuses solely on pharmaceuticals while quietly endorsing alternative breathing retraining programs such as Buteyko reveals the great lengths to which both Czech and New Zealand patients, parents, and medical providers go to enable more comprehensive mind–body therapeutics. The work of nurses, asthma educators, scientists, and activists in both countries, moreover, raises troubling questions over governments', corporations', and individuals' responsibilities for ensuring structural conditions conducive to health and well-being. Opening up our analysis beyond how patients and doctors cope with the self-management of pharmaceuticals thus reveals a much more comprehensive understanding of what "asthma care" requires and the multiple avenues that must be explored if we are to curb this epidemic.

Competing Responsibilities

One way that I have found productive for examining these dynamics is through the concept of *competing responsibilities*, which underscores how, even in contexts where advanced liberal reforms are seemingly widely embraced, attempts to blanket out other forms of obligation and accountability can never be complete. Elsewhere, Catherine Trundle and I have noted that "responsibility" has become a key word in twenty-first-century social and political life, coming to dominate a range of conversations about not only health but also education, fitness, work, arts, and leisure (Trnka and Trundle 2014, 2017a). But we also argue that the notion of responsibilization is in danger of colonizing responsibility, so that when we think about or enact "responsibility," we end up referring to a one-size-fits-all model of autonomous personhood. In fact, neoliberal policies exist within cultural and historical settings that always contain preexisting ties and obligations, some of which necessarily counteract them (Trnka and Trundle 2017b). In New Zealand, for instance, physician-activists' attention to the need for healthy homes and the problems of child poverty are examples of attempts to actively and self-consciously broaden the medical and political gaze beyond self-responsibility. Conflicting ways of responding to health and social issues such as asthma are even easier to spot when we look at sites where neoliberal policies are strongly contested. In the Czech Republic, the commercialization of the health-care system is in tension with the socialist legacy of *solidárnost* (solidarity) under which health care remains a collective concern. There is also a strong emphasis on privileging medical professionals' expertise that neither patients nor doctors appear willing to jettison. Moreover, self-care does not necessarily equate to responsibilization and the creation of autonomous subjects; as some of the Czech environmental activists in this book explain, self-empowerment is often seen as a necessary precursor to becoming an active, vocal participant in civic society.

Medicine and the care it entails are a particularly fruitful domain for examining responsibility. Despite the drive to inculcate patient self-responsibility, enactments of care often involve individual and collective responsibilities and obligations that far exceed the boundaries of responsibilization. Whether it be intimate forms of care that take place within families or between doctors and patients (Mol 2008) or more formal collective mandates for care enshrined in the social contract ideologies that underpin the very notion of states and citizens, care encompasses a variety of different kinds of rights and responsibilities, duties and obligations.

Although there is no limit to the medical conditions that may be productively analyzed in terms of competing responsibilities, some, such as asthma, lend themselves especially well to highlighting the multiplicity of ways that responsibilities (and rights) are framed. As asthma is one of the most significant sites for promoting self-managed care, it is not surprising that it provides insights into discourses and practices of responsibilization and the effects of neoliberal ideals of autonomy. Yet the social, medical, legal, and political facets of how this disease is lived out are much broader, requiring us to consider other aspects of health and citizenship. Alongside the encouragement of new forms of patienthood and revised notions of citizenship, asthma care is shaped by long-standing ideas of social justice, relations among states and nations, and distributions of economic power. It also requires a look inward at relationships within the family, as well as between the self, the body, and the mind. Neoliberalization frames many of these experiences but does not determine the scope of their content. Understanding asthma therefore requires a wider lens, one able to capture the range of everyday experiences of people with asthma and their families that anthropological research brings to our attention.

In offering a comprehensive perspective on the way asthma is lived out in families, in schools and medical clinics, in the scientific lab and on the floor of Parliament, and in the bodies and minds of those who suffer from this condition, *One Blue Child* departs from the growing body of social science and public health studies of asthma concerned with assessing the impacts of policies promoting self-management programs and advising on how to improve on them.[3] Instead, my focus is on locating therapeutics in the wider context of interrelations that are pivotal to constituting care. These necessarily include not only relations to the self, be it in the form of self-management programs or other enactments of self-care, but also relations among patients and medical providers, their family members, the environment, companies, and the state.

Childhood is a particularly important site for examining these issues. Asthma tends to emerge in families, with multiple generations often suffering from this condition. Shared familial responses both highlight the interrelationality of how asthma is lived out and demonstrate divergences in how individuals cope with it. Furthermore, at the same time that asthma rates among children have skyrocketed, in many Western nations there is growing awareness and acceptance of children's rights to self-determination, particularly the need to enable children's active roles in determining their own well-being. In many societies, our expectations of children, understandings of what they are capable of, and the value attributed to their perspectives on their lives and their health care have radically shifted over the past two decades (Streuli, Michel, and Vayena 2011). Children have, moreover, not escaped the new social emphasis on self-management—on the contrary, they frequently bear the brunt of socialization processes intended to instill such moral framings. And yet, children are by definition dependents, requiring the care and nurturance of others. The emerging tensions between listening to children's and young adults' voices, teaching them to better self-manage, and recognizing their limitations and attending to their needs result in childhood constituting a particularly fertile site for examining neoliberal health-care policy, enabling us to recognize how interrelationality and dependence, as well as knowledge, autonomy, and self-responsibility, lie at the heart of how families, societies, and governments foster and curtail health and well-being.

Politicizing Asthma in the Czech Republic

Since the Velvet Revolution of 1989, widespread political-economic reforms have been reshaping Czech society. In health care, the shift from fully state-supported care to a mix of private and public health care with state-supported mandatory health insurance has radically altered the terrain of medical practice. Policy reforms have resulted in citizens shouldering increasing personal responsibility for their own health and medical care as well as, more broadly, for their overall individual and familial economic and social well-being.

Nevertheless, although moves toward greater patient empowerment and autonomy dominate current discussions of health-care policy making in Western societies, they play a more subdued role in discussions of health policy, and even more so medical practice, in the Czech Republic. Publicly, demands for increased patient rights are muted, with notable exceptions in the areas of childbirth (Hrešanová 2010) and end-of-life care. This is not to say, however, that this is not an important theme in medical encounters. As medical care is increasingly privatized, doctors and other medical professionals are necessarily redefining their roles and relationships with patients. And although patients frequently grumble about wanting more say in their health care, they also expect to have frequent access to intensive, highly regimented, specialist care. Together, doctors and patients are resisting the dilution of professional expertise while attempting to accommodate increasing patient demands and responsibilization.

For the most part, however, Czech patients and doctors are engaged in debates involving a very different kind of conceptualization of rights to those of patient autonomy and empowerment, focusing instead on the rewriting of health policies to ensure citizens' rights to have access to particular kinds of services and protections from the state. Within these debates, asthma has a distinctive public profile. Respiratory illnesses, particularly in children, are a frequent topic of discussion on TV and radio, often raised as part of political debates that pit one side of the public, keen to protect the environment, against those focused on promoting industry. As such, government responses to childhood asthma are widely represented as something that should be of interest across the nation.

Though the language used may vary, the need to protect "one blue child" from the perils of rampant industrialism is frequently deployed to mobilize broad segments of society. Indeed, at the EU-funded Institute for Experimental Medicine in Prague, an entire scientific team devotes itself to documenting the effects of air pollution on children living in the industrial city of Ostrava. In academic papers, on TV, and on the floor of Parliament, these scientists argue that asthma should be understood as a disease of civilization and more particularly a disease of industrialization. They have furthermore contended that emissions from the largest steelworks in the Czech Republic, ArcelorMittal Ostrava, have resulted in Ostrava having the highest rate of childhood asthma in the world at 37 percent (Šrám et al. 2013). Several high-profile legal cases have been made by citizens' groups as well as by the city of Ostrava against ArcelorMittal and against the Czech state for allowing excess emissions. The fear, however, is that enforcing emissions policies will drive away industry, and without industry there will be no jobs. Without jobs, people with—or without—asthma will suffer even more. Here then, economic rights come to be pitted against health-care rights.

In public consciousness, moreover, the role of the Czech state in addressing childhood asthma takes us far beyond standardized biomedical asthma treatments employed in the West. Indeed, public debates revolve around not only how to weigh up the right to live in a healthy, unpolluted environment against the desire to attract lucrative foreign industry but also how to resolve citizens' rights to receive residential spa cures versus the need for government to focus on balancing the health-care budget. Popular therapies range from hourly stays in "salt rooms," or climate-controlled rooms where children inhale heavily salinated air, sometimes also called "salt caves," to more intensive treatments such as two- or three-week visits to the coastal areas of Croatia and Greece. The most coveted are insurance-subsidized multiweek stays in health spas renowned for their clean air, curative waters, and medicinal "procedures" such as massages and steam inhalations, which also offer a respite from urban life. Embraced by the majority of the medical establishment, such therapies are specifically intended to temper the central role of pharmaceuticals in asthma care. A March 2014 ruling by the Czech high court, moreover, found that all Czech citizens have a legal right to spa treatments, ensuring that popular therapeutics that lie outside the scope of worldwide asthma guidelines and evidence-based medicine will be used in tandem with international biomedical protocols. Some environmental activists contend that the state needs to go even further in countering industry and protecting citizens' rights to a healthy environment, whereas for others such a ruling sends a clear message about how the Czech state considers itself to be ultimately responsible for overseeing and ensuring its citizens' access to medical care.

Individual Responsibility, Health, and Asthma in New Zealand

When Dr. Veselá called for a "changing of society," she had a very specific view of what that change should entail. In New Zealand, a different mode of "changing society" is taking place. It too is underpinned by a particular kind of politics with its own associated understandings of personhood, rights, and responsibility. It too grew out of radical political demands but today is largely viewed as neither political nor particularly contested, except by a relatively small minority.

New Zealand has the world's second-highest rate of childhood asthma, just behind the UK (Ministry of Health 2013; Asher et al. 2006). Curiously, although Czechs widely view asthma as a national problem and generally believe that their asthma rates (at 10 to 15 percent of children) are extreme, most New Zealanders are surprised to hear that their country ranks so high in asthma cases. To a large extent, this blindness is due to New Zealanders' intensely individualized approaches to health care. With the patient in the "driver's seat" of care, it becomes increasingly unclear what role doctors should play. Policies promoting self-management and patient-centered approaches to asthma have generally translated into pharmaceuticals becoming the centerpiece of care. In some cases, the role of physicians has become reduced to a knowledgeable pharmaceutical broker, as they are the only one in the doctor–patient "partnership" able to hand out prescriptions. The result is not only the stripping away of medical authority and expertise but also a loss of medical oversight. Sometimes, the loss is extreme, as some of the asthma society representatives I spoke with estimated that up to 90 percent of patients do not receive the minimum guidance of a personalized asthma action plan, much less coordinate their use of it through regular routine visits to a physician (see also Crengle 2008).[4] Less alarming but more common are patients who received action plans long ago and have spent years phoning in requests for repeat prescriptions; experimenting with various doses, timings, and combinations; cobbling together their own pharmaceutical regimes; and consulting their doctors only in cases of emergency.

More structural problems, and solutions, tend to be ignored. From the world-renowned epidemiologists who led the ISAAC study to global experts on the impacts of poor-quality housing on health, New Zealand physicians have been very vocal about the need for structural changes to help curb the alarming rise of asthma, advocating for the right of all New Zealanders to live in "healthy homes" with heating and insulation, as well as for economic relief for children living in poverty (Holt and Beasley 2002; Howden-Chapman et al. 2007). However, although many asthma nurses, particularly those working in services tailored for members of the minority Māori community, embrace the need for poverty alleviation and economic change, overwhelmingly their services focus on providing one-on-one patient education and support.

Although there are many shortcomings to focusing interventions primarily on individual patients, policies promoting self-management also have a number of merits in terms of encouraging patients to speak out and articulate their own perspectives, especially on the topic of medication use. The implementation of self-management in New Zealand is, moreover, not accidental but developed out of patients' rights movements in the 1970s. Tired of "patronizing doctors" who dismissed their concerns, mothers such as Angela Scott, who later became a central figure at the Asthma and Respiratory Foundation, founded patient-focused asthma societies whose goal is to both educate and empower people suffering from asthma. As a result, a country of under 4.5 million people now has an extensive system of close to two dozen regionally focused asthma societies, all of which provide outreach and education to patients and parents of children with asthma.

But how did moves to promote patients' rights turn into ten-year-olds being, in some cases, held responsible for managing their own health conditions? What strengths might we draw from patient-centered care in order to offset the more authoritarian and paternalistic relations that make a number of Czechs feel stripped of the right to determine their health care? In turn, how might a more collective focus on care that incorporates but also limits pharmaceuticals counter some of the detriments of the self-management model that has come to dominate international policy guidelines? These are some of the questions this book endeavors to answer.

How This Research Came to Be

This book "follows a policy" (Shore and Wright 2011) as the primary focal point of analysis. It tells the story of how self-management has emerged as the global policy standard for asthma care, examining both the intended and unintended effects of its implementation. But it also goes much farther in tracing the myriad of ways that governments, medical professionals, corporations, activists, parents, and children actually take up, recast, or ignore responsibility for mitigating asthma.

Using an assemblage approach to policy (Greenhalgh 2008), this book tracks the interrelationships among policies, people, rationalities, technologies, affects, and values that are enacted across various domains of social and political life. Part of this task requires stepping outside the confines of a "policy world" (Shore and Wright 2011) to reflect back on where and how its boundaries have been drawn. It means asking what lies within the sphere of asthma self-management and how might other approaches to childhood asthma differently delineate what is, and is not, understood as the "problem of childhood asthma." It also means taking a close look at both the benefits and shortcomings of self-managed care.

Cross-cultural ethnography is a vital tool for achieving such insights as it starkly illuminates how things we take for granted as being necessary or "true" in one context might not even occur in another. Cross-cultural ethnography also demonstrates the well-known ethnographic rule of thumb that a very effective way to investigate "big issues," particularly global ones, is to look closely at what is going on in "small places," where researchers can establish face-to-face relationships with people and, through the depth of their encounters, produce nuanced understandings of phenomena under investigation (Shore and Trnka 2013). In wanting to understand family dynamics, doctor–patient relations, and such intimate concerns as what constitutes "good care" of children with asthma, ethnographic methods prove invaluable.

In many ways, researching a medical condition as ubiquitous as asthma has its advantages. When I embarked on this project, it seemed that everywhere I turned I encountered people coping with asthma who were eager to discuss their health or that of their family members. In the Czech Republic, during the first few weeks of this project my new landlords shared their confusion over what might be triggering their young son's respiratory difficulties, an old family friend recounted a gripping tale of a midnight drive to the hospital when his sister suffered a dramatic asthma attack, and the husband of a local academic I was keen to get to know related how his mother had nearly died of asthma. In the days and weeks that followed, it seemed that almost everyone I met had a story to tell about asthma and its impact on their lives.

In New Zealand the stories were even more common. The primary school my children attended regularly sent home notes asking parents to pack their children's inhalers with them when they went on excursions off school grounds. On a recent school field trip, a mother accompanying the class was surprised when she was handed an allergy emergency kit, complete with a syringe and rescue inhalers, which she was supposed to carry with her in case one of the boys under her care had an allergy or asthma attack. After asking the other parents if they knew what to do with the items (no one did), she ended up quizzing the six-year-old boy himself about how to use them. In the same class, one of my children was selected as a "buddy" to assist another classmate in getting to the nurse's office whenever he had an asthma attack. Parents I met and friends of my children regularly told me about their experiences of getting and learning how to use inhalers and then being diagnosed with asthma—often in that order. For every three or four parents I met who shrugged off asthma as just another "hassle" they have to deal with, there was one who was vociferous in her or his denunciation of the pharmaceutical industry and the insistence that alternative therapies—usually Buteyko—were the solution to her or his worries.

These are only a few of the encounters that frame the analysis of asthma that appears in this book. In the course of four years of research (from 2010 to 2014) in New Zealand and the Czech Republic, I met and spoke with adults, youths, and children who suffer from asthma; mothers and fathers of asthmatic children; respiratory specialists; family physicians; pharmacists; physiotherapists; emergency room doctors and ambulance staff; asthma and pediatric nurses; child psychiatrists and psychologists; health spa directors; alternative health providers; directors of asthma societies; physical education teachers; health and environmental activists; scientists; pharmaceutical company representatives; the heads of health insurance companies; leaders of corporate social responsibility programs; members of Parliament; and government policy consultants. Much of the research consisted of formal interviews, but I also spent large amounts of time with families of children with asthma and allergies, joining them in their homes; on trips they made to the doctor, playground, or sports field; or on special excursions to the zoo. While I conducted the Czech research on my own, in New Zealand I had a team of seven graduate research assistants. Altogether, we met and spoke with over 200 people, each of whom shared with us his or her perspectives on childhood asthma.

Their accounts form the backbone of this text. The pages that follow move back and forth between New Zealand and the Czech Republic, examining global concerns through the lens of local realities. Chapter 1 examines more closely self-management discourses and practices in New Zealand, as well as the local and international scientific and activist histories that underpin self-management approaches. Chapter 2 spotlights how New Zealand patients and parents of children with asthma engage in their own "domestic experiments" with drugs and other therapies, in some cases engaging in "noncompliance" as a radical critique of the pharmaceutical industry. Together, Chapters 1 and 2 underscore the discrepancies between how physicians and other medical personnel picture self-management to work in principle and the ways it is actually played out in New Zealand health care. Chapters 3 and 4 take us to the Czech Republic to focus on how medical responsibility, patient agency, and patient–doctor communication are being reshaped in an increasingly commercialized therapeutic landscape. Here, agency and responsibility are cast not only in terms of one-on-one care for the self or others but also the work it takes to compel experts, including physicians, to take an interest in providing quality care. Responsibility for individual children's well-being vacillates between resting in the hands of the family and the nation, just as the nation vacillates between full-heartedly embracing neoliberal reforms and maintaining the legacies of solidarity.

Chapter 5 considers the phenomenology of asthma and addresses how two nonpharmaceutical forms of therapeutics—sports and Buteyko breathing retraining—open up spaces for New Zealand sufferers to address the experiential overlaps between breathlessness as a physical disorder and a manifestation of mental distress. Chapter 6 looks at similar forms of nonpharmaceutical therapeutics, albeit under the auspices of state biomedicine, that take place in summer camps and health spas across the Czech Republic. Although some critics contend that these activities constitute indulgent "holidays," I examine how pleasure is actually pivotal to their efficacy. Chapter 7 considers the political effects of scientific claims that the Ostrava region in the Czech Republic suffers from the world's highest rates of childhood asthma. Tracing socialist and postsocialist histories of environmental activism, I analyze how Czech children's respiratory health has come to constitute a citizenship issue, acting as a contemporary litmus test for the viability of state–citizen social contracts in a newly democratic nation. The Conclusion returns us to the questions of how asthma is problematized, arguing that self-management must be understood as one possible framing among many others and outlining the policy implications that expanding our analyses of asthma beyond self-management would entail.

At the beginning of this project, I could not have anticipated the wide range of therapeutic responses and sites that would emerge as the fieldwork led me from respiratory hospitals to health spas and salt caves, from group lessons in how to lengthen breath exhalations or play the didgeridoo to scientific seminars, activists' protests, and parliamentary inquiries. In this book I draw on these various facets of what can be broadly termed "asthma care" to consider the contemporary reshaping of citizens' rights, patient knowledge, and experiences of chronic illness. I suggest that as advanced liberal reforms redefine the obligations of the government, the public, and collectivities such as corporations and activist movements in insuring health and providing medical care, they raise crucial questions, including what role should people have in overseeing their own bodily and emotional states and those of others? If the provision of care isn't about helping people when they cannot help themselves, what in fact does it constitute? And if the social contract is not about providing things like health care, then what is the purpose of the state?

In addressing these issues, my examination considers the broad terrain that responsibility for health necessarily entails. Looking across multiple domains, I trace the ways that a variety of different kinds of personal and collective responsibilities—from individual patients compelled to become responsible subjects and doctors and nurses redefining their professional obligations to corporations' implementations of social responsibility programs and the reciprocal responsibilities between states and citizens—come into play in how care is conceptualized and enacted. The result is a much more complex, and at times conflicting, set of practices than the image of the patient-expert promoted by self-management policies would have us believe. Indeed, by moving beyond the rhetoric of self-management and undertaking an empirically focused cross-cultural analysis of the lived realities of childhood asthma, this book reveals both the many pitfalls and the many possibilities that advanced liberal reforms offer us as we reshape our understandings of what it means to be a doctor, a patient, and a citizen in the twenty-first century.

Chapter 1

Democratizing Knowledge

Patients Caught between Compliance and Self-Management

Why Asthma Still Kills

In mid-2014, the world's largest assessment of self-managed asthma care was published by the British Royal College of Physicians. Titled *Why Asthma Still Kills*, the review set out to determine what led to the deaths of 195 people with asthma in the United Kingdom over a one-year period in 2012–2013. The commission's findings are a damning assessment of how health policies promoting self-managed care are failing patients. The detailed report suggests that there is an array of problems in contemporary asthma care ranging from doctors' excessive prescribing of reliever medications to inadequate specialist oversight. A disturbing number of patients with asthma are not receiving adequate preventative care: only 23 percent of those who died had ever received a personal asthma action plan, the cornerstone of self-management programs, and only 43 percent had seen a family physician or a specialist for a review of their asthma in the year before they died. Even more frightening is the number of patients who either don't appear to know they are in danger or seek out care too late, as nearly half of those who died did so without asking for medical assistance or before emergency medical services could be provided (RCP 2014: ix–xi). Figures from smaller-scale studies in the United States paint a similar picture (Hartert et al. 1996; Murphy et al. 2012).

All of these are important factors to take note of, particularly as self-management has become the standardized approach for asthma care, enshrined in GINA guidelines. But just as important as the specific steps that weren't carried out in these cases is the shift in practices and relationships that has led to action plans becoming required items in asthma care and preventative reviews being viewed as a difficult challenge in the first place. Indeed, in the report's brief foreword, one of the members of the review's steering group, Dr. Martyn R. Partridge, Professor of Respiratory Medicine at Imperial College

London, hints at some of the broader changes in contemporary health care that have set the stage for the statistics listed above. Partridge asks his fellow medical professionals:

If our patients do not always take medication as we advise, is that their fault or our failure to involve them in a process of shared decision making? If the patient fails to attend for review or to collect a repeat prescription, is it because our processes, methods of follow-up or their convenience was suboptimal, or indeed was it the quality of the consultation and the expertise experienced that failed to impress? Our continued failure to provide meaningful support as patients self-manage their condition needs to be rectified. (RCP 2014: vii)

Partridge's reflections indicate some of the larger issues at stake here. This is not just a story of action plans that were never handed out or follow-up appointments that were never scheduled: it is part of a much wider historical revolution in the nature of doctor–patient relations. The changes comprise shifts in medical professionals' authority and expertise, on the one hand, and the individualist drive for patients to have more control, authority, and responsibility over their own health care, on the other. Patients who were once seen as readily "impressed" by "the quality of the consultation and the expertise" of their physicians—at least sufficiently enough to follow their advice—have been replaced by independent "patient-experts" who are expected to take the central role in managing their care. How then are physicians to "impress" them to take up their instructions?

There is, moreover, a third player here, who creates a silent backdrop to the Royal College of Physicians' report, namely the pharmaceutical companies that sell the medication that is the basis of much of asthma care. Although many doctors focus on the changing nature of their relationships with patients, many patients situate their physicians' advice in a context where pharmaceutical companies are seen as even more powerful than doctors in determining the form and content of contemporary health care. The result is indeed a terrain in which "asthma still kills."

This chapter takes up what one New Zealand asthma patient refers to as the jettisoning of "old-fashioned ideas that your doctor knows everything" to probe how New Zealand's system of health care and associated ideas about responsibility, personhood, and the body structure new forms of patienthood and medical authority. These ideas are not top-down impositions of advanced

liberal reforms but come from a number of sources, including grassroots movements to divest responsibility to patients. In the 1970s, New Zealand took part
in a wave of radical patient activism sweeping through many Western countries,
culminating in a revolution in patients' rights. Part of this sea change was the
acknowledgment that patients' experiences of health care matter and that their
voices need to be included in medical decision making. Just how much authority, however, patients have been granted to shape their care is something this
chapter will investigate.

In the process, we will examine how new assumptions about the inherent
limits of medical professionals' knowledge rub up against the desires of physicians and other medical professionals to instruct patients in what they see as
the best possible avenues for asthma care, creating a tension in medical practice. Doctors, many of whom embrace the ethics of "patient-centered medicine," are torn between empowering patients to be more responsible for their
own health and providing the necessary care and oversight to enable therapeutic success. This tension, I suggest, is central to the actual implementation of
self-management policies and programs and results in an inherent contradic-
tion in what "self-management" actually comes to mean in daily practice. Contrary to what its name suggests, self-management frequently does not enable
patient *initiative*, much less patients self-defining their conditions, but often
ends up being another way of attempting to achieve patients' compliance with
doctors' directives, albeit with significantly less direct oversight. Moreover, in a
context where doctors are losing formal authority and patients are vested with
increased responsibility but have less access to expert advice and one-on-one
care, pharmaceutical companies have not lost their mandate to make a profit
(Abraham and Lewis 2002). The result is a skewed playing field in which strict
adherence to pharmaceuticals becomes seemingly the only viable solution,
raising concern among patients, and often nurses, over whether the drive for
increased patient adherence to medications is responsible and justified.

This raises some serious questions about what we mean by "personal responsibility." If patients are supposed to *self*-manage, then surely this would
mean that they should be free to determine when and how much medication to
take? In such a scenario—under the logics of neoliberal health-care policies—
physicians and other medical professionals would be cast as advisors but not
burdened with the responsibility of compelling recalcitrant patients to do other
than they choose. In actual fact, responsibility for health remains—as it must—

intensely interrelational: patients suffer from particular conditions, doctors use their medical expertise to attempt to ameliorate them, and, out of their collaborative efforts, care is enacted. Although the rhetoric has changed and the balance of power in doctor–patient relationships has shifted more toward patients, medical professionals have not given up either their legal or moral obligations to provide the best possible care. Just how the self-responsible, autonomous subject can be cared *for* is something on which neoliberal discourse is largely silent. Empirically, however, we can see the opening up of a new terrain of negotiation, and sometimes outright struggle, as doctors attempt to act responsibly to provide good care while promoting patients' rights and autonomy.

A second set of questions concern what exactly we are losing through our overwhelming focus on the individual patient. Despite the efforts of patients, scientists, health-care activists, physicians, nurses, and other medical professionals, many of the structural impediments to ensuring health and well-being are being increasingly overshadowed by solutions focused solely on the individual. Class differences, in particular, have come to be subsumed under a rhetoric of personal responsibility that assumes an equality of opportunity that is not always manifest in people's lives. Simply stated, it is much easier to mitigate respiratory distress when the walls of your house are not covered in moldy toadstools.

As David Hess (2004) has eloquently argued, the political underpinnings of science (and medicine) shape not only the solutions scientists arrive at but also the very questions they are compelled to ask. In turning our focus to how scientific problems are made, Hess and other scholars of science and technology studies reveal how the complex interplays among government policies, public perceptions, and the interests of scientists themselves make some problems worth investigating while leaving others "undone" (Frickel et al. 2010; Latour 1987; Latour and Woolgar 1979). In the New Zealand context, asthma emerges as an individualized problem, one that demands weighing up patient empowerment against the value of professional medical expertise, rather than a collective or structural question of, as one activist aptly put it, ensuring that the social and structural environments in which patients live are made to "comply" with the aims of enabling better respiratory health.

From Patient Experience to Patient Expertise

For asthma sufferers and their families, the shift from being considered a patient to a patient-expert can be both liberating and damning. Barbara is an asthma nurse-educator and a parent of an asthmatic daughter. She enthusiastically re-lated how different things are today from when her daughter was growing up in the 1970s, when "nobody ever told you anything much about asthma at all. You went to the doctor, you were diagnosed, you were given stuff, and you didn't really inquire too much about it. Nowadays you'd be on the Internet, or you'd be talking to support groups—you'd be finding out about it."

Other patients, however, underscore some of the difficulties of being in charge of their own health. Sybil is in her mid-twenties. She recently moved from a relatively poor rural community in the Far North to Auckland and is having trouble finding her footing financially. Having suffered from asthma since her early childhood, she reflected on her ongoing experiences of public health care:

You need to know how to work the system. It sounds bad, but that's actually what I think! What happens is that there are ways that you're *supposed* to do it, but no one knows about them because there's no training on how to *talk* to doctors. There's this old-fashioned idea that your doctor knows everything, but when you get educated, you real-ize that your doctor *doesn't* know everything and they *can't* know everything because there is a lot to know. I guess you get more proactive with your health and with seeking solutions and that is where I'm at, so I'm in a reasonable position to help my kids.

As Sybil noted, it takes both an ability to seek solutions and the knowledge of how to do so—knowing how to "work the system" and "talk to doctors"—to be in a "reasonable position" to get what you need. Not all patients can, however, undertake the strategic efforts to communicate and gain access to resources that Sybil describes. But regardless of how they respond to the challenges of "work-ing" the medical system, more often than not people with asthma and parents of asthmatic children voice a similar understanding to Sybil's that the onus of care rests firmly in their own hands. Some express considerable concern over the possible challenges this might lead to in dealing with medical professionals, whereas others embrace overseeing their own health.

After decades of increasing medical professionalization (Freidson 1970, 1986), the recasting of medical expertise out of the privileged hands of medi-cal professionals has been described as the deprofessionalization of medical knowledge (Hardey 1999). But it does not necessarily follow that deprofes-sionalization will result in the *democratization* of medical knowledge. Jeanette Pols has recently argued for the need to radicalize and democratize medical knowledge by turning patient knowledge, which she refers to as "practical knowing in action"—that is, the knowledge accumulated through patient experience and patients' everyday experimentation with techniques and technologies—into another source of scientific knowledge (2014: 75). To do so would necessitate a rethinking of what we mean by medical *knowledge* to enable first-hand accounts of the experiential realities and survival tactics of sufferers to be transformed into a knowledge base from which other patients and medical professionals can draw. Pols is, however, unclear on the steps needed to differentiate between patients' *perspectives* and patient *knowledge*—an important distinction, as we cannot always take for granted the accuracy and widespread applicability of what all patients hold to be true (see Prior 2003).

Perhaps more significantly, however, the affirmation of patient experience as *expertise*—that is, not only as knowledge but as *expert* knowledge—requires *social* recognition of the patient as the holder of a privileged perspective over a particular domain of knowledge and practice (cf. Carr 2010). In fact, social recognition of patients as experts is not always forthcoming, particularly during clinical encounters. Although there are circumstances in which physicians embrace the collaborative production of both knowledge and care practices with patients as part of daily clinical practice (Park et al. forthcoming; Jutel 2011), it appears that most New Zealand medical professionals working with asthma patients are more focused on getting patients to listen to them and follow their instructions. There are a number of reasons that this is so. Whatever the attractions of "putting patients in the driver's seat" of their own care, doctors remain legally accountable for the integrity of their advice. Most professionals are, moreover, understandably eager and concerned about providing the kinds of care they have spent years of training trying to master. Not only are their practices socially recognized as being for the most part efficacious, they have also been professionalized in a medical establishment that emphasizes the benefits of very particular ways of seeing and knowing the world that are distinct from the firsthand, experiential perspectives of patients (Foucault 1980; Good 1994). But even professional *experience* is no longer sacrosanct in medical practice. Doctors and other medical professionals are under pressure to move away from their own experience-based knowledge of medicine and follow streamlined, evidence-based guidelines (Adams 2013; Berg 1998). It is not surprising, then, to find that patient experience is rarely vested with the power to subvert increasingly standardized models of care.

Physicians are thus placed in a difficult situation as they struggle to retain authority and help shape, if not determine, the course of action that their patients will follow. The result is often a complicated dance between the rhetoric of patient empowerment and the drive to achieve patient compliance. Patient experience is acknowledged as important, but the rhetoric of patient empowerment is often turned on its head so that experiences that do not readily conform to the models of self-management are delegitimized. Patients are enabled to be experts *as long as they follow the rules laid out by (evidence-based) medical guidelines.* Although these dynamics underlie a range of patient–doctor interactions from maternity and birth (Bryant et al. 2007) to end-of-life care (Kaufman 2005), they come to a head in self-management programs for chronic illnesses that are explicitly designed to encourage patient oversight of care.

Initiating Self-Management

In the late 1980s and early 1990s, New Zealand wholeheartedly embraced neoliberal policy reforms, including those designed to induce patients to take increased responsibility for their own health care (Fitzgerald 2004; Barnett 2000). As part of what some critics have referred to as the "New Zealand Experiment," the country became "a paradigm case of neo-liberal political reform . . . regarded as remarkable for the purity of its new state managerial design, the speed of its implementation, and the ideological certainty with which it was pursued" (Lewis 2004: 161; see also Kelsey 1995). In the area of health care, the government oversaw two major restructurings of the health-care system: a radical marketization in health-care provision in 1993 and then a step back from the market-based model in 2001. Surprisingly, the cumulative result has been a largely unchanged mixed-services model, characterized by the availability of state-owned and private hospitals, free or largely subsidized pharmaceuticals, and mostly private primary care with government subsidies for low-income groups and children (Ashton, Mays, and Devlin 2005). As Toni Ashton and colleagues describe,

Now, as before and during the reforms . . . most patients must pay a fee for visiting their general practitioner (GP) or for an item on prescription, must get a referral from the GP to see a specialist, will receive public hospital services free of charge, and are likely to wait for some services provided in public hospitals and outpatient clinics. Now, as before, they can choose to pay either through voluntary private health insurance or directly out-of-pocket if they wish to access the services of a private specialist or attend a private hospital without altering their right to use the public system. (2005: 255–257)

One area that did undergo radical changes was New Zealand's adoption of new managerialism policies that aimed to reframe health-care delivery into a consumer service (Fitzgerald 2012). As part of a desire to combat "the perceived excessive paternalism of health professionals" (Ibid. 46), this shift included the expectation that patients would take increasing responsibility for their own health. As in other parts of the Western world, this was achieved through the rolling out of self-managed care.

Today, there are self-management programs for a wide range of conditions, from diabetes to bipolar disease (Ferzacca 2000; Martin 1997, 2009). Internationally, some of the earliest programs were, however, developed for children with asthma. Although there is evidence of an asthma self-management program trial in New York in the early 1960s (for example, Feldman et al. 1962), the full-scale development of asthma self-management took place in the late 1970s and 1980s and is generally attributed to the pioneering efforts of Thomas L. Creer, the director of the Division of Behavioral Science at the Children's Asthma Research Institute & Hospital in Denver, Colorado (Lorig and Holman 2003).

In the 1970s, new ideas about self-regulation and self-control were taking hold in American psychology. Texts such as *Self-Control: Power to the Person* (Mahoney and Thoresen 1974), *Behavioral Self-Management* (Stuart 1977), and "Self-Efficacy: Toward a Unifying Theory of Behavioral Change" (Bandura 1977) promoted a range of self-care strategies for overcoming afflictions ranging from low self-esteem to alcoholism and insomnia. As a trained psychologist, Creer was particularly interested in the usefulness of such methods for curbing the anxiety associated with asthma attacks. His groundbreaking move, however, was to adapt such methods of self-regulation to focus on *physical* self-management, engaging children in measuring, interpreting, and acting on both the physical and emotional symptoms associated with asthma (Taplin and Creer 1978). Developed at Creer's center in Denver, asthma self-management was popularized through a series of national conferences, most notably the Self-Management Educational Programs for Childhood Asthma conference in Los Angeles in June 1981 and the Workshop on Self-Management of Childhood Asthma hosted by the National Heart, Lung, and Blood Institute and the National Institute of Allergy and Infectious Diseases in 1983.

From the very beginning, self-management was hailed as a money-saving measure. In the introductory paragraph to a scientific paper launching the new method, Creer and Paul Taplin note: "It is clear that solutions to the problem of rising health care costs must be found; self-management of physical function has the potential of providing a powerful remedy" (Taplin and Creer 1978: 15). Asthma, in particular, they argue, is "an expensive affliction" and therefore an excellent testing ground for self-management techniques (1978: 15).

As these early publications suggest, the purpose of self-management was explicitly to redistribute responsibility and, by implication, create a new kind of patient. Expressing frustration over the ways that "chronically ill and handi-capped children" were unable to manage their own conditions, Creer and his colleague Walter P. Christian suggested that through proper training in self-observation, children could learn to "pace" themselves and thus keep their asthma in check (1976: 106). One of the key elements of this training was the creation of individualized "self-management contracts" signed by both the child and an adult that clearly outlined "target behaviors," terms of agreement, "payoffs," and consequences for breaching the agreed conditions (Creer and Christian 1976: 110). Creer encouraged children to modify and regulate their own behavior as well as oversee their own medication intake, enabling them to be in charge of their own care. If the children were not (initially) up to the task, their parents could step in. Either way, children and their families would learn how to take control of their illness and the physical and psychological behaviors associated with it.

The basic philosophy and financial reasoning behind Creer's vision still resonate with current policies promoting self-management. In practical terms, however, contemporary asthma self-management approaches have largely streamlined the wide-ranging behavioral and psychological training that Creer envisaged to focus more squarely on promoting the correct use of pharmaceuticals.

Although the exact combinations and timings of drugs differ, most people with asthma are prescribed a reliever inhaler (a bronchodilator that relaxes the muscles in the airways, facilitating airflow when there is an asthma attack) such as Bricanyl, Salamol, or Ventolin to use when they are having trouble breathing. When their asthma is particularly acute, patients may also receive an oral steroid such as Prednisone, usually used over a short time period. Alongside this, many are likely to receive a preventative inhaler (a corticosteroid anti-inflammatory medication) such as Beclazone, Flixotide, Respocort, or Pulmicort or a combination inhaler that combines reliever and preventative medications such as Seretide or Symbicort, either of which they may use once or twice a day. Often young children, and sometimes adults, are given a "spacer"—a plastic tube into which the inhaler is inserted—to assist them with inhaling their medication. Depending on their specific symptoms and the suspected cause of their asthma, they may also receive antihistamines, nasal sprays, or other medications.

Most guidelines suggest that patients be given an "action plan" filled in by their physician to guide them through the process of monitoring their medication intake and determining when to seek professional help. Action plans are usually a simple pamphlet or card, one side of which specifies symptoms, such as wheezing or waking up at night, which patients should watch out for. Some symptoms require the adjustment of pharmaceutical doses, as prespecified by a physician. Others indicate an impending emergency and require the patient to phone his or her doctor or go immediately to the emergency room. The other side of the action plan has the same information but based on lung capacity measured through a peak flow meter, a rudimentary cardboard and plastic tube that patients puff into. In New Zealand, peak flow meters are freely given out to patients by doctors, usually along with a graph on which patients should record their daily measurements (see Figure 1.1). One set of measurements delineates an acceptable reading, another indicates a warning and the need to adjust one's medication as specified on the plan, and a third indicates that patients have entered the danger zone and should seek immediate emergency care. Action plans are often coded in green, yellow, or red to facilitate patients' understandings of the relative dangerousness of their conditions. Though the format of action plans has changed over time, the activities of understanding one's symptoms, accounting for them (literally, through keeping track of peak flow measurements), and adjusting medication rates based on these remain at the heart of the self-management system.

The streamlining of care that asthma action plans represent was made possible, in large part, by the development of new kinds of anti-inflammatories, improved corticosteroids, and more selective beta-agonists in the 1980s (Jackson 2009). A decade later, the combination inhaler, which combines preventative and reliever medications, and Diskhalers resulted in even greater ease and efficacy in asthma care. Since the late 1980s, although the number of asthma

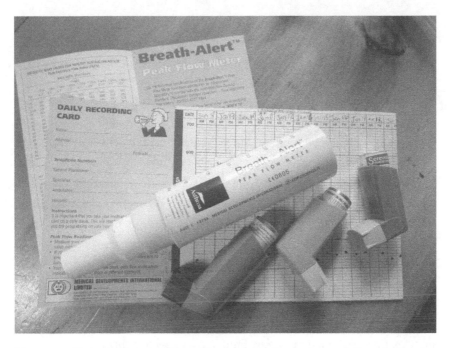

Figure 1.1   Technologies of asthma self-care: a peak flow meter, peak flow chart, and inhalers.

Photo by Revena Correll Trnka.

cases has risen, hospitalization and death rates have significantly diminished, and asthma has generally been viewed as a less onerous condition (Holt and Beasley 2002).

Physicians versus Big Pharma: From Fenoterol to Action Plans for Asthma

Perhaps ironically, self-management policies became popular not only because of pharmaceutical advances but also due to physicians' concerns over the negative effects of some of the new drugs. In the late 1970s and early 1980s, New Zealand had the highest per capita use of asthma drugs in the world (Pearce 2007: 45). It also had the highest rate of asthma deaths in the world, at three times that of other developed nations (Pearce 2007).

One of the new drugs was fenoterol, a high-dosage, short-acting beta2-agonist used to counter bronchial tightening and open up the airways. Never approved for use in the United States, fenoterol was introduced to the New Zealand market in 1976. It quickly cornered 40 percent of the national market share of beta-agonists, becoming more popular in New Zealand than anywhere else in the world. Almost as soon as the drug was introduced, however, New Zealand's asthma death rate began to rise, tripling over the course of the first three years (1976–1979).

A Wellington-based research team composed of clinical and epidemiological specialists Julian Crane, Richard Beasley, Carl Burgess, and Neil Pearce set out to study whether fenoterol might be responsible for the rising death rate. By early 1989, having completed the first case-control study of the spike in New Zealand's asthma mortality, they were persuaded that fenoterol was indeed responsible for the epidemic. But their findings initially met with resistance and even hostility among some members of the scientific community. According to Pearce (2007), fenoterol's manufacturer, Boehringer Ingelheim, actively attempted to suppress their results.

Many family physicians also expressed considerable resistance to the team's findings. Pearce later interpreted this as due to both physicians' natural reluctance to admit fault and their warm relationships with Boehringer Ingelheim, noting that, when the team's findings were made public,

We heard many reports of patients who had asked to be taken off the drug, but had been persuaded to stay on it by their doctors. Many doctors were expressing sympathy for the company rather than for their patients, and were concerned that the New Zealand branch might have to close down if the drug were withdrawn. . . . I heard people saying, "You don't bite the hand that feeds you." . . . The company's many years of advertising, funding of research and conferences, and regular contact with doctors were paying off. (2007: 128)

It wasn't until 1990 that fenoterol stopped being widely prescribed. In what has been called "an experiment in prevention" (Beasley et al. 1995), it was taken off of the list of government-funded drugs by the then minister of health, Helen Clark, effectively ending its use in the country. The effects were almost immediate: asthma deaths plummeted (Pearce et al. 1995).

At the same time that the team was working on proving the tragic effects of fenoterol, some of its members began to develop the first asthma action plans. Dr. Julian Crane explained to me the link between the two projects:

After we finished with fenoterol, we were big drivers for self-management to come in because nobody knows their asthma better than the person who's got it. And so we were very keen to drive [patients to take their own] peak flow measurements and when their peak flows change or their symptoms change, increasing the level of inhaled corticoste-roids and work on your asthma yourself. . . . We were doing things in New Zealand long before they were in Britain in terms of getting people to use peak flow meters [and] in the 1980s, the concept [of using action plans] got quite good traction, I think, as people did realize that when their bronchodilators stopped working, they needed to see some-body quickly because they were in trouble.

The person patients were supposed to see was a physician, and, hand in hand with action plans, there was an intensive drive to raise the skills of family physicians in their knowledge of asthma. This was the start of the present-day system in which family physicians are the linchpin of asthma care, with special-ists reserved for only severe or difficult cases.

What was initially a measure to get patients to the doctor in time soon be-came the standard for adjusting medication use. Patients and doctors became increasingly accustomed to the idea of patients making their own changes to dosage, ostensibly based on the instructions laid out in their action plans. Dr. Crane[1] is clear that widespread patient self-management is an outcome he ap-proves of, telling me, "I don't think many people in New Zealand would believe that [asthma] management is best done by the family doctor."

But whatever the strengths of self-management philosophies and policies, there are many faults in current self-management practices. As the Royal College of Physicians' review underscores, questions remain as to how care should best be divided between patients and doctors and at what point is medical expertise not only advisable but vital for ensuring adequate care. Self-management poli-cies give an indication of how self-management *should* run, but both experi-mental studies and clinical practices offer a different picture of it in practice.

Experimental Evidence: When Self-Management Becomes Collaborative Care

A surprising number of the scientific studies that proclaim the effectiveness of self-management do not actually leave patients alone to monitor and manage their asthma but assign a leading role in asthma management to physicians, nurses, or other medically trained professionals. Specifically, they provide test subjects with frequent, regular access to trained medical professionals who not only guide them through the tasks of "self-monitoring" but also offer one-on-one responses to their health needs. Indeed, reading across the grain, one of the key findings to emerge out of medical and social science studies of self-management programs is that *self-management works most effectively when it is no longer self-management but collaborative care.*

A British study by Ian Charlton and his colleagues (1990) purports to show the effectiveness of two aspects of self-management: patients measuring their peak air flow and charting their symptoms. In fact, the test subjects had weekly interviews with a nurse who checked their inhaler techniques and coached them on self-care strategies, giving advice on topics such as emergency care and how to stop smoking. Patients were offered even more frequent contact with the nurse "if she considered it necessary." (Charlton et al. 1990: 1356)

Similarly, in Wendyl D'Souza and his colleagues' New Zealand–based study of patients' use of credit-card-sized action plans, test subjects had continuous access to community health workers who "maintained contact with the participants, encouraged them to complete their diaries [documenting their asthma symptoms] and provided transport to attend the clinics if necessary" (1994: 1262). In their conclusions, D'Souza and his coauthors note that their study involved "longer, more informal clinic visits" than those usually available in the New Zealand health system. The authors conclude, however, that this did not influence the success of the trial as "all of these factors should be considered an essential element of any asthma management plan" (ibid.: 1264). In fact, "long, informal clinic visits," coupled with regular, routine outreach by community health workers and much less free transport to medical clinics, are facets of health care far removed from the experiences of most New Zealanders.

Neither of these clinical studies (and others like them, for example, Smith et al. 2007 in Australia) openly reflect on the fact that "self-management" seems to work best when it becomes a misnomer, involving frequent, and in some cases almost uninhibited, access to medical professionals. The literal and active *erasure* of the crucial role of professional guidance in studies supporting asthma self-management has, however, been demonstrated by Henriette Langstrup and Brit Ross Winthereik (2008). Langstrup and Winthereik analyzed a new online asthma self-management program in which Danish patients entered their peak air flow measures and respiratory symptoms online, following which they received automatic preprogrammed information on how to adjust their pharmaceutical intake. Patients' information was also made instantly available to their physicians, who could choose to intervene if necessary. When the online tool was made publicly available, Langstrup and Winthereik discovered that neither patients nor physicians found it useful. Physicians did not want to take on the extra workload of daily monitoring their patients' pharmaceutical use, and without their physician's input patients' interest in recording their symptoms quickly waned.

This was a surprise because in its trial phase the online program was tremendously popular. Its success, however, hinged on the intimate personalized relationships created between the researcher testing the program and the test participants. During the trial, participants used a "question box" feature to send questions or comments directly to the researcher, who proved to be both highly attentive and deeply concerned about their health and well-being. Exchanges between the researcher and the trial participants ranged from detailed recommendations on adjusting medication doses and one-on-one counseling on avoiding specific triggers to wishing a participant well on her upcoming university exams. When the online program went public, however, the question box feature was removed. This aspect of the trial was, moreover, erased from the published results as it was deemed inconsequential. In fact, Langstrup and Winthereik argue, the question box was key to the program's success and, when speedy one-on-one expert advice was eliminated, the success rate plummeted.

As these various studies reveal, self-management often works best when undertaken collaboratively rather than individually. The need for sustained professional involvement in "self-management" has been acknowledged through some asthma guidelines broadening of the term into "guided self-management" (Brussels Declaration on Asthma 2007) or "supported self-management" (British Thoracic Society 2014). What urgently needs to be clarified, however, is what this "guidance" or "support" should consist of, that is, what sort of regular input is needed from trained medical professionals, be they nurses, medical researchers, pharmacists, or respiratory specialists. Only when that is established can patients engage in more rigorous and complex forms of self-care, knowing that they have real avenues for seeking expert advice as needed.

Thus far, self-management guidelines have been unable to capture the complexities of real-life care practices. But although it is easy to be critical of any standards for oversimplifying a complex situation, to stop here would be to miss the point. Standards *must* simplify, or they cannot be effective (Timmermans and Berg 2003). What is more significant, however, is how such necessarily simplified standards come to motivate behavior by delineating morally laden ideals. The standard becomes not only something to be strived for but something that is expected to be achieved.

Activism for Empowerment

The ideal of patients engaging in self-care, as well as its practical manifestations in policies promoting self-management, did not come into being solely due to the efforts of scientists and medical professionals. A second strand of self-management's history lies in grassroots movements for patient empowerment. Just as health care for asthma was being devolved into the hands of patients, many patients (or, in the case of children, their parents) were actively seeking more control over their care. In New Zealand, in their campaign to engage patients in monitoring their own symptoms, Dr. Crane and his cohort had an unlikely set of allies in a group of parents, primarily mothers, of children with asthma who were intent on combatting the "patronizing" attitudes of medical professionals through the establishment of patient-run "asthma societies." In the process of educating themselves, some of these women became so intensively involved in health-care education that they later joined the ranks of the health professions.

Angela Scott was one of the earliest advocates for increased patient autonomy. In the 1970s, she lived in the small coastal city of Tauranga, raising two young children, one of whom had asthma. Frustrated by what she felt was an oppressive and elitist medical system, she was inspired by the activist spirit of the times to take a stand for patients' rights to self-determination. "The International Year of the Woman came," she recounted, "and it was the most exciting time, we were all doing things," and it felt like a real "'I can do anything' time." She became one of the founding members of a local asthma society and eagerly dived into the controversy they generated:

I used to go to and fro to these meetings and argue with these professors. It was full of doctors in Wellington [who] used to talk about these nice little societies, [where the women] can help make you cups of tea, and raise money ... And, I used to go down there and *argue* with these professors ... [as] it seemed to me ... that what we had to have was *more* than a group of people just supporting [the physicians]. *We* could manage asthma. You know, if *we* were given the right information about how you use inhalers and what they did, ... then these asthma societies could actually give information to the people themselves ... and *empower* the people to actually do something themselves.

One of the steps toward greater patient empowerment was the development of asthma action plans. Their introduction, according to Angela, was fraught as "doctors were never very happy about [action plans based on] peak flow meters. They think people are too silly to do [them properly]!... And a lot of people don't, of course.... So there's a fair bit of friction over who can be in charge." Nevertheless, Angela explained that the asthma society did not waver: "Our view was, and is, the patient is in charge."

Angela became so involved in the asthma society that she went from being a volunteer to becoming a paid respiratory educator. She described the move as an easy one, based on her strong belief that "you can learn anything. You don't have to be a nurse to learn. You know, you're not going to diagnose, but [do] all of the [other] things that need to be done." After putting herself through basic training in respiratory health care, she guided the society in applying for a contract from the local health board, following which they began to extend their services, conducting spirometry tests and providing advice and training to not only patients but also medical professionals. Angela recounted that, at first,

The doctors were patronizing.... But then, eventually, the doctors have come round now, and you'll find local doctors will say, "Just go to the asthma society—they'll do your spirometry for you and come back and tell us [the results]." Or they'll ring up and say, "What do I do about so and so?" And you know, we look up the notes or say, "Send them to us" and go back and advise them.

However, as today's local societies are staffed primarily by medically trained nurses, along with a few community health workers, when "doctors ring up" to get advice, they are no longer talking to parent-activists but fellow medical professionals. Political radicalism and the feminist movement energized mothers like Angela to demand more rights over their children's health. But as they became more vocal, their roles shifted. Along with the responsibility and oversight they demanded came not only accountability but *professional* accountability as qualified asthma educators.

Currently, approximately two dozen asthma societies are scattered across the country (see Figure 1.2). Their work is often paid for by regional health boards and other grant agencies. Financially, it is a precarious existence, and, although many of their representatives are intensely passionate about the care they provide, they are also very up front about not being able to cast their net widely enough. Two societies admitted to us that they keep relatively low public profiles because, if everyone who needs their services knew about them, they would be overwhelmed by too many clients.

Figure 1.2   Asthma Auckland, one of many asthma societies around New Zealand.
Photo by Revena Correll Trnka.

Angela's story depicts, in very gendered terms, how the initial hostility of (mostly male) doctors slowly gave way to begrudging acceptance of (mostly female) parent-activists, promoting the idea that patients should be active participants in their own care. And just as the activists were fighting for a dispersal of obligation out of the hands of physicians and into the hands of parents, scientists such as Julian Crane's group were trying to get patients more involved in their care. The results in both cases were the same: an emphasis on the patient as increasingly responsible for their own health.

Doctors for Patients' Choice . . .

Dr. Patrick McHugh is a general practitioner in Gisborne. With over two decades' experience working in family medicine, he is a very strong advocate for patient choice. "I aim to work from a patient-centered perspective," he explained, "and part of that is trying to guide patients regarding the different things they're doing that contribute to their health or disease, and giving them options as to how they can control or manage that. It's about developing more opportunities and approaches and choices for patients as to how they manage things while also reminding them of the consequences of behaviors that aren't so healthy. So instead of just closing one door and saying, 'You shouldn't be doing this,' we should really be opening other doors to give them more options."

Dr. McHugh went on to illustrate how this view is, in his thinking, a significant step forward from more traditional perspectives on medical authority. "If someone is coming from a doctor-centered framework, then they'll be perceiving themselves as the ones in charge, so they'll feel that they're responsible for the health outcomes, whereas in a patient-centered framework, the patient holds responsibility for their own health and the doctor's more of the advisor than the guru."

Katherine, a nurse and asthma educator, has a similar but more succinct description of her relationship to those who use the asthma societies' services. She explained, "I guess we give them the information [about various ways of coping with asthma] and then leave it with them to choose."

Some health-care professionals take a more extreme position. Dr. Mark Morris, a British- trained physician who has been practicing in New Zealand for over twenty years, argued passionately for the right of the patient to decide if and when he or she is ill. He explained,

From a medical perspective, one has to respect the fact that there's a lot of people out there with symptoms who never go and see a doctor, and they have the right to those symptoms. I don't have any right to intervene with somebody I see in the street because I think they need to be on treatment because they've not been to see me. The first step is seeking *permission* [to treat them]. In other words, [you wait until] they've made that psychological [step] and they say, "I think that I've got a problem that I want solved." And then there's a *contract* between the patient and the doctor where you come to see me and I try to help you with the symptom involved because you want [me] to.

Though often not as rhetorically colorful as Dr. Morris, many patients and parents of children with asthma offer similar perspectives on the importance of choice, autonomy, and patient–doctor partnerships, and indeed, as we shall see, some come to take charge of defining their own diseases, though often in ways that frustrate doctors. Although asthma educators and medical professionals speak highly about *partnership*, very few patients or parents of children with asthma express a desire to work *in partnership* with physicians. Instead, they are much more impassioned about the themes of choice, autonomy, and individual responsibility. For doctors, this often puts them in the position of either watching their patients take charge of their health even if they head off in directions they think are inadvisable or attempting to do what they can to wrestle back some modicum of control.

... and Doctors for Patient Compliance

Dr. Laura Wong, who recently completed her medical training and took up a position in an Auckland emergency room, was very frank about the struggles she faces in getting parents of children with asthma to follow her advice. "Sometimes," she sighed, "the daunting task with parents is that they know so much more about—" she stopped and corrected herself. "Well, maybe not so much the *disease* in general, but . . . about *their child's* own response to it and the disease *as it is for them*. It can be quite daunting because there's a lot of information out there and a lot of it is really bad information, so it's about sifting out false, popular beliefs . . . when the parents declare that *this* is obviously what they need. There is a balance you need to strike between them having a preconceived idea and them listening to your two cents' worth." At the same time, Dr. Wong is an enthusiastic supporter of self-management—although her description of it is one in which patients become very adept at carrying out their doctors' instructions.

Like Dr. Wong, many medical professionals describe self-management as a mixture of patient compliance and alertness. Patients can be in the driver's seat as long as they drive the way they are expected to. Despite the rhetorical emphasis on patient choice and autonomy, as in much of classic neoliberal theory, one is deemed only so "free" as to do what he or she should (Miller and Rose 2008).

Several decades of anthropological and sociological analyses of health have examined the ideologies inherent in discourses of *compliance* (and, in its later iterations, *adherence* or *concordance*). Soon after the concept of compliance became popular in the 1970s, sociologists and anthropologists suggested that the term *compliance* in and of itself assumes that the only appropriate behavior for patients is to follow or comply with doctors' demands, labeling those who do otherwise as "deviant," "careless," or "ignorant" and thus eliding patients' capacities to make reasoned, and reasonable, decisions about their care that may in fact differ from medical professionals' directives (Conrad 1985; Donovan and Blake 1992; Lerner 1997; Rouse 2010). As Peter Conrad asserts, the very term *compliance* mistakenly privileges the patient–doctor dyad and does not consider the range of social experiences that shape patients' decision making about pharmaceutical use. Rather than being noncompliant, patients may simply be reacting to social factors other than their doctors' care (Conrad 1985).

In contexts of increasingly neoliberalized health care, the already morally overburdened concept of compliance has taken on a new set of meanings as rates of patient compliance have become a benchmark for health-care audits (Dumit 2010) and even, in some cases, a key factor in calculating physicians' annual bonuses (Oldani 2010). Significantly, the widespread drive to improve patient compliance with pharmaceutical regimes is also a means of ensuring more robust pharmaceutical sales (Applbaum and Oldani 2010), leading pharmaceutical companies to have a direct interest in compiling their own noncompliance statistics.

The medical professionals we interviewed in New Zealand expressed their distress over patient noncompliance as part of their broader concerns over their patients' well-being rather than with respect to clinic or hospital audits or the prospect of salary bonuses. But regardless of the motivations driving their concern, its effects are to construct a Catch-22 in which patients, parents of children, and often children themselves, are expected to assume increasing amounts of responsibility over the daily monitoring and care of their conditions and yet also align not only their behavior but also their decision making with doctors' directives. When this is not the case, they are deemed noncompliant.

From Empowerment to Compliance:
The Work of Asthma Societies

Ironically, it has come to be the responsibility of asthma societies, which were founded out of the pursuit of patient empowerment, to compel patients to adhere to the medical regimes determined by their doctors. In most asthma societies, patient education is fundamental, and combating "patient noncompliance" is often the number one priority.

Significantly, although all patients are seen as potentially noncompliant, the primary groups singled out in discourses of noncompliance tend to be Māori and Pacific Islanders, both of whom are overrepresented in New Zealand's lowest economic strata. A few of the asthma nurses we spoke with were very blunt about their opinions on what they referred to as these "problem groups," whereas others expressed similar opinions in more circumscribed ways, by, for example, offering up descriptions of "noncompliant" patients, all of whom happen to be Māori, or in their depictions of "brown children" struggling to breathe.

That said, discourses of noncompliance are used more broadly to point the finger at any person from any ethnic group or economic background who is not using his or her medication as specified, for here, it is assumed, lies the answer to the problem of why their respiratory health is not improving. As Jean, a nurse-educator, encapsulated it, "We say [to patients], 'You're supposed to use your preventer night and morning, so if you look across the last few weeks, how many times, of say fourteen times in a week, do you use it?' And they say, 'Oh, six or seven.' Right. There's your first answer about why their asthma isn't under control—they're not compliant."

Such behaviors are often depicted as a personal failure on the part of patients and parents of children with asthma. The very term *noncompliance* is taken as indicative of a *lack* on the part of the patient or parent, a lack varyingly described as a shortcoming in understanding, desire, or discipline. In each case what is lacking is perceived as something within the persona of the patient who is deemed an inappropriate, irresponsible subject: if only these shortcomings can be overcome, there is the promise of achieving a "normal life" through the revolutionary capacity of drugs. As Jean bluntly stated, today "asthma can be really so well managed that it doesn't interfere with your life *at all.* It can be as simple as having the education and the understanding to manage it." Dr. Morris similarly argued that families need to stop looking for alternative remedies and resisting the use of steroids as it is only through regular medication use that "we're going to *make your life normal* so you can be exactly the same as all your mates."

One approach for countering patient complacency is to stress the potential negative effects of mismanagement. Jean explained, "I think that people are too accepting. So many people have asthma that it's 'just asthma,' and they don't actually realize that we lose about a hundred people a year in New Zealand through asthma deaths. And people with asthma themselves sweep it under the carpet." Katherine, another asthma nurse-educator, has a similar point of view, stating,

Some really don't understand the severity of it at all, saying, "It's only asthma, it's only asthma." . . . And some people are quite shocked, really, when you talk to them on the effects asthma has on the airways if it's untreated—you're *gonna* get scarring and remodeling of the airways . . . and some look as if they feel quite bad, like, "Oh gosh, I didn't know, oh gosh, I wish I'd given [my child] the preventer."

The other tactic is to highlight the positives of well-managed health. A number of nurses suggest that once people actually take their medication, they will see how healthy they can be. Jean offered a vivid example:

We had a ten-year-old Māori boy who came in. A normal NiOx [a test measuring exhaled nitric oxide level which indicates airway inflammation] is under twenty, and his was in the nineties. In those first visits, we do all those tests, and we speak to the parents and the child and go over how they're using their inhalers and the importance of the preventer. They go away with a little diary, and . . . they use their preventer every night and every morning for a fortnight. A fortnight later, he was like down in the fifties, and then down in the thirties. And the dad says to me, "We have a new son," because he's sleeping, he's concentrating, he's more energetic. There's a lot of people out there with asthma that's not putting them in hospital, but it's like having a little bit of a headache every day. They just don't know that they can breathe easier, you know.

The challenges, however, of compelling *unwilling* patients to adopt what nurses deem to be appropriate regimes of asthma management often lead to frustration and exasperation. "I don't know if they're against medication or if they believe in other methods of calming [their asthma]," Katherine stated, "But it *is* difficult. Because you're trying to persuade them into your [way of] thinking, aren't you . . . They just take the reliever as and when they need it, but [to get well] they just *have* to take the inhaled steroid every morning or every night."

Taken together, discourses of compliance relate a story of how combining efficacious drugs with well-informed patients who are willing to comply ensures that the lives of people with asthma remain "normal." In other words, the image that these discourses cast up is of a problem that *could easily be solved* if patients would only cooperate.

When All Care Is Emergency Care

But even for those who do their best to comply, self-management often poses an insurmountable set of challenges, many of which are structural. For families at the bottom of the financial scale, one reason why self-management often fails is fairly straightforward: patient–doctor partnership is unrealizable when patients are financially unable to see a physician. This is not because they do not have access to health care per se. New Zealand's public health care system ensures that hospital and emergency care is available to any citizen or resident.

Children under the age of thirteen receive free physicians' visits, and pharmaceuticals approved by Pharmac (the government's Pharmaceutical Management Agency) are either free or heavily subsidized.

Financially strapped families with older children or adults with asthma are, however, restricted by lack of funds from regularly having access to family physicians, most of whose work is in private practice. As a result, a significant number of patients, particularly from the Māori community, report not receiving medical care unless they are having an acute asthma emergency or are building up to one (Crengle, Pink, and Pitama 2007). Alternatively, families with limited resources will resort to using emergency services even when a crisis is not imminent (ibid.). As emergency room (ER) physician Dr. Wong explained, "The thing with the emergency room is [that] you'll find a lot of the time, it isn't *critical* per se. People come in because they ran out of medication at home and just need a prescription." Stopping by the ER to get a prescription might be free, but it means that these families usually do not receive sustained care from medical staff who can work with them over time to find the most appropriate solutions. Sandwiched in between emergency cases, such patients also often raise the ire of physicians and other staff for distracting attention away from more acute cases.

Even families with more financial resources often receive basic asthma care through the ER. Sometimes this is purely because the speed and severity of many children's first (or first few) asthma attacks necessitates emergency care. In other instances, however, families' lack of knowledge about the basics of how to treat asthma leads them to live through one emergency after another. Alley, a young, first-time mother, described that when Michael was two, his asthma "got much much worse, so that we were having to take him to hospital every two months or so. . . . [My] mum and dad said—because Dad had had asthma quite badly—that Michael was having to go to hospital way too much, and I needed to do something about it." It was thus family members, rather than hospital staff, who prompted Alley to visit her local physician.

Moreover, because of the costs charged by private physicians, many patients do not engage in follow-up care. Seeing physicians only when they are unwell means that patients often end up taking high doses of medication indefinitely as there is no mechanism for "stepping down" or scaling back their medication when they are feeling better, except for their own experimental attempts to do so. As Brenda, a nurse-educator, explained, "All too frequently, patients don't ever get reviewed about dropping their medication back down again. . . . A lot of people can be on a lot lower [doses] than what they are."

Indeed, many nurses and asthma educators make trenchant criticisms of what they refer to as physicians' lack of ongoing supervision of the patients in their care. Many of these criticisms center on the perceived laxity in dispensing pharmaceuticals, echoing some of the reasons patients give for not wanting to take medication. Jean, a nurse-educator, offered a personal example:

I had an experience with my daughter who is living in Wellington. She has a lot of sinusitis problems and went to an after-hours doctor who said to her, "Do you want antibiotics? Do you need an inhaler?" My daughter was twenty, and she said, "Well, you tell me," more or less. So this doctor prescribed a Ventolin inhaler and antibiotics. [He offered her] no education. Rachel went to the pharmacy and then she rings me up and, and says, "I've got this inhaler, what do I do with it?" And I said, "Are you wheezing?" And she said, "No, no, no, it's just my sinuses." So I explained how to use it if she needed to, but she actually didn't need it. She just used the antibiotics, and she came right. I asked her if I could ring the pharmacy and the doctor and blow them to smithereens—[they gave her] no spacer, no education, absolutely no advice on what to look out for or what to use.

Jean concluded, "It's nothing against our doctors generally—there's some *very* good doctors out there [who] are very proficient in asthma. But, if the patient goes back to the doctor and they say, 'Look, you know, it's not working for me, I'm using it ten times a day,' generally their answer will be to step them up [that is, increase their medication]. The physicians don't actually say, 'Can you show me how you're using the inhaler?' and check that they are using it right."

When physicians are unable to take on such responsibilities, it often ends up being the patients'—or in the case of children, their parents'—role to actively seek out information on when their medication should be lowered. This is hardly, however, the picture depicted by self-management guidelines, which clearly stipulate that regular reviews of medication by primary care providers are indispensable. The GINA guidelines, for instance, state that "ongoing monitoring" by medical personnel "is essential" for maintaining control of asthma symptoms, indicating that "typically, patients should be seen one to three months after the initial visit, and every three months thereafter" (GINA 2012a). Instead, it is not unusual for New Zealand patients to go for long periods phoning in requests for prescription refills and not having an asthma review for years at a time.

The lack of sustained relationships between patients and doctors is evident in how few New Zealanders mention a doctor by name. Many describe their medical care without referring to a specific doctor or practice, much less reflecting on the personality of "their doctor," underscoring that they might not have a sense of there being a specific doctor or set of doctors responsible for their health care. Unlike Czechs, who are intensively interested in the training and personality of "their doctor" and go to great lengths to cultivate good relations with them, here the "doctor" in the patient–doctor partnership model appears to be missing, filled in by the anonymous, faceless role of "medical services." Charlotte, a mother of two asthmatic children in her forties, was one exception, who noted with sadness the retirement of her favorite physician, precisely because of his very pragmatic, patient-centered approach. She said,

He was really good. If you went up on a Friday and kids were *starting* to get sick but they weren't quite bad, he goes, "Look, if they drop here's a prescription so you can go get what you need at the weekend, but if you don't use it, just rip it up." He was really good about giving you the information and letting *you* make the choice. . . . It makes a big difference having a doctor that doesn't just try and shove drugs on you.

Charlotte's concern over having "drugs shoved on you" by a nameless, faceless entity with whom one has no relationship, much less a sense of trust, reappears throughout New Zealanders' narratives of living with asthma. It is a product not of physician neglect but of a health-care system that prioritizes acute emergency intervention over sustained care, without recognizing the centrality of relationship building in health-care practices. It raises huge challenges not only for patients but also for doctors dealing with trying to convince people that they or their child have asthma and how best to attempt to treat it.

Politicizing Asthma

Much of the passion that first motivated Angela Scott to become involved in asthma societies continues to be voiced by the nurses who run the societies today. Indeed, many of them view their work as a form of political practice. Today's health-care system is, however, very different from forty years ago, and for many asthma educators the battle no longer consists of empowering patients to stand up against "patronizing doctors" but of empowering patients to get the best care within a financially driven medical system that is short on both time and money. The issue at hand isn't a state that *takes over* one's health care but rather a state that sometimes might not seem to *care enough*.

Many asthma society representatives laud the societies' free services, which allow them to step outside the monetary framework that underpins most of New Zealand's primary-level medical care. Julie, a nurse-educator in Christchurch, articulated this eloquently when she spoke, with a tone of almost angry defiance, about the importance of resisting the imperatives of profit-driven medical care. She said,

There is *quite* a lot of complacency about asthma in New Zealand, and people just live with a level of unwellness without realizing how much better it could be. As a practice nurse [in a physician's office], I never saw people for asthma education. When I came to this job [at the asthma society], the people that sought me out for asthma education had been to the same physicians' practice that I had come from, and I was totally unaware that those people had asthma. So [at the physicians'] they were going in, they were getting their inhalers, they were paying at the front desk and walking out the door. Nobody was ever saying, "Do you understand? Why don't you go to the practice nurse and she'll help you use your inhalers?" The cynical part of me says [that's because] it's just not income generating.

Other educators similarly describe their work as driven by their commitment to empower patients through education. Some of them take on the role of patient advocates, writing letters to housing courts to have clients moved out of damp, moldy homes or working on petitions to limit the spread of privet (a flowering plant whose pollen can cause breathing problems). Their political visions are often, however, curtailed by the societies' individualized approaches, the overriding focus on achieving patient compliance, and the fact that their work is often funded by government grants that are geared toward providing health services, not supporting political advocacy—factors that make using asthma societies as sites for political agitation a difficult challenge.

Tu Kotahi Māori Asthma Trust

One society that seems to have circumvented these barriers is Tu Kotahi, the only asthma society that focuses primarily on providing culturally sensitive respiratory care to Māori. Tu Kotahi conforms with the general attitudes of patient empowerment and compliance but adopts a significantly broader stance on what "asthma services" should entail.

Based in the Hutt Valley, near Wellington, Tu Kotahi was established as a result of the 1991 Māori Asthma Review, *He Mate Huango*, as part of an array of Māori-led initiatives to improve access to health services in Māori communities (Ellison-Loschmann and Pearce 2006). In addition to training clinical and nonclinical staff in culturally sensitive approaches to working with Māori, Tu Kotahi carries out its own patient outreach. The society's manager, Jeanette, is both passionate and philosophical about the effects that such patient education can have. "Small changes are okay," she explains. "It's not going to happen overnight when someone hasn't been taking their medication all their life. You're not going to be a miracle worker—they're not going to suddenly come to you in a week's time and be compliant."

Although Jeanette sometimes slips into the language of compliance, for the most part she avidly attempts to avoid the concepts of both *compliance* and *management*. The key in providing asthma care, she asserted, is for families "not to 'manage' as such but be able to live with their asthma so it doesn't become a burden on them." It is therefore important to her that Tu Kotahi's health workers actively engage in "turning some of the terminology around. So we used to get referrals that say *whānau* [extended families] aren't compliant. But now we often go out of our way to say it's not the *whānau*, it's the environment they live in that's uncompliant."

Some of this shift in attitude and focus onto *an environment that is uncompliant* appears to have arisen from Tu Kotahi's philosophy of keeping the door open to other issues that arise as part of asthma care. If, for example, a family is unable to regularly administer medication, Tu Kotahi's nurses approach the children's schools and identify staff who are willing to provide them with their preventative medication during the school day. They have also been known to call up physicians to request later appointment times for patients who can't make it to an early morning consultation, or to pick people up at home and drive them to their medical appointments.

But Tu Kotahi's purview goes far beyond making sure people get to the doctor on time to address some of the underlying structural issues that exacerbate their illnesses. Nonclinical staff at the society facilitate a wide range of services. As Jeanette noted, the need for budgeting services is particularly acute:

Most of our families couldn't afford to fill prescriptions or . . . go to the doctor. Or they *couldn't* go to the doctor because they had a bill and the doctor wouldn't see them until it was paid, and that can't happen. . . . [So we help them with] setting up realistic budgets, working out how much money's owed and advocating between the power companies or maybe the phone companies or maybe Housing New Zealand to set up payments so they can start paying off their debts. We even deal with evictions, going to court [on their behalf]—all of that has happened in the past.

In addition, some staff are involved in directly helping to ameliorate clients' living situations, setting up a free curtain bank to help keep homes warm and, at one stage, funding free home insulation. What is striking about Tu Kotahi is how much of this work is done in-house, by the staff themselves. Through the rubric of asthma, they are in fact addressing much wider issues of structural inequalities and the effects of poverty.

The Need for Structural Solutions:
Collective Versus Personal Responsibility

Many of the areas of need identified by Tu Kotahi—access to primary health care, creating healthier living environments, addressing the economic constraints of care provision—have been raised by health workers around the nation. As an Auckland asthma educator noted, many people with asthma are living in homes not fit for purpose, houses that "are moldy, damp, cold. You know, we've seen toadstools growing out of the walls. Sometimes there is no heating, [or] not enough money to actually *use* the heating. You can't expect patients to become well-managed even if they're compliant, living in that kind of ongoing dampness."

Some medical professionals put together their own piecemeal solutions to these problems, bending the rules as necessary. An ER nurse, for example, told me she gives out her private cell phone number to families who can't afford medication. By getting advance warning before they turn up in the ER, she can steer them through the process in a way that puts the least amount of strain on already stretched emergency services. This kind of advocacy, although laudable, works one patient or family at a time and is difficult to translate into larger-scale solutions. However, such structural issues require more comprehensive responses, and over the years there have been repeated moves by small groups of New Zealand scientists and other medical professionals to galvanize collective action, calling for better government policies to tackle poor-quality housing and other issues of deprivation associated with poverty (see, for example, Howden-Chapman et al. 2007).

Dr. Nikki Turner is a primary health-care specialist who focuses on children's health. She is also a member of the Child Poverty Action Group, a lobby group that advocates for broad structural solutions including changes in the tax structure, social security, and the minimum living wage, as well as more targeted health measures such as reducing the costs of children's health care. In many ways, the structural changes the group promotes address class disadvantage in general rather than the plight of children per se. The move to highlight *child* poverty is, however, a politically motivated effort to pressure the government to act in the interests of the seemingly most innocent members of society who are often unable to take responsibility for their own care and are thus most in need of government protection. But, as Dr. Turner points out, this effort is not always successful, lacking in luster when put up against the ideal of personal responsibility.

When we met at her office in the Otago Medical School buildings in Wellington, Dr. Turner explained that one of the key obstacles to garnering wider support for new social policies with respect to childhood asthma is the government and the public's shared attitudes about collective versus personal responsibility. As she sarcastically put it, "The government feels it doesn't need to worry about kids' health as it will be taken care of by the family and, if not by the family, then this is the wrong kind of person to worry about." Ironically, she described current campaigns to promote policies addressing the structural factors that have an impact on children's respiratory health as running up against the very value that asthma activists once worked so hard to promote: personal autonomy. "One of the big drivers around asthma in New Zealand would be parental responsibility," Dr. Turner noted. Public attitudes, she suggested, tend to be "that asthma rates in New Zealand are crap . . . because parents are feckless. . . . Every now and then you hear of someone dropping dead and people think, 'Oh, their parents didn't manage that properly,' rather than looking at the bigger issues."

Indeed, holding the family responsible for children's health is part and parcel of neoliberal approaches. Neoliberal philosophy may foreground the autonomous, individual subject as the master of their fate, but, as Rose (2006) has argued, there is often an implicit assumption in policies promoting responsibilization that, when in need, individuals will in fact be supported by other family members. For the most part then, within neoliberal discourses, children come to index *familial* responsibility, representing neither the idealized (but unrealizable) individual neoliberal subject nor the concern of the broader community as they do in some other cultural contexts. Not everyone, however, has a family that is willing, or able, to provide a support network, and those who don't come to bear the full brunt of such individualizing solutions.

Personal and familial responsibility are, according to Dr. Turner, the values that drive the typical middle-income white New Zealander's resistance to viewing children's respiratory health as a collective issue. She explained,

If I'm reasonably well off and my kid has got asthma, [I see it as] an illness [that can be treated very simply] like a broken leg. And if that poor little snotty-nosed brown kid down the road has got asthma—that's nothing to do with me. It's *their* living conditions . . . it's the parents' fault that those kids are [sick]! [Most people think], "I am not responsible for that little poor brown baby down the road. It's *not* my responsibility those parents can't sort their shit out. They're just lazy and not working hard enough." *That* ethos, I think, still runs through New Zealand *very* strongly.

In the slippery confluence of race and class, financial stability, and moral worth that runs through the response of Dr. Turner's imagined "New Zealander," we see one of the end points of neoliberal discourses of personal autonomy. Although there are many in New Zealand who do actually care about the fate of "the child down the road," Dr. Turner's depiction of the harsh logic of personal responsibility conjures up a bleak image of the flip side of patient empowerment: whereas some are indeed empowered through the control granted to them by self-management, others not only find themselves unable to cope but are effectively cut off from the possibilities of making collective demands on the state for the care they need.

*   *   *

In the Royal College of Physicians' review, Dr. Partridge concludes that it is the responsibility of physicians to take up the challenge of fighting against "complacency" and do all they can "to ensure that good care is equally available to all" (RCP 2014: vii). But to do so would require attending to issues that lie outside of the scope of empowering patients and consider the limits of self-management policies, both in terms of the diversion of public attention away from structural problems such as poverty and the ways in which self-management has come to be redefined, often by the most ardent supporters of patient rights, as another route to compliance. Medical practice has indeed broadened to include patients' voices. But although strategies such as self-management offer tools for increased patient engagement, in practice, the overwhelming focus on pharmaceutical compliance overshadows the possibilities of enabling patients to reshape their care, much less to be "drivers" in control of the process. The asthma societies that were founded across New Zealand as a radical move to democratize medical practice have ironically become professional providers of medical services whose work focuses predominantly on compelling patients to adhere to their medication. And yet, their radical potential remains, as seen through the work of nurses and other activists who rally around not only patient education but also the need for broader, structural change. Health reforms ostensibly focused on increasing personal responsibility have, in fact, opened up a new set of struggles around how to best ensure effective health care. Patients may now have more of a voice in their care, but the crucial questions of how to negotiate between patients' desires and their lived knowledge of their bodies and their health and medical providers' professional expertise remain unresolved, instead shifting into another register.

There is, of course, another actor in this story from whom we have heard little so far: the asthma sufferer. Like doctors and nurses, many patients embrace self-responsibility, but they often have a very different perspective of what it entails. Although some are daunted by the intricacies of "working the system," others come to terms with self-management by searching out medical knowledge and also taking on increasing amounts of personal oversight for their own care. In fact, many describe making their own medical diagnoses, experimenting with pharmaceuticals, and independently stepping up or down the dosages of medication. In doing so, they extend the limits of "self-management" in ways that doctors and policy makers often cannot envision.

Chapter 2

Domestic Experiments

When Parents Become "Half a Doctor"

NEW Zealand's embracing of neoliberal policy reforms has created a society in which the values of patient autonomy and self-responsibility go nearly unquestioned. Despite physicians' and nurses' interests in enforcing "compliance," patients today have much more of a say in how they and their bodies are treated than they had in the past. In many cases, they have become not just recipients of care but authors of their own care. They do so, however, without any formal training in basic health care, relying primarily on their own ever-evolving experiences and experiments with pharmaceuticals and other medical resources.

For many New Zealand families, the centerpiece of how they respond to childhood asthma is through the development of familial regimes of care that focus not only on keeping children well but also on preserving cultural ideals of "normal" childhoods. These regimes underscore widely held social assumptions that the primary onus of responsibility for ensuring care rests within the family, with health-care activities predominantly taken up by those whose preexisting ties are based on relations of love and care. Care thus has two valences here, indicating both health *care* and *affects* of care.

Although the child with asthma is the focus of attention, a key figure in this dynamic is the "parent-expert" who negotiates and undertakes their child's care; if a certain kind of child is being cultivated in this process, so too is a certain kind of parent. Much has been written about the rise of the "patient-expert" who takes command of his or her illness and shares authority with medical professionals (Dumit 2012; Epstein 1995). But in cases involving children and youth, both legally and practically, authority, accountability, and responsibility for dealing with health care are differently distributed. In suggesting we think about the figure of the *parent*-expert (Trnka and McLaughlan 2012), my intention is to explore the privileged role of the parent in creating a terrain in which pharmaceuticals become part of the medico-normality of childhood. I argue that in the case of asthma, care practices are not only *vested* in kinship networks but often *arise* out of familial experiments aimed at determining how to preserve normality. The child is an important subject in these processes of trial and error, as are his or her siblings, aunts and uncles, grandparents, and father, but most often the central figure is the mother. Although many parents are, moreover, initially overwhelmed by and even fearful of being in control of their children's asthma care, most rise to the challenge, many in ways that make them feel in control and even empowered, despite the ongoing struggles and confusion that taking on such responsibility often entails. It is not uncommon for parents to openly confront medical professionals over their differing perspectives on care, with the most frequent point of contention being pharmaceutical use.

In some respects, parents' views on medication echo those of medical professionals as they often employ drugs as the easiest means of enabling a "normal" childhood. Like doctors and nurses, parents look at markers such as being able to play sports or school attendance as indicative that their children are thriving and becoming the children, and ultimately the adults, they should be. But although doctors tend to wholeheartedly promote the *efficacy* of pharmaceuticals, many parents are caught in a conundrum. The *efficaciousness* of drugs is usually not in question—most parents generally agree that taking drugs, including corticosteroid preventative treatments, will at least temporarily improve their child's respiratory function. A few want more or different drugs (such as antibiotics) or different modes of delivery (such as nebulizers), convinced that they know their child better than any medical official.

A significant number are, however, worried that taking too many drugs is effectively subsuming their child's health and overall well-being to the profit-motivated prerogatives of pharmaceutical companies. Parents who have these concerns are questioning not necessarily the efficacy but the responsibility of using long-term prevention regimes; they wonder whether, in allowing the daily use of these drugs, they are joining doctors, nurses, and asthma societies in acting irresponsibly toward their children by setting them on the path of seemingly never-ending daily drug consumption. In doing so, they contest medical authority and aim to subvert what they see as the dominance of pharmaceutical companies in determining health-care measures, from diagnosis to ongoing preventative care, based on profit margins. Another way of looking at parental "noncompliance" is thus to consider how some parents are attempting to act responsibly in the face of an irresponsible and unaccountable medical establishment that promotes drugs as the solution without enabling adequate processes for "stepping down" drug doses when necessary and thus potentially endangering children's health.

In this respect, many parents engage in what Italian philosopher Antonio Gramsci referred to as "good sense" critiques of hegemonic structures. Gramsci argued that, as part of everyday practice, (lay) people develop extensive understandings of the worlds in which they live. Although some of these remain in the domain of immediate, knee-jerk "commonsense" reactions to their surroundings, others are refined through critical reflection, forming the basis of what Gramsci referred to as "good sense" or a homegrown "critical and coherent conception of the world" (1971: 324). Such viewpoints provide a counterpoint to the hegemonic or dominant perspective that promotes pharmaceuticals as the sole solution to illness and clearly merit further consideration than the label "noncompliance" suggests.

Much has been said of the downsides of neoliberal relations of care, in particular the way they can leave those who are in need of care without ongoing medical support. One of the most influential arguments is Annemarie Mol's *The Logic of Care* (2008), in which Mol demonstrates how health-care policies that promote concepts such as "choice" and "empowerment" can burden patients with the task of decision making when they are least able to do so. Moreover, as Mol and other authors have shown, despite concerted attempts by health authorities and patients themselves to embrace more patient autonomy and choice, in many cases such rhetorics prove illusory, masking the more open-ended nature of relationships and, in some cases, dependencies that are desired by both patients and medical providers (Davis 2012; Kaufman 2005).

Although many of these dynamics are evident in asthma self-management in New Zealand, there is also an undercurrent of proud authority in how parents and patients engage in their own care. Self-management policies can and do lead some families to take charge of their own care in ways that affirm their abilities to steer through childhood coping with a potentially life-threatening illness. Responsibility here cuts both ways—it can overwhelm those unable or unwilling to manage their own care, and it can lead to granting more control to those who rise to the challenge, in some cases acting as a mode of empowerment as parents tailor health-care routines, determining what constitutes emergencies and what is just part of normal, everyday living. Taking matters into their own hands, parents refute, embrace, or demand pharmaceuticals, and in some cases recast diagnoses—all in ways that radically extend the meaning of "self-management" beyond what health authorities and policy makers have in mind.

Parent-Experts and the Crafting of Domestic Policies of Care

Chronic illness in childhood requires a distribution of responsibilities. On the one hand, there is a widespread social desire and often the *need* to involve children in their own care, particularly as children transition out of the home to attend day care or school. On the other, as in all cases involving children and dependent youth, legal and social accountability are vested across a range of actors, and, in most contexts, parents or other legal guardians remain socially and legally responsible for accessing treatment for sick children and enacting home-based care (Buford 2004; Rich, Patashnick, and Chalfen 2002).

In New Zealand, mothers tend to take up the majority of these tasks. Sally, mother of nine-year-old Adam, explained that in terms of her son's care, "It pretty much has always fallen to me. . . . My husband will do stuff, like hear him coughing in the night and go and give him his Ventolin. But in terms of deciding the *policy* of what we do as opposed to the immediate treatment, that's pretty much me."

Another example is Charlotte, a stay-at-home mother in her forties who has three daughters under the age of five, two of whom have asthma. Charlotte is married to Daniel, a police detective whose long working hours often keep him away from home. She explains that Daniel knows how to deal with the girls' asthma, "but I always have to tell him how much they need . . . I tell him, 'Look, just give her two puffs through the spacer, or give her six puffs and break them down into three rounds.' . . . I'm with the kids all the time, so I know where they're at."

The gendered nature of care is partly due to the fact that, in families with young children under the age of five who are not in day care, it is most commonly the mother or another female caregiver who contributes most of their daily care (Mariskind 2014). Even with school-age children, however, health-care decision making tends to remain a predominantly female activity, with asthma educators and medical personnel noting that they see many more mothers than fathers accompanying their children into doctors' offices.

But mothers—and fathers—do much more than bring their children to doctors. Indeed, for many parents, taking care of a child with asthma is less about enabling access to medical professionals than it is about becoming an ultimate authority on their child's health. To do so, they develop family-specific knowledge and expertise. Becoming a parent-expert, moreover, is not just about gathering generalized advice from books, magazines, or the Internet, but about developing an in-depth knowledge of the personal and familial shape of asthma, relevant to oneself and one's children. The basis of such knowledge is often kin-based experiments in care, engaging in trial-and-error processes that become guides for coping with both chronic and emergency situations. Jane, for example, described regularly doubling her son's dose of Ventolin based on her sense that he wasn't able to inhale enough of it. Other mothers spoke of preempting doctors and ordering antibiotics off the Internet.

There is a distinct sense of experimentation at play here. Parents, not receiving the instructions they need or eschewing the limited written action plans that doctors give them, discover for themselves what combinations and timings work for their children. Akin to Annemarie Mol, Ingun Moser, and Jeanette Pols's notion of "tinkering," they engage in "attentive experimentation" (2010: 13) with pharmaceuticals and other measures, crafting together a regime of practices they can rely on. The "expertise" of these parents thus transcends their immediate responses to health-care crises to involve a focused and attentive cultivation of knowledge or "good sense" through acts of experimentation that, it is hoped, will provide adequate guidance for future care. The results of their experiments are, however, never generalizable, nor are they intended to be. Rather, they are intended to determine a highly specific set of practices that works to keep one child well and one family functioning within the bounds of normalcy. However, what exactly is seen as "working" and providing a good, or "good enough" (cf. Mol, Moser, and Pols 2010:13), result often differs from what asthma educators and medical professionals might deem as markers of success.

Intimate Ties: The Bodies of Mothers and Children

Faced with mastering new and often frightening situations, parents and children cobble together shared familial regimes of care. Often these regimes develop out of parents' (and in particular mothers') knowledge of their child's individual condition and responses, as well as their own embodied respiratory experiences.

Mothers frequently describe how they acquire very intimate knowledge of their child's asthma symptoms. As Charlotte put it, "My kids aren't the ones where you have a severe asthma attack and have to dial an ambulance. It's all a slow, progressive [change in] their breathing—they start sucking in at the base of their neck. It just creeps up on them slowly, and their breathing gets a bit more labored, and labored, and labored."

Jane, a "postie" or mail carrier who was raised on a farm in the South Island and is now in her early fifties, remembers well her son's struggles with asthma as he was growing up. She can still describe the onset of John's respiratory distress in minute detail: "You would usually first detect the wheeziness—you would hear this kind of *eeeeeeeeeee, eeeeeeeee*, but also you would often be able to tell just from his demeanor. He was starting to kind of tighten up. When he was starting to fight for breath, you couldn't touch him. He didn't like you coming near him."

Jane is one of many mothers who noted her children's tendency to hide their symptoms. As Alley, a stay-at-home mother of two children, ages five and three, related: "The thing with both of them is [that] they just go really quiet at the start of an attack—it's not like they run up to me and say anything! So I have to really listen out for the wheezing—they will just be sitting quietly and wheezing. I also lift up their shirts, and if they're having an asthma attack . . . you can see they're trying to suck in air." Children's secretiveness over bodily distress has been documented in other New Zealand contexts. Julie Park (2013), for example, describes how young boys with hemophilia hide the effects of a bleed from their mothers, who similarly engage in acts of watchful attentiveness.

Mothers often view their failure to spot their child's predicament, even when it is being concealed, as a dereliction of their maternal obligations. One mother who didn't recognize her daughter's condition was Iris, whose daughter Wei Ming suffered from a mild form of asthma as a young child but was not diagnosed until she left home at the age of nineteen. Iris expressed deep regret over having missed the signs and even chided Wei Ming, who is now in her mid-twenties, for not sharing with her her symptoms. In trying to explain how the condition came to be overlooked, Iris and her daughter engaged in the following exchange:

Iris: [*To the interviewer*] We weren't particularly [physically] active—we walked the dog together, she did dancing. [*To Wei Ming*] Did you ever have pain when you danced?

Wei Ming: I don't think so. I used to have it on cold mornings sometimes.

Iris: You never told me.

Iris's dismay over not knowing her daughter was suffering is suggestive of both the limitations that mothers face in their efforts to keep tabs on what is happening in their children's bodies and the daunting sense of responsibility many of them take on.

It is perhaps easier for mothers who have asthma themselves and can draw on their own experiences to set up care regimes for their children. Mary, for example, described how her own asthma helped shape the care of her twenty-year-old son:

Up until [his first asthma attack] he would wheeze from time to time, but he never needed Ventolin. But this one time, he was *really* bad—so bad that I said, "He needs a nebulizer." *Fortunately, because I've been through it, I knew what to ask for and what to do.* So I took him to the emergency room, and there he was given the nebulizer and Ventolin. . . . He used the Ventolin for a couple of days, but now I keep telling him that he should carry it on him, because *I know* how difficult it is if you have [an attack].

Mary shifted between describing her son's condition and her own, often melding the two together. Other mothers who don't have asthma themselves similarly cast themselves—both discursively and sometimes physically—into the position of their children in order to respond to their conditions. In describing her infant daughter's asthma attack, Sangeeta described *herself* as "coughing nonstop," stating,

Angela was six months [old] when she got her first bout. It was nonstop coughing . . . You wait for four, five days, and it doesn't go [away], and you're coughing nonstop. You're awake; you can't go to sleep because you're just coughing, coughing. And then her breathing—I used to check her breathing. . . . It's horrific, I tell you, when they're so young and they can't say whatever they're feeling. You feel so helpless. You feel like *you're* feeling breathless. You actually do.

Alley, on the other hand, described practicing breathing exercises taught to her by an asthma nurse to simulate the sensations of an attack. "You just keep on breathing in, again and again, without breathing out," she recounted. "It really helps with trying to understand what they're going through."

Sometimes, however, the focus on personal experience and personal knowledge can backfire when new symptoms and new trajectories are not recognized, even in oneself. Charlotte described her shock when an asthma attack she had while pregnant landed her in hospital on a nebulizer: "When I was a kid, I never, ever had a major asthma attack. If it was uncontrolled I just ended up with bronchitis, because it would slowly, progressively get worse, but you never sort of see it as an emergency! . . . I didn't even realize that could happen until I was grown up—it was like, 'Crikey! That can happen?'"

Stroppy Mothers

Although most of mothers' decision making is carried out behind closed doors, direct confrontations with medical professionals are not uncommon. Often they are described as leading to an increased sense of authority and power on the part of parents who successfully assert their perspectives on their child's care. Jane told a vivid story of her family's emergency room encounters to which she attributes subsequent changes in the policies governing her local hospital's intake procedures, allowing children who are known to have asthma to go directly to the children's ward for care:

Whenever we knew that John was really bad, we took him straight to hospital, but then we would find that we would have to sit in A&E [Accident and Emergency] and wait until it was our turn and answer all these questions. After the second or third time, we knew he needed to go to the children's ward and be put on the nebulizer, but there was this obstacle in the way. So one day, out of sheer desperation and bloody-mindedness, we bypassed A&E and went straight to the children's ward . . . The matron came out and said what were we doing there? We said, "He needs to be dealt with. We've been here before and we know what you need to do for him." And she said, "But you've got to go through A&E first," and we said, "That's really silly, we know he needs to be up here." . . . And they reluctantly took him.

Jane finished her story by recounting how "when we went back for checkups, we'd [often] get a registrar [a specialist still in training] who often didn't really know [enough] . . . and you found that actually after a while *you* were telling the registrar what it was that you needed a prescription for."

For mothers like Jane, their intimate knowledge of their children's asthma and responses to medication leads them to view themselves as being as competent as, or even more so than, the physicians they deal with. They are also, however, very aware of the negative effects of their behavior on physicians or nurses who often find them overly demanding: a number of mothers declared, "I became a bit of a pushy mum!" or "I was getting quite stroppy with the doctors." But such "pushiness" is, they feel, justified when their knowledge of their child matches or exceeds the knowledge and capabilities of medical staff. Like Jane, many described their demands as being highly effective in changing medical personnel's treatment plans.

These dynamics are encapsulated in a story recounted by Sangeeta, whose infant daughter was frequently in and out of hospital. The process of learning exactly what her daughter needed when she suffered respiratory distress and standing up to physicians to demand it felt so significant that Sangeeta characterized herself as having become "half a doctor." She described her typical interactions with medical personnel when her daughter was having trouble breathing:

I've told her doctors, "Look, if she needs an antibiotic, she gets an antibiotic. I don't want to wait!" Because when we went to the hospital, they just kept giving her Panadol [paracetemol] and [putting her on the] nebulizer. . . . But the minute she's got a fever, I know that you need to give her the antibiotic because I know how bad it can get. . . . [But] initially the GPs [general practitioners or family physicians] were not prescribing antibiotics, and so I told them, "I want her to have antibiotics." I was not going to take that chance. *I was half a doctor by then*, because you know your child. And then they realized that she needs it, so after that it was no problem.

Minimizing Threats

As with Sangeeta and Jane, usually the focus of parent-experts' activities is on figuring out the most appropriate use of pharmaceuticals, though some families also put effort into recognizing and minimizing triggers. Despite the wide availability of allergy tests, most parents describe this process as similarly built out of years of familial experience, developed out of trial and error.

Having a family regime does not mean that everyone in the family who has asthma treats his or her asthma in the same way, as what triggers one family member may not affect others. In some cases, moreover, families engage in competing interpretations about what triggers a particular family member. In the Prasad family, both thirteen-year-old Kavita and her father, Ajay, suffer from asthma. Although everyone in the family accepts that Ajay, unlike Kavita, reacts to an unidentified plant in their garden, the possibility of the family cat also being a trigger is still in dispute:

Ajay: Every time I work in the garden, I get it [an asthma attack]. I can't throw out all my plants, no way, so I'd rather take a puffer. I wear a mask . . . [but] it's no use. I can't identify the source of this pollen in the garden.

Nisha (Ajay's wife): It's different things. Sometimes he'll come down in the morning and Aces [the cat] will come in, and he'll pick up Aces and hug him and next thing you know he starts sneezing. So Aces sets it off sometimes.

Ajay: I know it's not Aces.

Nisha: I think sometimes, *sometimes* it is.

Ajay: No. It's not the cat.

Nisha: No? I think sometimes you pick him up and you start sneezing straight away.

Kavita: Aces might just have pollen on him though.

Ajay: You've got a point.

Discovering triggers is not always straightforward and can, particularly when involving family pets, be fraught with unwanted emotional consequences. Some parents and asthma sufferers never manage to identify which particular triggers are at work, whereas others are unwilling to reorganize their lives to avoid them. For those who do, this can involve a careful weighing up of different options. As Nisha said of Kavita, "A lot of people would tell me, 'Uh! Your girl has got asthma and you're keeping a cat in the house.' And I'm thinking, 'Well, you know, you've got to weigh it.' I mean she's able to manage it, and as long as we can stay on top of it, I think the enjoyment she's going to get out of having a pet is going to far outweigh [any negative effects]."

Pharmaceutical Solutions

Like Nisha and Ajay, many people find that using pharmaceuticals is by far the easiest way of coping with asthma. New Zealand nurse-educator Brenda expressed frustration over the Australian government's advice to asthmatics to close their windows in the evening and thus reduce the amount of pollen entering their houses when one could just "keep things normal and use an allergy spray." Similarly, many parents consider it crucial to retain the ability to partake in "normal activities" by means of using relievers and/or preventers. This is hardly surprising given the rapidly increasing acceptance of long-term use of pharmaceuticals across Western nations (Dumit 2012; Martin 2006).

The standard of care outlined in GINA's asthma care protocols usually in-volves "the daily, long-term use of controller medications to keep asthma well-controlled" combined with a reliever medication, such as Ventolin, used on an as-needed basis (GINA 2014: 92). In actual fact, patients' use of pharmaceutical remedies frequently proceeds in one of two divergent directions: either they engage in routinized compliance with daily regimes of preventative medication or they craft together their own approaches, foregrounding the use of emergency reliever medication.

For most families, daily preventative drug regimes are the preferred means of keeping things normal. This is the case not only in New Zealand but also in the United States (Clark 2012) and the United Kingdom (Prout, Hayes, and Gelder 1999). It is important to note, however, that often the incorporation of daily drug regimes into one's life is *initially* seen as anything but normal. As with anything that is *consciously* constructed, achieving normality through pharmaceutical intake stands, in and of itself, outside the unreflective norm until the drug use becomes routinized and fades into the background, a dynamic that most doctors and nurses and many parents actively strive to achieve. Asthma nurses frequently describe struggling to explain to families not only how inhalers work but also how to insert an inhaler into a spacer, the importance of rinsing one's mouth after inhaling steroids, and the necessity of carrying Ventolin with you wherever you go. None of these habits is seen as easy at the outset; they are techniques that need to be learned and mastered and then routinized to be effective. Asthma nurses are not the only ones focused on this task, and there are a number of other means for making drug regimes and inhaler techniques both familiar and comfortable.

One very overt method used by drug manufacturers is child-friendly marketing. Laura, one of the research assistants on this project, has very fond childhood memories of her brother's asthma inhaler embossed with the figure of Dr. Beco, a cartoonlike character of a doctor with green hair. During the interviews she conducted, Laura sought to find someone else who shared these memories and finally found a willing subject in James, a student in his mid-twenties:

Laura: Do you remember Dr. Beco?

James: Oh yes!

Laura: And his green hair?

James: And he may have had a spaceship.

Laura: And he came with those little Becotide magical discs.

James: That's right, and it really went to the next level with Dr. Beco because your inhaler could be embossed with your name if you sent it away to the Beco Club . . . I had an inhaler named "James" . . . And I *really* enjoyed it.

Although highly effective with children (and sometimes their parents), this kind of targeted marketing that links symbols of childhood with asthma care can be ironic for adults who get forced into a world of cartoon characters when they are in medical distress. The perceived connection between asthma and childhood in New Zealand is such that twenty-six-year-old Samantha related that when she goes into the emergency room suffering from an asthma attack, "I feel silly . . . because it's usually little kids they expect, and last time I was in there the nebulizer had Thomas the Tank Engine on it. I'm sure the doctors are like, 'What are *you* doing in here? You're a grown-up, you should be over this by now.'"

Regardless of whether inhalers are embossed with Dr. Beco, they are the preferred way that families keep things "normal." And when it works, many parents are delighted with the outcome. Sally, whose son Adam suffered from very severe asthma for a number of years, credits her son's reliever with allowing him to have a normal life like everyone else. When asked if she takes any other measures to protect him from having an asthma attack, Sally laughed and replied, "Oh no, no, no, we don't like, heat the house all winter or anything. He runs around in the rain, in the cold, like everyone else. He goes swimming whenever he wants to, even if it's freezing. He does those sorts of things. But that's because we *can* control it with Ventolin and Flixotide. . . . We just take his Ventolin with him, and he does everything that everybody else does."

Indeed, in many ways, Sally's actions uphold the values widely associated with the typical "Kiwi," or New Zealand, childhood. Going barefoot and swimming outdoors even in cold weather are both aspects of how many New Zealanders envision childhood should be. (See Figure 2.1.) Emphasizing the importance of not "cotton-wooling" children but allowing them to develop a rugged, physically robust constitution that can survive the outdoor elements (Tap 2007), the role of caregivers is to step back and allow children to grow into what are seen as their "natural" capacities. In local terms this is often described as "leaving well enough alone," on the basis that as long as a child can get by, in

Figure 2.1   One of the facets of a "normal Kiwi childhood": youth at a popular swimming spot.
Photo by John Michael Correll.

the end "she'll be right" (everything will be fine). Like many other parents, Sally strives to see her son achieve this normality, even if it is a normality dependent on the ingestion of drugs.

Inculcating Medico-Normality

"Medico-normality" refers to the routinization of pharmaceutical regimes as a means of achieving perceived notions of normality. This sort of routinization is a learned behavior, taught to children by their parents, who keep tabs on how often they take their medication and also teach them how to respond to symptoms with pharmaceuticals. Medico-normalities can focus on emergency-only care, preventative regimes, or a mixture of both—either way, "being normal" comes to be seen as most easily achievable via the use of foreign substances. Across a number of health systems, there is an acute awareness of the need to "unclog" medical offices and keep patient–doctor interactions—and costs—at a minimum, resulting in a growing social and medical acceptance of relying on increased levels of pharmaceutical use (cf. Fitzgerald 2012; Luhrmann 2000). In many cases, families also welcome pharmaceuticals for their efficacy, speed, and ease of use.

But no matter how normalized pharmaceuticals have become, incorporating them into one's routine is not always straightforward. Often parents go to great lengths to teach children how and when to use these substances appropriately. Many mothers spoke of repeatedly cajoling their children to take their medications. Others had to go through their own struggles to accept medication as a daily part of their children's lives. As one mother put it, "A lot of people don't like taking [preventative inhalers] because, at the end of the day, it is a steroid. But if it's going to help you with your everyday life, go ahead and have your Flixotide or your Seretide . . . You've got to do whatever works for you."

After a while, many parents welcome the sense of ease they derive from maintaining drug regimes. Charlotte explained how it works in her family, where she and two of her children are asthmatic: "You get repeats on your prescription, and so you get a prescription for three [people] and then three repeats, so you actually get a prescription for nine [inhalers at a single doctor's visit]. It's quite good because I have one for me, one for Jesse, and one for Caitlin, so if I run out, it's quite handy. . . . And I've got four or five of spacers. I've got one in the car normally this time of year, through the autumn and winter months, and I carry one on me at all times." At home, administering Ventolin has become almost automatic for Charlotte: "It's like at the point now where if they are a bit wheezy in the night, I can give them the Ventolin in their sleep and they don't actually wake up anymore." Not only has Charlotte laid out a strategy for making sure that the inhalers and spacers she needs are always on hand, but asthma drugs have become so routinized in her family's life that they can be administered to her children while they sleep.

The Responsible Child

Although parents often remain central in negotiating the dispensation of drugs to young children and teenagers, they also speak of the importance of handing over the oversight of daily care to their children. Inculcating self-responsibility is widely seen as a positive attribute, albeit one that poses a difficult, if not impossible, challenge, as parents recount fearing that too much responsibility might have a negative impact not only on their child's health and physical well-being but also their emotional development. For many parents, *care* thus emerges as a multifaceted practice that entails a careful reckoning of just how much responsibility for health care should be divested to a child at any given point (cf. Buford 2004).

The notion of the entirely self-managing child appears alluring but often more in a rhetorical sense than a practical one. Chris Trawley, father of an asthmatic son and a Buteyko specialist who works with asthmatic children, related, "When someone comes in at the age of fourteen, the first thing I say is, 'Whose asthma is it?' And they go, 'It's mine.' 'Okay,' [I say], 'so who should be mostly responsible for it?'"

Similarly, Ajay vests responsibility in his thirteen-year-old daughter Kavita, complimenting her as "a pretty good kid as far as we're concerned, because she's kept herself well over the years." Nisha, Kavita's mother, elaborated: "She has managed it herself. I'm constantly dinging into her head that it has to be managed by you, not by me. I'm not up there with you in school. You have to take responsibility. . . . We had a form I put up on our little corkboard for her to look at [to track her medication intake]."

In some families, this kind of self-responsibility is encouraged at an early age, with the first and easiest step being requiring a child to recognize when she or he needs to use a reliever. Many mothers described children as young as three or four approaching their teachers at day care with their inhalers in hand, declaring, "I need it." In Jane's family, by the time her son John was five,

You very rarely needed to remind him—he knew himself when he was getting tight chested, especially when he started school, and he would know to reach for his Ventolin and take it if he started to feel wheezy. But he was often at home anyway when he had asthma . . . so we would probably be managing it a lot for him because, obviously, we were the ones that were taking him to the doctor when he needed a new prescription or when there were issues to discuss. But probably by the time that he was around the age of ten, I would say he was managing it pretty much himself. He'd know when he'd run out of something or when he needed something.

In most cases children's self-management is more limited, and parents describe heavy involvement in not just initiating but also regulating and maintaining the drug regimes of children, from infancy up through their teens or even their early twenties. Sally, who described how her son at age nine will bring her Ventolin when he thinks he needs it, followed this up with the strongly worded caveat, "But it's not up to him to protect himself. *We notice* if he can't breathe properly. He might get the Ventolin and bring it to us, but he won't be able to save his own life."

In a few cases, however, the onus of accountability falls more heavily on the child. When hoped for and even expected health outcomes are not achieved, the ideals of self-responsibility are so deeply ingrained in some young people that they blame themselves for their inability to stay well.

Samantha's Story

Samantha, who is in her mid-twenties, has suffered from asthma since she was five. From about the age of ten or eleven, Samantha was expected to take charge of her own asthma care. She and her mother Pamela, a primary school teacher in Auckland, recounted how this came about:

> Pamela: I had four children, you know, so in many ways we left it up to her, didn't we?
>
> Samantha: I was very independent, and I sort of ran my own life from quite young [turning to her mother, who is nodding in agreement]. I always took care of my own homework and my school lunches and took responsibility for that kind of stuff.
>
> Pamela: And I expected it and expected all the other kids to do it too! That's because I'm a slack mother, obviously.
>
> Samantha: No, it's not. Because if your daughter is willing to take responsibility and is *able* to take responsibility, it's probably a good thing to encourage that. . . . So you did leave me alone to manage my own asthma, really. I just wasn't very good at it . . .
>
> Pamela: We just had to pick up the pieces every time you had an attack in some strange place. . . . Sam's forgetfulness [to bring along her medication] was *annoying* more than anything else.

Today, Samantha appears to view her asthma as solely her problem, while expressing a great deal of self-blame for the deterioration of her condition, something her mother does not contest.

> Samantha: I think I've been my own worst enemy, and I haven't managed my asthma as I should have, so I really blame myself, not the GP who's told me what I should be doing. I don't know if there's a way that they could've incentivized me to do this better. I'm just generally a slack person.

Pamela: She always loses things and [is] not self-managed ... She'd put her jersey [pullover] on back to front and not notice.

Samantha: I don't know, I'm just *slaaack*. And then I got a boyfriend [who has asthma] who started stealing my inhalers all the time, so when I did want to use my inhaler, it wasn't there. They'd always disappear ... And I'm very untidy, which doesn't help. But, yeah, I don't really know what more the doctor could've done.

Throughout the interview, Sam's mother Pamela oscillated between calling her daughter irresponsible, referring to herself as similarly "slack," and justifying why she has never taken her daughter's asthma too seriously, as if to exonerate herself from any blame over Samantha's condition deteriorating as she grew older. At the same time, both Pamela and Samantha fluctuated between describing Samantha's condition as serious and life threatening and depicting it as a petty annoyance, like putting on a pullover the wrong way round.

Pamela explained that when Samantha was first diagnosed, "The only thing I knew [about asthma] was that my mum was an ambulance nurse and she was called out once to a child who had it and died, and I know how badly that affected her. So I knew that you had to be a bit careful of it. But Samantha ... didn't seem very bad—[she] just [had] problems breathing." She turned and said to Samantha, "I didn't know enough about it, and I didn't sort of ... *ha ha* [laughing loudly] ... take much notice of it, because it was only when you had a cold so I didn't notice much difference at all. But it did get worse, didn't it?"

Later Pamela recounted a moment when she consciously fought off being frightened by her daughter's asthma even though many of the medical personnel attending to her daughter seemed very concerned:

I never worried because it never really seemed *bad enough*. The only time I really worried was when you were in the doctor's office already on a nebulizer ... and you started turning blue [because the nebulizer wasn't working]. They were panicking a bit, but as far as I was concerned you were *there*, where you were supposed to be. . . . Her fingers started going blue. I think that's what they were panicking about.

At other points, particularly when the turning point of the story is how Samantha yet again forgot to take her inhaler along when the family traveled somewhere, asthma was described by both Samantha and her mother as an annoying interruption of the flow of everyday life. Mirroring attitudes of families of New Zealand boys with hemophilia (Park 2000), a potentially life-threatening condition is made seemingly more manageable by being downgraded to a mere "nuisance," "hassle," or "inconvenience":

> Pamela: I remember going down to Rotorua once, and you'd forgotten all your inhalers, and that was a *real* hassle. Then you had to find a doctor who was open, and it was a weekend so there were no doctors, and you couldn't just *buy* an inhaler [over the counter].

> Samantha: To me, asthma has just been a giant hassle. I just want to reduce the hassle as much as possible, which unfortunately has meant not taking my inhalers properly and getting even more asthma. So yeah, it's been an inconvenience and a nuisance more than anything else.

At least part of the "hassle" for Samantha is the fact that her doctors insist she take preventative medication even when she does not feel unwell. Speaking of her asthma as something that comes and goes, she explained that taking medication for an illness she does not *feel*—and therefore assumes she does not *have* at the moment—seems like a waste of time to her:

The thing is that when you *don't* have asthma, you go, "Oh, I don't need that, I'm fine." And when you *do* feel a bit wheezy you go, "Oh, maybe I should be taking it." . . . My boyfriend, he won't take his [inhaler] for weeks and then when he takes it, he'll take like twenty puffs. It's like, "*Noooo*! It doesn't work like that!"

Madison, Sam's younger sister who also has asthma, chimed in in agreement: "Oh, I'm really bad at taking the preventer. I pretty much don't take it. And I'll only take it when I actually *have* asthma: I'll take the reliever and then I'll take the preventer as well."

Despite their dismissal of the importance of regularly using preventers, Samantha and Madison live in a household that is depicted as being littered with relievers, although sometimes it might be hard to locate the one prescribed to them. Samantha related how by the time she reached high school, she and her father shared the same reliever: "I think by that stage I was on Bricanyl[1] instead of Ventolin. And that was the same one Dad was on as well, so I always used to steal his inhaler when I lost mine."

Together, Madison, Samantha, and their mother recounted how inhalers circulate from person to person through the family:

Madison: I remember that time that I was sick. I had the flu real bad and I had to go downstairs and ask Samantha to use her inhaler because I couldn't breathe. It was really uncomfortable. And that was when Mum was like [*in a nagging voice*], "Go to the doctor and get an inhaler." But I didn't.

Pamela: I used to keep all your ones in a drawer upstairs, because I knew that you would never find yours whenever you were panicking, so I knew where *I* would, I knew where there *was* one . . .

Samantha: Oh, my backup was always Dad's one in his sock drawer.

Pamela: Yeah, but then after that [the divorce], *I* had to keep them all and in the same place! But I don't have any more, by the way.

Samantha: That's all right, I live with Alex now, and he's got one.

In contrast to the inhalers that are shared and passed along among family members, Samantha spoke disparagingly of the school inhaler she sometimes had to use in high school. Handed out in physical education class, the inhaler made the rounds among children who forgot to bring their own. Her face scrunched up in disgust, Samantha exclaimed, "I wonder if they still do that? I wonder how many people used that inhaler before me, *eeeeew*!"

Samantha's unease over using the school inhaler stands in sharp contrast to the comfort created by the shared family inhaler that has come to link siblings as well as father and daughters, even after their father has been long absent from the family home. In Samantha's family, asthma is portrayed as a life-threatening nuisance that unites them not only in a shared symptomology but shared ideologies of the body and health enacted through collective regimes of coping, including at times using the same inhaler. The intimacy created is so palpable that at one point during the interview, younger brother Ethan, age thirteen, who has never been diagnosed with asthma, eagerly suggested that he too might have the condition.

Cultivating Noncompliance

Samantha's family is a particularly vivid example of how asthma gets constructed as something that can be dismissed and normalized and yet simultaneously requires constant surveillance and, at times, the use of quite intensive medical intervention. Asthma is cast as both a hassle and a force of intense disruption in Samantha's life, impeding her ability to fashion herself as a capable child and now as a capable adult.

In a similar way, other parents discussed the "slackness" they exhibited when teaching their children how to routinize medication use. When asked if Adam, who had been repeatedly hospitalized with severe asthma five years ago, takes daily medication, Sally replied, "Yeah, he does have to—well, he *sort* of does it every day, *if* I have noticed he's been coughing. Then I put him on the Ventolin and the Flixotide straight away, and I suppose I would tend to keep him on the Flixotide for a week or two. And then if he seems completely better, I drop the Flixotide again, because sometimes he can go six months without needing it."

Sally is one of those parents whom physicians and asthma educators are likely to deem noncompliant due to her refusal to keep Adam regularly on a preventer. In fact, Sally is very pleased that he can go for up to six months relying only on what most medical professionals would consider much too frequent doses of Ventolin. And yet she is also one of the parents who proudly narrated her son's improvement in terms of her own emerging self-education, which allows her to take over responsibility for his care.

Rather than engaging in the rhetoric of choice and partnership, Sally invoked a growing sense of knowledge and authority. She described the differences between the days when Adam's asthma saw him in and out of hospital and today when, despite its ongoing severity, his asthma is considered to be under control, in terms of her own evolution into someone who is intimately acquainted with and can respond to her son's particular condition. Initially, she explained, "it was frightening and meant his life was potentially in danger. If for some reason he didn't receive medical attention, he could've died." Sally noted the lengths medical professionals went to to give Adam the care he needed after he was first hospitalized. With a tone that suggests a hint of surprise, she explained,

The medical wheels did kind of spin into action, and there was actually communication between the hospital and his physician and the asthma society, which means he did actually get *reactive* treatment. Like they did actually at the time take steps to make sure he did have an asthma management plan. . . . And the Asthma Society came to see us and made a lot of recommendations for what we could do.

Five years on, the situation is quite different. "We're so much more onto it now," Sally explained. "I can look at him and think he's *gonna* need this . . . and I bump up the Ventolin a lot sooner, before [there is an attack]." Visits to Adam's physician are irregular and up to Sally to organize. She feels confident, however, that she now knows what she needs from her son's physician:

Well, we don't have an asthma specialist; we just go to the physician. And if I think about it, we don't get anything proactive from her—we have to go to her, and then she will prescribe. But you know, he's had it a long time now, and *I kind of feel like I know what I need from her.* . . . If I was hopeless, then he could quite easily go a long time without getting treated, though I guess if he had a severe attack, maybe they'd start [actively treating him] again.

Sally's move from a mother feeling out of her depth to one who feels like she knows what she needs from her child's physician is characteristic of many New Zealand parents for whom being a responsible subject is less about following the regularized pharmaceutical regimes promoted in self-management plans than about adopting the position of a parent-expert in charge of her child's care. If Sally has engaged in a partnership with her son's physicians, she described it as largely on her own terms of learning how to care for her son and effectively use their services, in particular their ability to authorize medication refills.

Although many parents have come to terms with administering daily corticosteroids to their children, others like Sally and Pamela strive to see their children "do everything that everybody else does" *without* taking part in a daily drug routine. Although they refer to their actions as due to "slackness," such slackness is often coupled with a strong distrust of the necessity of long-term medication use as well as of the very diagnosis of asthma itself.

Diagnostic Controversies

Asthma is not an easy disease to diagnose. Recent research has suggested that a range of conditions are clustered under the "asthma" category, making diagnosis especially problematic (Brasier 2014; Pearce 2011). In some biomedical systems, one response to these difficulties has been to rely primarily on technological readings of lung function capabilities, such as through spirometry tests or newer eNO (exhaled nitric oxide) tests, both of which have been accepted as the gold standard of objective measurement. In New Zealand the use of eNO is relatively rare; although spirometry is gaining in prevalence, it remains uncommon. A leading study of spirometry use in New Zealand found that "despite almost 60% of doctors having direct access to spirometry equipment, primary care doctors . . . markedly underused [it]" (Eaton et al. 1999: 422). Training in conducting spirometry tests, moreover, has not been as robust as it could be, with quality control studies revealing that less than 15 percent of the spirometry tests undertaken in primary care practices were up to standard (Eaton et al. 1999). It is thus not surprising that, aside from respiratory specialists, many New Zealand medical professionals describe spirometry as simply too challenging. As one service leader in respiratory medicine who teaches physicians and nurses how to use spirometers noted, most medical professionals he sees who have spirometers "use them badly or not at all." "I am well known," he added, "for berating practitioners who use spirometers but don't use them properly. I stand up in front of them and say, 'Put it in your filing cabinet and lock it away if you're not going to use it properly . . . You're not helping anyone.'"

The perceived difficulties of using spirometers became quickly apparent when nurse-educator Katherine of the Auckland asthma society walked us through the process. "So we bought this huge machine," she said, pointing to the society's spirometer. "It cost hundreds or thousands of dollars; I'm not sure. And there's all our readings, piling up, as you can see," indicating a small tower of paper at the end of the table. "And these great big things . . . it's like a three-liter syringe, and you attach it on the end, and you just go [*she pumped it*]— except it's stuck." Katherine struggled with the machine a little as she continued, "You calibrate it once a week, but not everyone can afford to. . . . They have these spirometers in general practices but can't use them because they can't afford the syringe." She continued demonstrating how the machine works. "And this turbine kind of thing is where you blow. And you have to blow like—" Katherine demonstrated, taking a deep breath and then expelling the first gush of air full force and forcing out the rest until all the air had left her lungs. "And you keep blowing till you can't anymore. You've got a maximum of eight blows, and if people are really bad, they find it really hard."

She held up one of the papers displaying a series of detailed graphs. "This gives you all the readings. You need three reproducible blows, so you need to keep doing it till your figures are reproducible. See, what she [the previous patient] blew is there, and it will give you a lung-age—so she's fifty-nine, and she's got a lung-age of sixty-one. And I'm fifty-two and I usually have a lung-age of between thirty-six and forty, which is strange really because I used to smoke. And I always thought my lungs were bad so . . . hmm. So even though I wheeze when I'm blowing, everything seems to be in working order."

Katherine was clearly uncertain of the validity of the readings. The difficulty of conducting and interpreting spirometry is similarly a concern for family physicians. An Auckland-based GP, Dr. Mason, noted of her own use of spirometry,

We do have a spirometer, but I probably don't use it so much in asthma. . . . I don't think I've ever used a spirometer with a child. . . . Most of us [in New Zealand] don't really use spirometry, and so we're not used to it, and it's very complicated what the machine spits out. You look at the picture and think, yes, that looks like an asthma curve, but actually, [when] you compare all the bits and pieces it's kind of quite complicated trying to interpret it.

It is thus not surprising that many of the New Zealand parents we spoke with, including those whose children's asthma is severe, had never come across spirometry, with many of them not recognizing the word *spirometer*. Indeed, the only parent who wanted her child to have spirometry is herself an asthma educator. Josie related,

I've got a daughter who's sixteen who I've never thought had asthma, but she coughs badly every winter. . . . We went to the GP [who] said, "Would you like to get some breathing tests?" and I said, "Wow, yes!" We're being offered a proper diagnosis here, rather than just trial medications, which is what we've always been offered in the past and which have never been conclusive.

Concerns over the reliability of how asthma is currently diagnosed are voiced by New Zealand patients, parents, nurses, doctors, and specialists alike. But instead of focusing on the low use of spirometry, many medical professionals explain the difficulties in diagnosis as due to the nature of the condition. As respiratory specialist Dr. Morris explained, asthma is

hard to define. I don't believe it's one disease . . . That's a bit like saying we should call anything that coughs *coughitis*. You know, you're not going to get anywhere there because it's a symptom; it's a sign of some sort of nonspecific disturbance of the airways that's associated with reactive airways. And in children it's *more* complicated because of the many variants of wheezing. Certainly with preschoolers, when they've been labeled as having asthma, I'm sure many of them do *not* have asthma. . . . We don't really understand what makes them wheeze so much . . . and some of those children will *not* respond to treatment . . . so the label doesn't fit well.

This has a significant effect on how Dr. Morris interacts with his patients. When asked about whether he uses the word *asthma* in his own practice with clients, he responded,

with older children, yes, of course, because apart from anything else that label is really useful from the perspective of giving them effective treatment. With younger children, personally I tend to avoid labeling them as asthmatic. I tend to say: "Your child appears to respond to a bronchodilator at the moment, and we don't know what that means." If there's a strong family history of asthma in other members of the family, then the family will often work it out for themselves, and those children will most likely go on to be consistent asthmatics.

The result, however, of placing on families the onus of sorting out their child's diagnosis is that diagnostics become even more fraught as patients, parents, and doctors second-guess one another.

Central to this is the deemphasizing of spirometry, which reveals the cultural and historical specificities of how diagnostics are practiced even within globalized biomedicine (cf. Smith-Morris 2016). In other countries, such as the Czech Republic, spirometry is viewed as offering "definitive" readings, according to which diagnosis is determined and medication levels adjusted. Its usage by medical professionals, moreover, attributes to them a level of knowledge and skill, as do medical technologies more broadly (Saunders 2008), developing trust between patients and doctors by assuring patients that their care is in the hands of experts who "truly know" the situation. In New Zealand, in contrast, with spirometry viewed as indeterminate, family history and pharmaceuticals take a pivotal role, with diagnosis often taking place, as one physician puts it, "by trialing patients on an inhaler while they're here [in the clinic], and if they have a response, then that makes the diagnosis of asthma."

Often, however, this diagnostic strategy is preempted by the patient's family. As the same physician commented, "Sometimes they'll have parents or siblings with asthma, and they will sometimes have tried their inhaler and be able to tell you that it works." Such was the process in Alley's family. After a few years of taking her older son Michael to the hospital to treat his asthma attacks, she described what happened with her younger child: "With Amy, she got wheezy and a bit breathless, and so we gave her Michael's inhaler, and it worked, and so that sort of said to us that she had asthma. Then I thought we'd better get her checked separately and they said that she had asthma, definitely. So then she got her own inhalers."

Others spoke of initiating their own diagnosis by going into a doctor's office and directly asking for inhalers. Helen, who is now in her mid-twenties, related, "I was diagnosed when I started university . . . I was at the doctor's, and I was like, 'Um, I think I have asthma, but I don't really know.' She gave me an inhaler and she said, 'Give it a go and see if it affects your breathing.'"

Although many of these diagnoses seem to be fairly straightforward, other people describe more contested, and often fraught, diagnostic encounters. Some end up rediagnosing themselves, simply refusing to accept their doctor's findings. In Samantha's family, three out of the four children have been diagnosed with asthma, and each of them has at times seriously questioned or refused their diagnosis, despite growing up in a family where asthma is a familiar condition.

When Samantha was first diagnosed, her mother had serious misgivings. Speaking both to us and to Sam, Pamela recounted:

The first thing I knew was that she had a cold. We went to the doctor, and it was a heavy cold, and you weren't breathing properly, but I never thought it was asthma. But [he said] it was asthma, and gave her some liquid. . . . We always thought that, *nahh*, it couldn't possibly be asthma, but then we went overseas, and you got it again when you got a cold, and the doctor over there said, "Yeah, it's definitely asthma," and started giving you inhalers and things. . . . I didn't really *believe* it to start off with, I suppose.

Since they've reached adulthood, both Samantha's brother Jack (now age twenty-nine) and her sister Madison (age twenty-two) have been diagnosed with asthma, but, like their mother's response to Samantha, both have refused their diagnoses. When Ethan, Samantha's youngest brother (age thirteen), interrupted to ask what asthma is and then proposed he might have it too, Pamela replied:

You've never had asthma. But [your brother] Jack, actually—the doctor said *he* had asthma, and he said, "I don't believe you," and he just refused. But, Ethan, the doctors have never told *you* that you've got asthma at all. See, sometimes you wonder about the doctors *because they say if you've got any kind of a wheeze, you've got asthma.* But see Jack just refused to believe that he had it. I don't think they even gave him any kind of a drug—though they might've done . . . But *he* didn't take it. His cold got better, and it never worried him. . . . So I suppose he grew up not believing half the things the doctors say.

In large part, such questioning of whether one really has asthma or not is motivated by the concerns of many patients, as well as some medical practitioners, over the possibility that asthma diagnosis has become too broad (cf. Whitmarsh 2008b). Akin to anthropologists' and sociologists' warnings about the expansive nature of medical categories more generally (Conrad 2007; Rose 2003), many New Zealanders feel that the sweeping character of the diagnosis ends up in non–asthma-related conditions being mislabeled and mistreated. The result is, as Pamela put it, that children grow up "not believing half the things the doctors say." They are not alone, however, in their skepticism, which is well supported not only by some physicians but by asthma nurses as well. As nurse-educator Brenda put it, "We went from not diagnosing asthma to everyone who got a cough being diagnosed with asthma when it wasn't."

Countering Chronicity

Just as the inhaler is often used as a means of determining diagnosis, some asthma sufferers reverse the logic and reason that as they are (momentarily) *not* using an inhaler, they are not asthmatic. This kind of assessment and active contestation of asthma diagnoses are based on two principles: first, that the relief granted by an inhaler is indicative of asthma being present; and second, that asthma is a situationally specific diagnosis, that is, that one can move in and out of states of *having* asthma.

Such is the case in Samantha's family, whose members regularly speak of asthma as something that comes and goes. Sam's sister recounted her surprise at having an especially long bout of asthma while visiting Australia:

I had the worst asthma I could ever remember. . . . [and] I still *had* asthma for quite a few weeks after that, even after I got back to New Zealand. And it kind of hasn't really gone away ever since. . . . I would count myself as being asthmatic *at the moment*, but I'm hoping it'll go away soon, when I get better.

In a similar vein, Mary drew on her own experiences with asthma to describe why her twenty-year-old son refuses to take his asthma medication: "He doesn't believe he is asthmatic at all—that's probably where it's coming from, because he just had one attack. . . . What happens is when you're all right, you feel you're fit. You don't feel you're an asthmatic patient. That's the difference. You feel, 'Oh, I can breathe.'"

Geoff, a forty-year-old health worker, offered a related explanation for why neither he nor his two sons take the preventative medication prescribed to them. Describing his own asthma, he downplayed its significance:

I was first diagnosed when I was quite young. I used to cry a lot when I was going to sleep as a little kid, and one night my crying suddenly stopped. Mum said, "Well, that's strange" and went in to check me, and I was blue. So they called the ambulance, and the ambulance rushed me down to hospital, and they said then, "Geoff's asthmatic." I had two episodes when I was older, when I was thirteen, and both times I ended up in hospital or in a medical center [where] I had to go on the nebulizer because it was quite a severe asthma attack. . . . But asthma's never really dominated my life at all. I've always been quite physically active. When I would start exercising on a very cold day, I might get a bit wheezy, so I'd just have a wee puff of my inhaler then.

Like many other New Zealanders, Geoff uses only Ventolin. Although he has been told to use a preventer, he explained, "I never did. Because I just didn't feel it was necessary to take medication every day for something that gave me a bit of a problem quite infrequently." His account emphasizes what he sees as the minimal effects of having just a "wee puff" of the reliever now and again, as opposed to using an inhaler regularly and, in doing so, effectively *becoming* asthmatic.

Geoff's, Mary's, and Madison's portrayals of moving in and out of states of asthma are based on an understanding of reliever inhalers as indicative of the presence of illness (and conversely, its ability to be absent). They also reflect a different kind of temporality of care. Physicians enact one kind of timeline of asthma, with the aim of stabilizing the condition and, they hope, keeping it stable in perpetuity. Pharmaceutical companies promote a similar kind of logic, focused on stability and minimizing exacerbations, albeit premised predominantly on profitability rather than patient well-being (Sunder Rajan 2012).

Patients engage in yet another line of reasoning. In line with philosopher George Canguilhem's ([1966] 1989) suggestion that a disease is always defined by the sufferer's experience of it, existing only when the sufferer feels the condition impinging on her or him, many patients resist the suggestion that they are ill when they do not feel their lives are compromised. Much like the patient described by Dr. Morris who determines his or her own symptoms before the physician can act on them, the temporality of illness as experienced by many asthma sufferers suggests to them that asthma is a state that comes and goes and therefore does not always require pharmaceutical amelioration—an activity that many patients consider as involving its own potential dangers. Calibrating their medicinal intake based on their own experiences of momentarily having, or not having, asthma, such patients privilege their firsthand knowledge over the advice of medical authorities precisely because of their concerns with overmedicalization.

As we have seen, medical professionals frequently refer to patients with asthma and parents of children with asthma who do not follow their advice in taking daily preventers as being "noncompliant." But taking a cue from sociologist Peter Conrad's (1985) seminal critique of how discourses of noncompliance mask patient agency, it is worth considering how, rather than simply being "noncompliant," many of these patients may be actively engaged in a different form of self-care. As Conrad argues, "The whole notion of 'compliance' suggests a medically-centered orientation. . . . It is a concept developed from the doctor's perspective . . . [But] noncompliance appears very different from a patient-centered perspective than a medically-centered one" (1985: 30). Even more provocative is Conrad's suggestion that "what appears to be noncompliance from a medical perspective may actually be a form of asserting control over one's disorder" (ibid.: 29). Here, I suggest, patients are indeed engaged in "asserting control" over their illness by means of resisting hegemonic framings of asthma that are not upheld by their experientially derived "good sense" views of the world.

"You Can Never Trust Drug Companies"

In light of the twenty-five-year-old fenoterol catastrophe as well as extensive international media criticism of the power of the pharmaceutical industry, it is not entirely unexpected to find that patients question the necessity of pharmaceutical treatments when they are not feeling unwell. Although most physicians shrug off outsiders' anxieties over the influence that pharmaceutical companies may have over them, indicating that they are well able to resist being seduced by free samples and other marketing strategies, many patients, parents, and asthma nurses express concern over the influence of what they view to be drug companies' misinformation campaigns. Nurse-educator Brenda gave an example, relating how after years of telling clients that "you should take your reliever to relieve symptoms only when you need it," the new combination re-liever-preventer inhalers mean that suddenly people are taking relievers every day. "So how do you explain that one? It's a bit tricky!" she noted, continuing, "Can you just say it's a drug company scam? Well, it might well have been. You can never trust drug companies."

Another nurse-educator, Katherine, is skeptical of not only drug companies but also physicians who, she suggested, need to "follow the bloody guidelines" rather than make use of free samples. "Whatever they've got in their cupboard, the GPs seem to just dish it out," she said. "They get samples from reps . . . and they think they're doing the patients a favor by giving them a free inhaler, but they're not following the guidelines very often. So a patient will get put on a long-acting agonist because it's just in the bloody drawer!"

Likewise, for many patients, pharmaceutical companies' relations with phy-sicians are an important reason to feel apprehension. Although many would like to trust the medical establishment, they feel compelled to question the easy use of remedies that are two sided in nature, being both potentially efficacious and seriously dangerous.

This double-edged nature of pharmaceuticals has been well captured by Jacques Derrida in his reflection on the ancient Greek term *pharmakon*. As Der-rida notes, in ancient Greece certain substances were recognized as being "both a remedy and a poison," thus underscoring the potential of drugs for being both efficacious and harmful (1981: 61; see also Biehl 2010, 2013). This intertwining of medicine's positive and negative valences tends to be publicly subsumed in contemporary Western perspectives of drugs as predominantly *positive* forces as long as they are used correctly. Drugs are, moreover, viewed as increasingly vital for the ongoing constitution of health (Dumit 2012). In the United States and New Zealand, the only two countries in the world where direct marketing of pharmaceuticals to the public is legal, decades of informing the public about drugs, first through print sources and later through radio and TV, have resulted in a consumer base well versed in the beneficial aspects of medication (Greene and Herzberg 2010). There is also, however, notable public opposition to the image of medications as imbued with almost "magical" healing properties (Van der Geest and Whyte 1989), as demonstrated by the growing public interest in alternative therapies.

The negative side effects of asthma medications are well documented. Vari-ous studies have demonstrated that preventative medications can cause oral thrush (fungal growth), and, in higher doses, minor growth suppression in children, osteoporosis, thinning of the skin and bruising, and a reduction in the body's overall ability to respond to severe illness. Reliever medicines may have side effects such as headaches, mild shaking, a racing heart, or restlessness. Steroid tablets, such as prednisone, can have even more serious side effects. When taken for three weeks or less, they may cause increased appetite, mood change, and occasionally fluid retention and indigestion. Longer-term use has been linked to complications such as weight gain, thinning of the bones, slowing of children's growth, a reduction in the body's own natural production of steroids, easy bruising of the skin and slow healing of cuts, puffiness or roundness of the face, indigestion or stomach ulcers, fluid retention with swelling of the ankles, and cataracts (Barnes and Pedersen 1993; Dahl 2006; Asthma Foundation n.d.[a]; Rossi, Cerasoli, and Cazzola 2007).

Most of the parents who worry about harmful side effects do not delve into such details, simply noting that "steroids are bad." A few others are more specific about what they fear to see, or think they have already seen, in their children. Charlotte is at the far end of the spectrum, confusing corticosteroids with anabolic steroids and convinced she saw the visible short-term effects of Redipred, a prednisolone sodium phosphate solution used for short-term treatment of severe asthma, on her five-year-old daughter's muscles. She recounted,

One dose of Redipred is the same as taking Flixotide every day for two years. So it's a huge dose of steroid, but she needed to get on it. . . . It worked *really* quickly with her asthma. You could always tell when she'd been on it as it took a bit to get out of her system. I mean, it was a steroid. She had abs of steel for a while. I don't know whether she was any *stronger*, but you could see her muscles.

But there is often another facet to parents' concerns: although many parents are motivated by worries over steroids' immediate or long-term effects on the body, they also express apprehension over what it means to embark on a regime of continuous medication intake. Their concerns are not only what steroids might do to the body but also what they signify: the creation of permanent patienthood.

In refusing the chronicity of asthma, patients take an inherently political stance of critiquing the pharmaceutical industry for attempting to make a profit from their ill health. Here patient noncompliance is not evidence of "patient defect" but rather a concerted act of resistance (cf. Rouse 2010; Trostle 1988). Yet most of the doctors and nurses who belittle this behavior do not seem to recognize what generates it. Focusing on patients' gross misunderstandings of how steroids work—fears of muscles of steel, for example—they often miss the political basis of their concerns. *Whatever their own perspectives may be of the pharmaceutical industry*, doctors, nurses, and other medical professionals regularly redefine patients' reluctance to take medication as having nothing to do with the politics of the for-profit pharmaceutical industry but rather as stemming out of individual patient *failure*.

Negotiated Fears

The desire to offset asthma by using pharmaceuticals while not allowing it to dominate one's life and one's identity articulates a tension in how many patients and parents describe the experiential aspects of the disease. Their struggles with asthma are dominated by a fear that doubles upon itself: in addition to the fear of having a severe, possibly life-threatening asthma attack, there is the fear that, in being frightened of such an attack, they might smother their (or their child's) capacity to have a normal life. These opposing forces pull at many of the New Zealanders with whom we spoke.

Some go through a temporary period of adjustment (cf. Buford 2004). For Jane, her son's asthma "was always really *scary* until you got to know that he was going to just be chronic all the time, and it wasn't going to get to a really acute phase where he would go into anaphylactic shock or anything." Others, however, never come to terms with it. Forty-five-year-old Jason, who himself has had severe asthma since his childhood, described his five-year-old son's asthma attacks as a mixture of the familiar and the terrifying: "He's had several attacks that require taking him to hospital. They put him on a nebulizer; they watched him overnight. . . . Terrifying stuff, but I've been through all that stuff myself . . . so I kind of know the drill. . . . [But] fuck, yeah it's still scary."

But often mothers and fathers worry even more about letting their fear run away with them. Charlotte explained, "I'm one of these *paranoid mothers* where if there is the slightest drop in temperature at night, [I get up to make sure] they're warm." Nisha offered a similar description of herself: "To be honest, I'm pretty paranoid, in the sense that the moment I feel there's a change in the temperature, the first thing I do is to tell her, 'Cover up.' The moment she sniffs—I mean she probably thinks I'm the *worst mother in the world* because

I'm always jumping down on her—the moment she sneezes, I ask her, 'Have you got a cold?'"

Whereas some engage in such pejorative self-descriptions, others recount making a real effort *not* to become overly concerned about their children's asthma. Most New Zealand parents undertake a carefully attuned balancing act between protecting their child from unnecessary distress and enabling them to experience the "normal" experiences of childhood. Nisha and Ajay reflected on how hard they try to not get too worked up over their daughter Kavita's asthma, noting that their position is similar to medical professionals', inasmuch as both are effectively powerless:

> Ajay: There's no point in getting paranoid over something you have no control over, correct? That's our basic principle. Even the doctors don't have control over asthma, let's face it.
>
> Nisha: You need to carry on doing your normal thing, do your normal stuff. Whatever everybody's doing, do it. Just take precautions where we feel you have to. Otherwise you dwell on it too much, and it becomes a bigger part of the action.

Nonetheless, Nisha described how, during Kavita's last hospitalization, she sat weeping at her bedside until a social worker came to comfort her.

Jane similarly moved back and forth between depicting her need to keep her son safe and her fear of being overprotective and cutting him off from having "a normal life," stating,

There's no doubt about it that he was a much more timid child early on, incredibly timid, and I'm sure that some of it was [his] personality, but I think some of it was living constantly with this sort of fear of not being able to breathe—that suffocating feeling. . . . When I look back at his really early years—a lot of it was pretty terrifying. . . . Just how much, psychologically, it sets you up further in life, it's hard to say. But I do think it would've had an effect.

In some cases, the specter of overprotectiveness results in parents embracing everyday activities to the point of allowing children to determine their own behavior even if it exacerbates illness. Such was the guiding principle in Pamela and Samantha's household:

> Pamela: You have some people that are very overprotective. You know, their child's got asthma and has to be *protected*.

Samantha: That's the whole cotton-wool generation. I wasn't [in the] cotton-wool generation, I was [in the] "let your kids run out on the road" generation.

Pamela: Some kids get colds easily and get asthma easily when they get colds, so they'll stay home when they've got a cold, whereas our generation, it was like, "You got a cold, well, hard luck, you're not dying yet."

Samantha: We used to go to school barefoot *all* through winter.

Family Choices

No matter where parents and children stand on the spectrum—slack or stroppy, noncompliant or engaged in the latest methods of asthma care—collaborative engagements between family members frequently result in distinctive familial regimes of care that are both tailored to the individual child and nested in familial dynamics that promote a particular sense of normality. Across New Zealand there is an emphasis on pharmaceutical usage as the key strategy for maintaining such normality. This does not mean that patients are somehow forced to engage in pharmaceutical treatments: rather, medical professionals' sole emphasis on drug treatments often coincides with patients' desires for a pharmaceutical solution that will allow them to otherwise keep life as normal as possible. Why drugs are deemed to be normal whereas other methods of alleviating or preventing asthma symptoms, such as eliminating triggers through more stringent household cleaning or getting rid of the family pet, are not, is a reflection of both the centrality of pharmaceuticals in New Zealand's healthcare system and other structural and cultural forces that make taking a pill or using an inhaler much easier than heating one's home. There are, however, those who view regular drug intake, especially of preventative medication, not as responsible health care but as an unnecessary and potentially dangerous demand driven by pharmaceutical companies' profit motives. But whether families embrace the daily use of preventatives or only treat acute exacerbations, either of these regimes needs to be contextualized within the broader dynamics of family life.

Love can drive parents to extremes in ensuring that appropriate medical care and support is provided for their children (Mattingly 2010; Rouse 2010), but it can also compel them to value other attributes of childhood above and beyond their children's health. In New Zealand, this includes the value of encouraging children to grow up feeling strong and capable. Although mitigating respiratory distress is important, so too is not frightening, coddling, or "cotton-wooling" one's children even if it ends up exacerbating their asthma. For many parents, drugs that enable their children to fearlessly run barefoot in the winter and swim in freezing cold water are thus seen as essential to providing normal childhoods.

Striving to instill the value of personal responsibility, parents encourage their children to engage in self-management by enacting the regimes of care that parents and children have collectively crafted. Most adults do not match the image of the patient-expert put forward by policy makers, that is, the patient who eagerly grasps the reins of self-care, collects (expert) information, and weighs up the objective evidence to make her or his own, independent decisions about how best to proceed. Instead, families work together to collaboratively assemble their own health regimes, based on their own experimental efforts to determine the effects of the pharmaceuticals supplied to them.

Those parent-experts who skeptically question their positioning as consumers of pharmaceuticals in a medical system that appears to them as more bent on enabling profits than providing responsible care do so not necessarily due to misunderstanding or lack of education. And while we should not reject calls for strengthening patient–doctor relationships and reinstating a more open-ended, negotiated relationality between patients and medical providers (Mol 2008), it is also crucial to consider how some patients and parents of children with asthma position themselves as critics of the pharmaceutical industry. For these parents, the key issue at stake is not so much the efficacy of drugs, as doctors and asthma nurses seem to imply, but their recognition that we need to employ the *pharmakon* responsibly, neither underestimating nor overusing it. As doctors are not always in a position to "step down" people's dosages, some parents have come to regulate this themselves. In doing so, they respond to the intricacies of clinical understandings of asthma in ways that push self-management policies to their extremes. Taking on the authority to self-define their conditions, in Canguilhem's terms, they choose which symptoms are symptoms and when and how they or their children have the disease.

Asthma in Cross-Cultural Perspective

Policies promoting self-management and increased personal responsibility among patients have initiated a new set of power dynamics between medical professionals, asthma sufferers, parents, and children in New Zealand. Although they have opened up a space for adult patients and parents of asthmatic children to have more say in their own care, they have also left many families hanging, unable to gain access to care when they need it or simply unclear on what steps they should be taking. This is not, however, an inevitable outcome of neoliberal health-care reforms. If we "follow a policy" (Shore and Wright 2011: 12) out of one cultural and historical context and into another, we can see some of the same sorts of issues alongside strikingly different concerns and challenges. Moreover, rather than merely tracing the *effects* of a policy outward as if emanating from the document itself (Colebatch, Hoppe, and Noordegraaf 2010), adopting an assemblage approach that considers policy as one node in a shifting assemblage of actors, technologies, rationalities, and affects (Greenhalgh 2008) enables us to see both how policies can shape subjectivity, health, and medicine and in turn are themselves adopted, reformed, or entirely rejected across distinct political and cultural milieus.

When a child is diagnosed with asthma in the Czech Republic, medical professionals make a point of using the same policy guidelines, most notably the GINA protocols, that are widely employed in the West for diagnosing patients' conditions and determining pharmaceutical treatments. But the social and political relations that underlie Czech approaches to biomedical care as well as the array of possible therapies promoted by physicians mean that a Czech child's treatment may very well run a different course from that of a child in New Zealand. Comparing asthma treatments across these two nations helps us to reveal the often-hidden cultural and political assumptions that determine what is considered adequate or appropriate care. Cultural ideas of personhood, gender, and family life as well as perspectives on the environment and power dynamics among citizens, corporations, and governments combine together to determine the shape of care, influencing the adoption of pharmaceuticals, the kinds of medical and bodily knowledge that are deemed credible, and the forms of political action (or inaction) that patients, citizens, physicians, and scientists take part in. Cross-cultural comparison thus enables a detailed accounting of how neoliberal reforms are reshaping health care on a global scale, offering up examples that are at times achingly familiar and at others startlingly different, as similar policies are taken up, resisted, or ignored in disparate settings.

Arguably the most significant aspect of asthma care in the Czech Republic is that it takes place in a context where professional medical expertise is very highly valued. As in other postsocialist countries, advanced liberal reforms are enabling—and indeed requiring—patients to engage in consumer choice over health care, necessitating that they learn about the kinds of services and standards of care available to them (Čada 2014; Hrešanová 2014; Speier, Šmídová, and Wierciński 2014). But the democratization of medical knowledge is occurring to a much smaller degree than in most Western liberal democracies: Czech patients are not encouraged to self-manage their care because most physicians are loath to suggest they are competent to do so. Instead there are intense processes of training or "enskilling" (Ingold 2001) patients into mimicking the methods used by medical professionals. Unlike New Zealand approaches to patient education, such lessons are usually not premised on the assumption that patients should be able to *manage* on their own but rather form another facet of instruction and surveillance.

From the perspectives of patients, both adults with asthma and family members of asthmatic children often denounce what they describe as the harsh treatment they receive from medical providers while simultaneously exalting physicians' expertise and specialized knowledge. Such deference is perhaps not surprising given that a recent Czech opinion poll found that physicians far outrank members of any other occupation in terms of the public respect accorded to them (Tuček 2013). Patients also, however, maneuver the medical system, making use of the resources on offer and actively lobbying for access to others by drawing on their social networks and making the most of market competition. A significant part of the work of care in this biomedical system is the building and maintenance of long-term relationships with medical professionals through engagement in unequal exchanges that show deference to medical professionals' expertise and attempt to keep them invested in taking active responsibility for their patients' health. Instead of moves to equalize the positioning of patients and doctors, neoliberalization here has resulted in a consumer model that both necessitates patients exercising choice over medical providers and encourages the establishment of long-term patron–client relations through nonmarket exchanges of gifts or bribes.

At the same time, the shift to a market-based medical system has not resulted in the jettisoning of socialist principles of ensuring solidarity in health care. Although there is an increasing focus on individuals' personal responsibility for their health, there is also a wider political will to view asthma as a collective problem and consider broader structural solutions. As in many parts of the world (cf. Biehl and Petryna 2013; Brotherton 2012; Petryna 2011), issues of how to safeguard equity and justice in health care within a market-based medical system have become deeply divisive topics that dominate debates about twenty-first-century Czech medicine.

The Czech situation showcases attempts to balance increased emphasis on patients' personal responsibility with a fostering of medical expertise and a focus on promoting social justice (that is, health care for all, underpinned by the principle of solidarity). This is by no means to suggest that the Czech health-care system somehow offers a "solution" to the problems posed by New Zealand's approach to health care; rather, Czech medical practice offers a contrast to the patient-centered model adopted in New Zealand, indicative of other ways in which neoliberal health-care policies can proceed. As such, it must be understood in terms of its own strengths and challenges.

Chapter 3

Patient Agency, Personal Responsibility, and the Upholding of Medical Expertise

"IT'S all based on the system of solidarity," Dr. Kamila Šoucová declared in the midst of her description of standardized asthma treatments in the Czech Republic. Once a practicing physician, Dr. Šoucová now works for the country's largest health insurance firm, VZP. With its Prague headquarters sprawled across multiple floors of an enormous, old-fashioned office building that occupies a full corner of one of Prague 3 district's main streets, VZP is a large-scale operation. It insures some 6.2 million people—more than half of the Czech Republic's population. As its full name suggests, Všeobecná zdravotní pojišťovna or the Universal Health Insurer builds its reputation on being the country's most inclusive public insurance company, extending coverage to the unemployed and elderly whose premiums are paid by the state.

Dr. Šoucová, who is in her late forties, spoke at length about VZP's underlying philosophy. Initially, her impassioned account of what she described as "the system of solidarity" that underpins VZP surprised me, as it had been a while since I'd heard anyone in this postsocialist country so enthusiastically invoke the concept of *solidárnost* or solidarity. "It's an old system, rooted in the Communist period," she acknowledged and then added, as if to preempt possible critiques, "but it isn't a *bad* system, and it will outlive me." She explained how she envisioned *solidárnost* to work: "Take, for example, an old pensioner—the state pays 550 crowns (approximately US$22) a month for his insurance, but his health care costs more than that, so those like me who are currently working help fund it by contributing payments to the VZP fund out of our salaries. One day I will be old and need care, and the fund will pay for me. It is based on solidarity, according to which we take everyone and cannot turn anyone away." Together Dr. Šoucová and her colleague, Mrs. Malinová, VZP's specialist on spa care who joined us during the interview, explained that *solidárnost* is an important safety net that lies at the center of VZP's health-care policies. Mrs. Malinová

Pavel extended this critique of an unfair shift in responsibility to the health-care system in general:

Before the revolution, the government thought about you, and you just had to do what you were told. So, the doctor would come to the school twice a year and do a checkup. If your child was unwell, the doctor would organize a two-week trip to Jeseník [respiratory spa] for him. And the doctor just *informed* you that your child was going. The state was responsible for asthmatics, and the parents didn't need to solve it [their child's health problem]. The doctor would also come and find you at your house to check on you if you hadn't been in to see him or else *he* would get into trouble. . . . Say you didn't want an inoculation—they would come and find you, and you had to pay a fine. This was good because the state thought of it *for you*. But now, *you* need to do it. And as a result, we have TB and whooping cough again. *Today, no one is responsible for anything.* I think it should be that the state still thinks for you, but it shouldn't be for *free* as under socialism. Instead you should *pay for the state to think for you*, in the same way that a client pays a private banker to think about him and give him *proactive advice*—in effect, the banker *thinks for him*. Today, the state should similarly think for its citizens.

Pavel and Dr. Šoucová clearly diverged in their assessments of how well VZP is managing to act as a proxy for a state that once took active responsibility for the health of its citizens. But that isn't the only discrepancy in their perspectives. Dr. Šoucová painted a direct connection between VZP's activities and the socialist models of state-supported health care of the past, highlighting how collective interests might need to supersede those of the individual. Although the state used to make such determinations, this is now the role of the (state-supported) insurance company, she asserted. In contrast, Pavel suggested that by divesting responsibility to insurance companies like VZP, the state has given up its fundamental responsibility to protect the citizenry. But Pavel also wavered between wanting back a state that takes over responsibility for *all* its citizens and is authorized to act on behalf of the greater good, making TB and whooping cough things of the past, and the vision of a new state that acts as a service provider that clients can choose to hire—or not—to act on their behalf. Not only does this new vision of the state sideline those who *cannot* pay the state for its services, it ultimately vests responsibility and the power of decision making in the individual.

Pavel's depiction of the state giving expert advice like a banker to a client speaks, moreover, to a deeper logic within the practices of advanced liberalism, namely that those clients who can afford to do so entrust the work of "self-responsibility" to a network of expert advisors. The true "patient-experts" thus become the ones who are forced to rely neither on the state nor purely on themselves or their social networks but rather who can hire and fire expert advisors at will. "The state," in Pavel's final articulation of it, becomes not the source of collective responsibility, much less authority, but an entity that caters to individual citizens' needs and financial abilities. The question of how to balance the respective needs of multiple and various constituencies that the concept of solidarity foregrounds is discarded for another kind of social contract that exacerbates, rather than diminishes, class difference in the name of individual rights.

Pavel and Blanka aren't the only ones troubled by the changes in the health-care system. Some doctors are similarly wary. Dr. Marie Bílá, a pediatric heart specialist, described how the well-developed system of health care that existed under state socialism is being worn away due to the rising costs of services. "What is left today," she said, "is much worse than the quality of care we had before, though it might still be more advanced than in other parts of Europe." The state socialist health-care system was, in her opinion, "very comprehensive and very good," though she admitted that some viewed it as "tyrannical" because of its strict medical oversight. In contrast, she said, today health care depends on what *you* as a patient make happen. In the past, Dr. Bílá suggested, you had to give doctors bribes to get decent service—"I was offered them from my first days as a young doctor," she recounted—"but now you need not just money but contacts and the knowledge of what sort of resources or treatment you require."

Others, perhaps depending on where they are located in the nexus of cash, patienthood, and medical care, offer a more positive view of current health services. Věra is a pharmaceutical company representative in her mid-forties. "Can you believe it," she told me, "of all Europeans, Czechs go to the doctor the most. The average used to be sixteen times per year!" When I express surprise, Věra explained, "Well, you know, older people go all the time. *Most* people go even if it's just minor. [It used to be that] a child would *cough* and her mother would drag her off to the doctor. *Now* people are learning to go to the pharmacy more and buy medicines for their ailments." In fact, while the frequency of doctors' consultations has gone down in recent years, decreasing from approximately 14.2 visits per person in 2000 to 12.2 in 2009, the Czech Republic and Slovakia (which together formed Czechoslovakia until 1993) remain among the top five nations in the world with respect to patients' utilization of physicians (OECD 2011).

But, despite her enthusiastic support of the idea that today's patients should act more independently, Věra unequivocally asserted the crucial importance of medical professionals, particularly specialists, in determining and overseeing care. In her own life, noncompliance with doctors' directives would, she asserted, be nonsensical. "I always listen to my doctors," she stated, "but then I go to very good doctors because I am in the pharmaceutical industry and I know who the *good* doctors are. So, I take their advice. I figure they know what they are doing."

In some ways, Czech health policies are adaptations of the widespread international trend of devolving responsibility to patients. But the reconfiguration of responsibilities over health also reveals a distinctly postsocialist ethos of care combined with longstanding cultural perspectives on the body, personhood, and childhood. The emphasis on expertise, technological measurement, and pharmaceutical solutions is balanced by a wide array of nonpharmaceutical therapies, including spa cures and health camps. These approaches are historical legacies from the days before there were adequate and effective bronchodilators but are also bolstered by contemporary concerns over the potential dangers of pharmaceuticals, especially steroids, shared by patients and physicians alike. The promises of technology offering seemingly irrefutable diagnoses and objective assessments of medication use are thus offset by concerns over possible misdiagnoses and fears over unnecessary, or unnecessarily high dosages of, corticosteroids. But rather than lending themselves toward more collaborative endeavors between patients and doctors, such concerns are played out in a resolutely specialist-focused health-care regime, characterized by physicians imbued with authority and expertise, managing bodies and behaviors such that patients are largely left making the choice of resistance or accommodation, rather than management.

Although the Czech health-care system has undergone more than twenty-five years of radical change since the dismantling of state socialism, in practice patient–doctor relations remain firmly anchored in a hierarchical model that promotes physicians' authority and expertise. As part of a more consumerist approach to health care, patients are no longer centrally assigned a doctor based on their area of residence, instead choosing from an array of public and private providers and changing their doctor as they see fit. Nonetheless, many patients and physicians are keen to continue cultivating long-term relationships. Patients, moreover, tend to treat their doctors with great respect and esteem owing to their medical expertise. Though many patients would prefer that medical professionals speak to them a little more kindly and explain to them what they are doing rather than reducing them to a body to be attended to (Read 2007; Hrešanová 2014), with the exception of select areas such as birth care and end-of-life care, there is little public advocacy for the models of collaborative care promoted in the West. Instead, there has largely been a continuation of what Eugene Raikhel has referred to in Russia as "a steeply hierarchical physician–patient relationship" (2010: 132).

This is not, however, to suggest that patients *lack* agency. Many of today's patients (or parents of children who are patients) draw on skills honed during state socialism when *solidárnost* wasn't always extended as in principle it should have been. They maneuver their way through the medical system through the cultivation of extensive personal networks and well-placed gifts or bribes, in addition to using the new tools of financial might (if and when possible) and a growing awareness of the importance of gathering their own knowledge about available resources and therapies. Taken together, these various forms of patient influence suggest that a new model of engagement between medical providers and patients and their families is in the making, just as a new set of relations between citizens and the state, lying somewhere in between *solidárnost* and neoliberalism, has taken force.

Expertise and Hierarchy

"So, you're finally getting to see him," Viktor Fraňk grinned at me. We were sitting in the offices of ČIPA, Česká iniciativa pro astma or the Czech Initiative for Asthma, waiting for ČIPA's former director and founder, the eminent Professor Václav Špičák, to arrive. I shrugged, a bit embarrassed that he had so openly acknowledged my persistence. "You read my emails asking for an interview," I asked. "All of them," he nodded. "But it was really the phone calls that did it," Viktor added, and when I look surprised, he explained that my meeting with Dr. Špičák was thanks to my two recommenders: a physiotherapist who worked closely with Dr. Špičák and a librarian who is his lifelong patient, both of whom phoned the office multiple times on my behalf. This sort of lobbying to gain someone else access to a medical expert was not something I was used to, and I thought through its implications as Viktor and I drank tea and waited for Professor Špičák's arrival.

We killed time by talking about rugby. A muscular, broad-shouldered man in his mid-fifties, Viktor is an avid sportsman who used to play rugby and trained at a well-known gym used by the much-idolized Sparta soccer team. Rugby is not popular in the Czech Republic, but given that I live in New Zealand, he expected me to have a bit of knowledge about the prospects of New Zealand's All Blacks in the upcoming Rugby World Cup. He was keen to recount his own participation in the game, including his job as a rugby coach and sports camp manager prior to meeting and going to work for Professor Špičák some thirty years ago. The skills he learned in these positions, he told me, have been essential to his role as ČIPA's general manager and summer camp director. Barely able to fit into his office chair, Viktor embodies the ideals of sport, discipline, and the maintenance of a strong physique that I encountered over and over in my interviews with medical professionals. And, despite his short stature, he seemed to almost overwhelm the thin, wiry, and rather tired-looking eighty-two-year-old Professor Špičák when he joined us.

After we were introduced, Professor Špičák seated himself next to Viktor. The chitchat between Viktor and myself was clearly at an end, but at the doctor's request the younger man stayed and attended to Professor Špičák throughout our discussion, frequently leaping up and fetching materials (pamphlets, journals, computer printouts) as they were needed. At various points, Professor Špičák reached toward Viktor, resting his hand on the younger man's shoulder or on his knee. On one occasion, when the professor reached out toward him but missed and his hand was awkwardly left hanging midair, Viktor leaned forward and held the older man's hand for a few minutes in a striking sign of affection and tenderness. I was reminded of my recent visit with the forty-five-year-old physiotherapist who spoke to Professor Špičák on my behalf, and the respectful, devoted way she walked up to her boss, a physician nearly in his nineties, and straightened out his collar and tie before he departed from the office. This sort of physical intimacy coupled with a watchful attendance to the needs of others is not unusual in the dynamics between junior and much older senior professionals and is indicative of how authority and respect in such contexts are not merely based on a senior person's power and influence over others but also involve a mode of deference displayed through acts of intimacy and care directed by younger people toward their elders.

Like many of the medical professionals I met, Professor Špičák began his conversation with an assertion of the "high standard" of Czech health care.

After a spirited explanation of how the measurement of asthma in the Czech Republic is much more rigorous and precise than just about anywhere else in the world—*all* Czech children, he told me, are assessed for asthma during their annual checkups, and those who have asthma are monitored across the country, repeatedly checked by allergists—he relaxed a little and slipped into describing his great passion: summer camps for asthmatic children. It is a subject, it seems, that he could talk about endlessly as he recounted over forty years of the history of summer camps, explicating their positive effects on children.

Through the course of the morning it became apparent that although "self-management" (*samostatná léčba*) is a part of the Czech Republic's official asthma policy guidelines, it isn't an idea that many physicians, much less patients, are familiar with. Although the Czech branch of the pharmaceutical giant GlaxoSmithKline encourages patients to undertake an online symptom-based self-test to see how well their asthma is under control, which initially looks very similar to the action plans handed out to patients in the United States or New Zealand, strikingly the only advice offered to those who are having problems is to "visit your doctor who will help you get your asthma under control" ("Test kontroly astmatu" n.d.). When I specifically asked how self-management policies are put into practice and if there are any situations in which patients are encouraged to alter their medication based on the self-test or on some other measures such as peak flow, Professor Špičák shrugged and replied halfheartedly, *We are teaching doctors that it is all right to ask patients do this, in terms of if they take one puff to raise it to two if they are getting a cold or something. Then after three or four months, when they next come in for a checkup, they can tell their doctor about it.*[1]

"So that sort of self-management *is* happening here?" I asked.

Professor Špičák adamantly shook his head and clarified: *We are still trying to* teach *doctors that this is possible.*

But if Professor Špičák is in favor of physicians engaging some of their patients in undertaking more self-focused care, he is decidedly opposed to moves to largely devolve asthma care out of the hands of specialists like himself. This is hardly surprising given that historically much of the care that in Western countries is viewed as belonging to the domain of "family medicine" or general practice has in the Czech Republic been carried out by specialists. As Lily Hoffman notes, under state socialism Czechoslovak, "Primary care doctors tended to function primarily as clerks and to refer most patients to specialists" (1997:

physicians' directives, as in the example of the mother who planned to buy her son a cat despite his allergies, as opposed to understandings of oneself and one's body, much less of one's illness.

"People Always Listen to Their Doctors Here"

Other doctors I spoke with complexified this picture but spoke in similar ways of the deference accorded to medical professionals. Some, such as a family of three physicians who invited me over to dinner, laughed over the very thought of self-management. Mirek is an oncologist in his mid-thirties. His wife, Jana, who is a few years younger, is an emergency room pediatrician who often cares for children with asthma. She herself also has asthma. At first Mirek was baffled when Jana and I tried to explain the concept of self-management to him. He then shrugged the whole idea off with the comment that

for the most part, patients will do whatever the doctors say. You commonly get patients who, when you ask them if they want an operation, say, "That is *your* decision, doctor, you tell me if I should have the operation or not." During the old [state socialist] system, people learned to listen to their doctors. It was said that the doctor knows more than the priest, more than the pope!

"Self-management just doesn't work here," Jana confirmed, "because Czech patients all prefer to come in and talk to their doctor rather than do it themselves."

Mirek's mother, a retired cardiologist, agreed: "People will always listen to their doctors here because a doctor is never questioned."

But counternarratives also proliferate. Out of earshot of her mother-in-law, Jana confided to me, "You know, I am one of those *noncompliant patients*. I *never* take *my* [preventative] asthma inhaler unless I feel very sick, or unless he [pointing at her husband] nags me." Although Jana may be unusually positioned by being both a patient and a medical authority, she is not the only one unable to reconcile her actual practices with received medical wisdom. Most Czech patients do not go as far as to refuse to take medication—the two people who told me they had are both doctors whose status grants them greater authority in questioning and contesting other physicians' medical judgments—but neither do they always unquestioningly follow their doctors' directives.

Patient Perspectives

It's not uncommon for patients to describe wanting to have more control over their health care. One area that is particularly contentious is preventative checkups. Although some patients are keen to take part more often in preventative visits, others expressed feeling overwhelmed by the amount of care they receive. Even Pavel, who spoke so eloquently of the state's responsibility to think for its citizens, laughingly criticized the thoroughness of his current family doctor, recounting that when his wife was in hospital and he stopped by the physician's office to pick up some paperwork, the doctor "grabbed me and pulled me into the consultation room." She promptly weighed him, took his blood pressure and a blood sample, ordered urine and stool tests, and then "sent me running all around Prague so that various other tests could be done." Were you OK? I asked. "Yes, the tests were all negative. I just hadn't been there for two or three years, so she grabbed the chance to check everything was fine," he explained.

An even more contentious area is patient–doctor communication. As has been widely noted by scholars, many Czechs complain of being belittled by doctors who never elicit their point of view (Benoit and Heitlinger 1998; Heitlinger and Trnka 1998; Heitlinger 1987; Hrešanová 2014; Read 2007). A case in point is forty-year-old Jitka, whose daughter has asthma. "There is one thing you need to know about the doctor who first took care of Alexandra when she started choking," Jitka bluntly recounted to me, "and that's that she was a bitch." "In this country," she continued, "when you ask something or try to get involved in your child's care, they treat you horribly. . . . They treat you as if you are so small, though of course when you come in for something like that you are already scared. And they make you feel like *nothing*." Jitka is unusual for trying to avoid biomedicine as much as possible and take her daughter's health care into her own hands. For the most part, however, although many people bristle at doctors' overriding authority, they do not necessarily envision themselves as equal partners in health-care decision making.

That said, even under state socialism there were two health-care activities in which patient agency was imperative: cultivating social networks and giving bribes. Despite the wide-scale marketization of the health-care system, both these activities remain key today in determining access to services as well as their quality.

The Legacies of Postsocialist Healthcare

Following the 1989 revolution, Czechoslovakia's health-care system, like other state services, underwent radical reform. Previously, medicine had been seen as a citizen's right, and services were provided for free (Heitlinger 1987). After the revolution, mass-scale privatization resulted in all public health-care services, with the exception of large hospitals, being sold into private hands.

In terms of the quality and general accessibility of medical care, prior to 1989 most observers rated Czechoslovak services as on par with Western European countries but with a distinct technology gap, particularly with respect to the shortage of pharmaceuticals (Čada n.d.). Czechoslovaks were, however, exceptional in terms of their very generous ratio of doctors and nurses to patients: in 1987 there were 36.6 doctors per 10,000 inhabitants as compared to 26.4 in Poland and 19.2 in Austria (Hoffman 1997: 350). As Hoffman notes, it was taken for granted that "more physicians and more beds meant better medical care" (ibid.). Quality of care was, however, inequitable, as sectors of the public deemed more valuable by the state, from high-ranking state officials to miners, were provided superior service (Lawson and Nemec 2003).

After the revolution, there were immediate moves toward the privatization of health care. As part of broad-scale changes in state–citizen relations, politicians such as Václav Klaus firmly embraced unfettered market-driven capitalism. Klaus, who was one of the principal economic advisors of the revolutionary Civic Forum and was finance minister in the transition government, later becoming prime minister (1992–1998) and then president (2003–2013), was particularly noted for promoting a "market without adjectives, . . . looking to the Thatcherite United Kingdom as its model" (Večerník 2008: 499). The result was a comprehensive shift in the organization of state services.

The restructuring of the health-care system included not only the introduction of new technologies but also the influx of more pharmaceuticals. Prior to the 1989 revolution, the range of available pharmaceuticals was severely restricted and access to commonly used drugs was concentrated in the hands of medical professionals, so much so that the dispensation of basic cough syrups required a doctor's prescription. After the revolution, the quantity and range of drugs grew exponentially. Although pharmaceutical companies receive very little public attention in the Czech Republic, working, as Colin Lawson and Juraj Nemec (2003: 223) note, largely outside of public notice, they are major actors in determining the pricing and availability of drugs. The Czech Republic has also become a significant site for international pharmaceutical clinical trials, with seemingly no shortage of patients willing to act as test subjects to gain access to the latest remedies before they are put up for government approval (Petryna 2009).

Alongside government and pharmaceutical companies, a third key player in determining health-care provision is insurance companies. Serious cuts in health-care funding took place during the 1990s. At the same time, in the interests of ensuring equity, the government supported the introduction of private health insurance companies with the proviso that no citizen be left uninsured. In 1992 VZP arose as a means of allowing state sponsorship of insurance for children, the elderly, and the unemployed, with the result that every citizen can now be insured. A number of other insurance companies—initially six, but later ballooning to twenty-six—were founded. In contrast, however, to many Western private insurance systems, coverage is underwritten by the state, creating a space for consumer choice but also ensuring that every person can have some sort of comprehensive health insurance—in other words, *solidárnost* alongside neoliberal consumerism.[2]

The state-supported consumer model is the most important aspect of a wider reform movement that emphasizes not only cutting costs but also the perceived benefits of increasing patient self-responsibility. As Karel Čada notes, "The wasting of money in health care [during state socialism] was associated [by reformists] primarily with personal patient responsibility. While the distribution of care provided by hospital professionals was considered reasonable, the way in which patients consumed health care was questioned" (2014: 431). Another means of attempting to instill increased individualized responsibility has been through the introduction of a system of small individual co-payments, on the understanding that if people need to invest their own money in their care, they will be more parsimonious and take only the services that they really need. Although medical care continues to be viewed as a citizen's right, previously free public services, including hospital stays, now incur small charges (not covered by insurance companies' payments). In 2008 patients were expected to pay 60 crowns (approximately US$2.40) per day spent in the hospital, and by 2012 the cost went to 90 crowns per day (approximately US$3.60).

From a patient's perspective, however, getting what one needs is not always a matter of being parsimonious, and often the differences in coverage offered by various insurance companies become extremely significant. Repeatedly, people pointed out to me the importance of being savvy as to these differences, in terms of not only costs but also the quality of care that results from different kinds of reimbursements. For example, when my middle-aged friend Vašek found out that he needed the bridge on his teeth replaced, he first visited a friend of his who is a dentist who told him exactly what he would need done and which insurance company would pay for it "the best." "You mean in terms of the amount of money you will need to contribute?" I asked him. "Oh, no," he clarified, "I mean in terms of what the insurance company will actually pay out to the dentist. You want to make sure the insurance company pays the dentist *properly*, so the dentist will *want* to work with this company and will do a good job."

For some, however, the sort of shopping around that Vašek and others engage in is seen as undermining the principles of *solidárnost* that are envisioned as being the very raison d'être of a system of universal coverage in the first place. As Dr. Šoucová saw it, solidarity only works when those who don't need a service contribute to help out those who do. "Some people have illnesses such as hemophilia that cost millions and that an individual can never pay for on their own, so we need to collectively cover them," she explained. "But all too often, you will find that people use VZP to cover a family member with a serious or chronic condition, even if the other family members are signed up with another insurance company. Take a family with three children: one of them needs glasses, so he is signed up with the company that gives the best coverage for glasses; the other needs to go to the health spa for asthma every year, so she is signed up with the company that has the most liberal payments for health spas; and the final child is very healthy and doesn't need much medical care so is signed up with a company that pays for him to go swimming and use the gym. It isn't right," she complained. "They *should* all be with one company. The principle of solidarity would *require* that they contribute into and be recompensed from the same fund. And solidarity should, after all, *begin* within the family. But there is no law requiring this."

Not only do insurance companies provide different amounts of coverage, but for a short while it appeared that the basic cost of public care would also be bifurcated along class lines. A two-tiered system of costs and services referred to as "standard" [*standard*] versus "above-standard" [*nadstandard*] care was introduced in 2011. How much a person was able to pay would determine whether he or she received basic (standard) or higher quality services. It was, however, widely feared that levels of payment would also determine the quality of interactions with medical personnel. As one woman explained to me,

If you go to the dentist for a filling, you will get the ugly, metal one for free [that is, with a small co-pay]. But the white one that looks nice or some *even nicer* kind, you will need to pay for. And then there is the care, too—they treat you differently, of course, if you are paying extra. If you are going on the standard insurance plan, they don't make any money off you, so they don't need to treat you well.

The policy promoting a two-tiered system of care was suspended after the Czech Social Democratic Party sued the government, arguing that public health care remains a fundamental right of Czech citizens and that differentiating between standard and above-standard care undermines citizens' equal access to health care. Although offering two tiers of *nonessential* services, such as standard versus higher-quality hospital food or better hospital accommodation, was found to be legal, the idea of providing above-standard *medical* care was deemed in these (and earlier debates) as contravening "the principle of solidarity" between citizens (cf. Mertl 2008).

Regardless of the legalities of above-standard care, such practices have openly continued under other guises. In 2013, the head of one of Prague's largest hospitals publicly declared his support for selling special cards that would allow so-called VIP patients more frequent preventative visits and access to after-hours care not available to the general public. In the future, VIPs would also have their own designated entry into the hospital, enabling them to circumvent the long lines in the waiting rooms and be seen directly by medical professionals (Petrášová 2013).

Clearly, for the few who have the means of paying extra for their health care, the possibility of making such kinds of consumer choices and being *able* to be exercise personal responsibility are very attractive. For most people, however, these kinds of opportunities are far beyond what they can afford. A much more common concern for most patients is how to build solid, and ideally long-term, relationships with doctors when money is in limited supply.

Networking for Care

When a person falls seriously ill, it is common for their family members or close friends to use whatever social networks are available to them to gain access to care. Sometimes this involves calling on other kin or close friends who are well placed in the health-care system. On other occasions, and particularly among those without any connections in the medical profession, people need to actively search out a connection. Jiří's story of how his wife got to see one of the top oncologists in Prague is emblematic: "I got the best care for her," Jiří recounted. "I asked all my friends and finally found a guy on my soccer team whose brother is a top oncologist, and he got her in to see him." Like Jiří, for many a crucial part of the work of care is not just what happens during or after a doctor's visit, but the time and effort it takes to get someone in through the door of the doctor's office in the first place.

Once a relationship with a doctor is established, it needs to be maintained, particularly if it will involve long-term care. Although such relations are often predicated on proximities of social relations (that is, being the friend of a friend), they are also lubricated through material exchanges. This might involve cash donations or bribes, though frequently it also involves gifts of consumer goods. One physician, offering an early evening drink in her office, asked, "What would you like?" before adding, "I have *everything*," and opening up a cupboard overflowing with bottles of alcohol—all gifts from thankful patients. For patients, the question of what to give often involves a good deal of thought and planning. When I thanked one of my relatives for a gift of porcelain and commented on its very fine design, she showed me a collection of various pieces she had purchased in a village on the other side of the country and brought back to Prague to distribute. Pointing to a particularly large and ornate bowl, she told me it is intended for the eye surgeon who carried out her mother-in-law's recent operation. "It's a way of saying thank you," she explained. "The surgeon did a really good job," her husband interjected, "*and* he wrote it up as a different kind of operation—one that the insurance company policy would cover all the costs for—so we need to show our appreciation."

The gifts that smooth such exchanges constitute hidden fees that help determine levels of care. This is true as much today as it was in the era of state socialism. Whether referred to as "presents," "donations," or "bribes," informal, under-the-table payments are commonplace and often get added into family accounting practices as part of the expected cost of service. But although the donation/gift/bribe might appear as yet another form of payment, it is more about creating a relationship than paying for a particular discrete service. As Marcel Mauss ([1925] 1954) long ago brought to our attention, at the heart of gift exchange lies much more than an exchange of objects (or money): through gifting, social relations are created and solidified.

Among Czech patients and doctors, relationships that involve bribes are often long term, with the gift an essential means of acknowledging appreciation and enabling ongoing interactions to take place on a friendly register. As many Czechs told me, getting good care is not all about paying a lot of money, it is also about whom you know, and although drawing on one's social networks is one way of tapping into connections, the gift is another avenue for creating connections that, it is hoped, will translate into better service (cf. Stan 2012).

There is a crucial difference to gift giving today in comparison to the days of state socialism. Previously patients were assigned a doctor and did not have any choice in whom they saw for their medical care. In such a context, the gift acted as a means of attempting to improve a preexisting and, for the most part, fixed relationship. Today, however, patient–doctor relations are subject to consumer choice. The gift thus takes on the added valence of introducing an element of anticipated longevity into what could otherwise be a limited service transaction: one who is not anticipating further exchanges is not as likely to give gifts for services already provided. The gift therefore assists in recasting patient–doctor relationships into a wider framework of ongoing care so that the doctor (hopefully) becomes invested in the relationship and takes seriously his or her responsibility for the patient's well-being.

Good medical care from this perspective is contingent not only on money but also on the *satisfaction* of the medical provider. Although Dr. Šoucová proclaimed that medical care is never dependent on a doctor's spite or anger, clearly many Czechs are motivated by the desire to make their doctor happy. The interrelationality inherent in care is central for understanding these dynamics, as on the one hand, patients see themselves as responsible for keeping their doctors content, and, on the other, doctors' responsibilities to their patients are thought to increase once they get to know their patients and become indebted to them through the logic of gift exchange. Unlike in models of short-term consumer choice, success is dependent on each party acting to solidify their relationship through the exchanges of goods and services, payments, and acts of respect.

This is not to suggest that medical professionals are only motivated by gifts, nor that there do not exist warm, much less caring, relationships between doctors and patients regardless of gifts given or not. The point here is that both access to medical care and the quality of care cannot be taken for granted. Instead of being passive recipients of care, as they are often portrayed by the press and in popular discourse, patients (and family members on their behalf) maneuver the system, using gifts to position themselves as well-meaning toward their doctors, in the hope of benefiting from a reciprocal exchange. As Sabina Stan has noted of similar dynamics in Romania, "Patients' insistence on their voluntary role in informal presentations is an attempt to re-place themselves, at least symbolically, in the higher position of gift-givers (Mauss 1989), as opposed to mere payers of services" (2012: 74; see also Polese 2014 on the Ukraine). Likewise, although many Czechs complain of the additional costs of gifts or bribes, even those with very limited incomes generally depict them as a positive means of asserting some level of influence in medical encounters.

At the same time, there is a widely held public understanding that many medical professionals are motivated to do their best for their patients not due to personal connections, much less a desire for gifts or money, but out of deeply held moral convictions, similar to what Koch (2013b) has noted of public perceptions of medical professionals in Georgia. Indeed, one man who grew up with severe asthma made a point of emphasizing that both of the very prominent doctors who have cared for him throughout his life are motivated by strong moral principles, one being a confirmed Christian and the other "a very devout socialist." But whatever else is thought to inspire medical professionals, some patients are inclined to shop around for the best insurance deal to keep their doctor happy. Many others engage in decades of exchanges with the same physician to ensure that their doctor is motivated to do his or her best.

Model Doctors, Model Patients

Jaroslav has been battling severe asthma for nearly all the forty-five years of his life. A university librarian, he had a systematic way of rendering his illness narrative, starting off by dumping the contents of a plastic bag onto the table of the cafe where we were meeting. Box after box of medication came rolling out, and he lined them all up, one by one, before telling me what each one is for and exactly how it relates to his asthma. From inhalers, nose sprays, and antihistamine pills to prednisone tablets and heart medication (necessary because of the detrimental effects of the asthma medication on his heart), each one spoke to the centrality of this disease in his life.

In some ways, Jaroslav could be the poster child for asthma. He has, in fact, contributed an account of his childhood experiences with asthma to a lay health magazine, a copy of which he sent me prior to our meeting. The key to dealing with asthma, Jaroslav declared, is ensuring the training of good doctors and nurses, and he held up his care as emblematic of this. From his early childhood up until the age of fourteen, he spent three to four months of every year in the hospital. He described the experience as one of "solidarity between patients" and the building of very strong ties with his nurses, his two specialists, and the support staff. "My two doctors helped me with everything, even the emotional side of dealing with these things," he explained. "We have built up a relationship over my lifetime, and they take *care* of me. Dr. Špičák takes care of *all* my health needs. Once I had a very bad attack, and he drove to my house and then took me in his car to the hospital because it would be faster than the ambulance."

I asked Jaroslav about self-management, but he didn't recognize the term, either in English or in Czech. After thinking about my explanation for a while, he said, "I think self-management is a mistake, even though my asthma was so extreme I did something similar, in terms of using a peak flow meter at home and managing my own medical intake instead of going straight to my doctor. But monitoring your asthma is the doctor's responsibility. No one else can know what to do, and it should be done by a specialist, not your average doctor." The main factors, he concluded, that determine your quality of care are your doctor and the medications at their disposal. He turned back to the array of drugs laid out across the table, carefully picking up another one and asking me, "Do you have this in New Zealand?"

Ongoing Oversight

Unlike Jaroslav, fifty-year-old Klára wasn't diagnosed with asthma until recently, and her case is very mild, usually requiring just a daily dose of Symbicort (a popular combination of inhaled corticosteroid and long-acting beta-agonist), which her specialist raises whenever she gets ill. She sees a lung specialist for a checkup and spirometry reading regularly. Her health insurance policy requires six-month checkups, but she explains that she goes every three months "just to be sure." "Of course my health insurance pays for this," she told me with surprise when I asked about the cost. "They like to support preventative health care," she added. And when her breathing isn't right, she can see the doctor as often as she needs to adjust her medication. "He will tell me to try and scale back to such and such an amount unless I feel bad. You can feel it when it gets tight in your chest, and so you use the medicine before you go to bed at night."

It took a long time for her to be diagnosed, she explained, as she spent four or five years "coughing and coughing" but had no other symptoms. Her regular physician was convinced she had asthma, but the specialists kept saying she didn't, until she was hospitalized with her first major asthma attack. "But we can't blame them," her husband Martin added, "as she is an atypical case, with just a lot of coughing." Ever since she's begun using an inhaler, her life has changed. "I get up and use it straight away, just one intake of breath, and I am good for the day," she recounted. Although the diagnosis might have been fraught, now that it is finally sorted out, Klára has found that under the close supervision of her specialist her asthma is very easy to cope with.

Despite the differences in the acuteness of their asthma, both Jaroslav and Klára make use of ongoing specialist supervision. Their relationships of care are based on trust (although even "good doctors" may sometimes be mistaken), respect for authority, and engagement in high-tech medical care. They engage in acts of self-care but under the intensive oversight of their physicians. Each of them also narrates an illness account that revolves around the personalities of their particular doctors as much as the power of pharmaceuticals. Having, at least momentarily, found solutions to ease their suffering, both are grateful for the steps taken by the medical establishment on their behalf, and neither one is particularly keen to take a greater role in determining her or his own health care. Although certainly not every patient experiences such satisfaction in her or his care, their stories are emblematic of what many Czechs hope for in their medical encounters.

For patients like Jaroslav and Klára, the "empowerment" offered by self-management would be largely seen as burdensome, particularly if it got in the way of retaining the attention and oversight of trained medical professionals. Although the implementation of neoliberal health-care policies has opened up both new opportunities (changing doctors at will) and new concerns (paying fees for medical care), it has not fundamentally reshaped their outlook on where medical knowledge lies nor on how patients and doctors should relate to one another.

Good care is, however, composed of much more than what happens in the medical clinic. As Mrs. Malinová recounted in her explanation of why even under state socialism an alcoholic was refused treatment in a health spa, another important element of care is what—if anything—gets brought home from the medical encounter. And although some families of children with asthma do their best to carry out a multitude of doctor's directives, others take a decidedly more oppositional approach.

Chapter 4

Knowledge, Discipline, and Domesticity

The Work of Raising Healthy Children

"WHEN Alexandra was about eleven months old, she had what at first looked like a normal cold, but then one day she started to wheeze," Alexandra's mother, Jitka, explained. "By the second night, I thought she was almost choking. *So what do you do as a parent?* You go immediately to the hospital. There they gave her corticosteroids, which opened up her lungs. They kept her there, on corticosteroids and some other drugs, for four days. They wanted to keep her in hospital longer, but I decided that that was enough . . ."

Although relieved that the treatment had effectively counteracted her daughter's breathing problems, Jitka found the days she spent beside her daughter's hospital bed increasingly hard to bear. She described Alexandra's doctors' reluctance to communicate with her, much less involve her in their decision making, as key factors in her resolution to seek an early discharge. "I don't like how doctors deal with people," she recounted. "They explain very little because they *are* the doctor; they don't want to hear from you. I want some discussion, some say in what happens. . . . Of course when she was choking, I didn't need an explanation [of what they were doing], but after that, I wanted to know." Jitka summed up the hospital experience: "After a while, you can't take it anymore, physically, as a person." And so she demanded to take her daughter home, an act that would have been not only unthinkable but illegal under the previous regime.

By the time of these events in 2007, a reconstructed political-legal system that places increasing amounts of responsibility and accountability onto parents rather than the state enabled Jitka to decide that a long hospital stay would be detrimental to Alexandra's health and that the best thing for both her and her daughter was to go home. "I had to sign a written undertaking [*reverz*] that I was taking her home at my own peril [*na vlastní riziko*]," Jitka explained, before describing her subsequent efforts to help Alexandra overcome the worst of her asthma. Despite repeated hospitalizations, she did her best to limit her daughter's reliance on state-authorized medical care.

In many ways, Jitka's decision to minimize biomedical interventions is extreme, and the steps she took set her apart from most Czech parents. And yet Jitka also exemplifies the tug between adhering to physicians' extensive instructions, oversight, and regimentation of care, on the one hand, and resistance against their authority and the assertion of her own knowledge and standing as a parent, on the other. This chapter is about how Czech women navigate the tricky terrain of following doctors' recommendations while crafting their own responsibility, authority, and accountability as parents of asthmatic children. It is a story of how motherhood, care, and domestic regimes are constituted in relation, and often in subordination, to doctors' expertise. It is also a story of parental concerns over how to raise healthy children with immune systems strong enough to cope with illness.

My analysis of these dynamics focuses on how parents, especially mothers, alternatively make use of and reject doctors' directives as part of their daily activities of tending to children with chronic or potentially chronic respiratory conditions. I suggest that rather than competing over expertise—claiming, for example, to be "half a doctor" as some New Zealand parents do—in the Czech Republic the attribution of medical knowledge to medical professionals is, for the most part, undisputed. Most parents want to be secure in the knowledge that their child's doctor knows much more about his or her condition than they do. But parents, and mothers in particular, also engage in other forms of knowledge that sometimes lead to contradictory conclusions from those advocated by medical staff.

Working through these contradictions can be fraught, as they link to larger issues of who is responsible and accountable for children's health, well-being, and upbringing. Under state socialism, the balance of power between parents and the state differed dramatically from today, as the state was able to directly intervene in children's lives to a much greater degree. The state's oversight included medical care, education, food, and housing, as well as inculcating children in socialist ideology (Tesar 2012). In families who opposed the regime, children sometimes struggled to reconcile two versions of reality, one taught to them in school and another experienced at home (Trnka 2012). As one woman said of her childhood in the 1960s, for some children the result was "chaos in our heads. We believed our parents, but at school they poured something else into our heads. There was much confusion."

Over twenty-five years later, in a democratic, neoliberalizing state, people continue to wrestle, albeit in radically different circumstances, with where responsibilities for and over children lie. These questions traverse both the very mundane and the intensely political: Who will make sure a child does not misbehave if she or he is left in a health spa for curative treatment for six weeks? To what extent is the state responsible for providing children with health care? Who is responsible for the air pollution that, it is assumed, makes so many children sick in the first place? At what point should children—and adults—start to be responsible for themselves?

These questions emerge out of a cultural terrain where medical and scientific expertise, maternal care, and bodily discipline are widely accorded to be key factors in successfully ensuring health. In the Czech Republic, knowledge about health is not often viewed as residing in the hands of lay people. It is also, however, widely accepted that to be efficacious, some of the knowledge that belongs to the domain of elite specialists must be turned into practical, realizable action. This is achieved via the inculcation of very specific practices and daily regimes that are passed down the hierarchy as doctors and other health professionals "train" mothers who in turn, it is assumed, "train" children in self-care.

Although this may seem similar to the activities of physicians, nurses, and asthma societies in New Zealand, both the intensity and the premise are different; instead of a few minutes or an hour of sharing knowledge and "empowering" patients to take charge of their own care and (hopefully) make the right decisions, this dynamic consists of rigorous, one-on-one training of mothers and children to carry out very specific activities in the precise ways shown by doctors, nurses, and other medical staff. Much like the training of an apprentice (Grasseni 2004; Ingold 2001), mothers are posited as novices in need of instruction on how to view the body and act appropriately toward it.

Although the Czech model is premised on deeply entrenched hierarchies of knowledge and authority, actual *control* over what children do and what is done to them has, since the end of state socialism, largely shifted out of the hands of doctors as representatives of the state over to parents. Whereas once parents did not have the authority to openly contravene doctors' directives, now they can. Moreover, in the daily lives of families, enactments of care frequently involve contestation as well as compliance between both parents and medical professionals, and parents and children.

Care for children with asthma is thus constituted within a cultural space in which knowledge and authority are vested in actors (medical professionals, mothers, fathers, and children) who are positioned within an explicit social hierarchy that is realized and reinforced through their everyday interactions with one another. And yet, this is also a space in which multiple kinds of knowledge rub up against one another—be it the formal and experiential knowledge of a medical specialist at the height of his or her career, the experiential knowledge of a mother dealing (repeatedly) with a sick child, widespread social understandings of powerful medicinal substances as inherently both efficacious and dangerous (that is, a *pharmakon*), or the "objective knowledge" that is presumed to be collected and made transparent through medical apparatuses such as the spirometer. Although each of these ways of knowing are seen as valuable within their own contexts, when juxtaposed with one another, they necessarily require acts of revaluation and reconciliation.

In practical terms, mothers engage in taking on, adapting, and resisting therapeutic practices based on perceptions of their utility as well as practical exigencies such as having the time and the ability to carry them out. Rather than struggling over who has medical knowledge and the capacity for medical decision making, as do some New Zealand parents, this then is primarily a struggle over the place of medical knowledge in constituting domestic care.

Mothers wield tremendous amounts of power and responsibility within the domestic sphere, viewing intensive care and oversight of their children, often up into their early twenties, as a fundamental aspect of appropriate motherly love. They also, however, often eschew openly asserting their abilities and power as part of their deference to medical professionals who are hierarchically superior. The result is that mothers often walk a careful tightrope of deflecting the appearance of power and responsibility while in fact consolidating and actively enacting it. One reason for their deference is their own respect for social hierarchy. Significantly, however, their willingness to show respect also serves another purpose: namely, to engage others in actively caring for and taking responsibility for their children. Raising a child comes to be a collective effort, overseen by a mother but not solely her responsibility. When it comes to health care, the ideal that emerges is thus far removed from the self-responsible patient-expert who is self-reliant and largely independent in making her own decisions about her child's health; instead, here the ideal parent is one who quietly makes behind-the-scenes decisions but also adeptly engages the interest of medical authorities to take good care of her children.

The Gendered Terrain of Domestic Care

These dynamics are rooted in deeply held assumptions about not only power and knowledge but also gender. When I spoke with fathers, as well as brothers and sons, of people who suffer from asthma, much of their focus was on how to *gain access* to medical care, in particular the social relations used to facilitate care for their family members. They spoke much less about actual interactions with medical practitioners and even less about everyday acts of care that take place within the family—both activities that are widely deemed to be women's responsibilities.

Even fathers who are seemingly responsible for managing households are often not well informed about the specifics of their children's health care. Albert, who is in his mid-forties, was widowed fourteen years ago when his son was eight years old. He remarried a few years later. He was keen to talk to me about his son's early struggles with asthma, regaling me with dramatic stories about rushing him to the hospital in the midst of a serious asthma attack. But he could not answer any of the practical questions regarding his son's health care, such as what the onset of his asthma was like, if he saw an allergist or respiratory specialist, or if he ever received allergy shots. "My (first) wife Nad'a would've done all that. I was busy working," he explained. He turned to his current wife and asked, "Do you think he went to an allergist?" "He must've," she said, nodding her head. "Nad'a was a very conscientious mother; she would've taken him on all the necessary doctors' visits."

Albert is not alone in not knowing much about the specifics of his son's routine medical care. The gendered nature of domestic care is such that when I asked two mothers of asthmatic boys if their husbands ever take their sons to the doctor, they both burst out laughing. "That would be great if they did, fantastic!" one cried out, while the other added, "Imagine that! The neighbors would say, 'What kind of a wife is that, that *he's* the one who takes their son to the doctor!'" Another mother, who is also a physician, similarly found the suggestion of fathers taking their children to the doctor ridiculous and stated point-blank that "it is self-evident that the mother takes care of the children, not the father. The mum takes care of everything."

In fact, some fathers prove the exception and take their children on doctors' visits or accompany them on longer-term health-care treatments such as multiweek spa cures. An increasing number are also becoming the primary caretakers for young children (Maříková 2008). But, for most people, it was and still is the women in their families who provide most of the day-to-day care.

In previous decades, however, the mother was often joined by maternal and paternal grandmothers who took on a significant share of the responsibilities for child care. When Petr Kocour, a retired physician in his mid-seventies whose mother was ill with tuberculosis for much of his childhood and later developed asthma, told me his life history, he related, "I was raised by my grandma. My father came home at 7 or 8 pm for dinner. I used to say, 'I have two mothers: my mother and my grandmother.'" Dr. Kocour's experiences are not atypical, as today's ideal of the mother at home was not always realized by previous generations, particularly during the period of state socialism when, except for when they were on maternity leave, women under the age of retirement were required to work outside of the home, resulting in grandmothers often becoming key caretakers of children (Heitlinger and Trnka 1998). Yet the image of the mother at home providing for all her child's needs is a particularly emotive one, and the role often described as that of a "traditional mother" (*tradiční matka*) is widely socially embraced by women across a range of class and educational backgrounds. Not surprisingly, then, most medical professionals and parents alike focus their discussions of home health care on the role of mothers.

Wrestling with Medical Expertise

The majority of the mothers I spoke with were quick to initially claim that they relied entirely on their physicians' guidance in dealing with their children's health issues. As part of the value attributed to experts, many women stated that they did not see why anyone would want to talk to them about their children's health instead of talking to their doctors. It was only once our discussions were well underway that they delved into describing the more nuanced aspects of their actual interactions with doctors and with their children.

Unlike New Zealand parents, who rarely comment about the personal characteristics of the doctors who care for them or their children, a key point many Czech parents emphasize is the character of their child's doctor. "A good doctor" is defined not only as someone who provides high-quality care in terms of his or her knowledge and effectiveness but also in terms of being patient and flex-ible, approving concessions that others will not. For example, Eva described her daughter's doctor as "very good" because he explains procedures to her daugh-ter and waits for her to agree to them. For Olga, a good doctor is one who al-lows patients to bend the rules, for instance allowing them to have a family pet: "We are allowed animals—some [doctors] don't even allow fish because the fish food has allergens in it. But our allergist is great—she doesn't ban us from everything," she explained. Significantly, Olga depicted the physician as having the power to not only advise on but to some extent *determine* her household's practices, as if the doctor could in fact ban her family from having pets. Such a view is informed by experiences under state socialism when domestic practices were indeed seen as open to state scrutiny.

Reflecting more explicitly on some of these dynamics, Alena, who is both the mother of a teenage son with moderate asthma and a physician, spoke about bending the rules with respect to a similar "no pets" policy laid down by his doc-tors. Alena not only openly discussed contravening the doctor's orders but also reflected on the limited nature of medical surveillance today, recounting,

It is true that the doctors in the hospital were very strict when we wanted to have an animal at home, despite [our son] not having tested positive to any allergens. . . . They told us that we were absolutely not allowed to have any . . . so as not to complicate his situation. They took it really seriously and said, "You should be happy that [your son's treatment] is going well, and if your other child wants to play with pets, have them go to the neighbor's house."

However, despite the doctors' "seriousness" and "very strict" instructions, Alena related that "we now have a hedgehog because we found him and could not abandon him. He has spines that my son could conceivably be allergic to, but there haven't been any problems. So who knows? But when you ask the doc-tor, they don't let you have anything at all."

Alena went on to suggest that not only were the medical professionals ap-parently unduly restrictive, they are also now powerless to enforce their judg-ment; she explained that her son's physicians do not know about the existence of their new pet and then added, "But they also didn't check that we cleaned up our house and got rid of the carpets [as they told us to do]. They probably took it that that was *our* responsibility to do that . . . "

Like many of the mothers I spoke with, Alena depicted her responses to physicians' advice in a way that depicts her actions as almost involuntary. The hedgehog, for example, was described as not acquired but found and "could not be abandoned." She vacillated in affirming her son's physicians' power, explaining how they required her to rid the house of allergens but also noting their inabilities to enforce their decrees—it wasn't, she suggested, as if the medical authorities could come to the house and check that she had actually cleaned it, in contrast to the state socialist period when such an action would not have been unthinkable.

Alena's behavior exemplifies how, in an intensely hierarchical system, the flip side to respect can often be passive resistance. In the Czech Republic, such behavior is popularly referred to as *švejkismus*, in reference to the popular literary character from Jaroslav Hašek's 1923 novel *The Good Soldier Švejk*. Švejk's claim to fame is bumbling through his career as a soldier in the First World War, misinterpreting his superiors' orders with hilarious results, much like the American children's book character Amelia Bedelia. But, in Švejk's case, his misunderstandings enable him to both undermine his superiors' nefarious objectives and save his life. There are heated debates in Czech culture about whether Švejk is an imbecile and his good fortune is due to luck, or if, as most Czechs assert, he is actually very cunningly engaging in passive resistance by pretending to misunderstand them (see Červinková 2009). Either way, Švejk always comes out on top, and—importantly—cannot be held to account for contravening instructions he ostensibly did not understand. He thus manages to evade both the tasks he doesn't want to undertake and taking responsibility for standing up against them. In a similar way, although mothers very occasionally describe openly negotiating with their children's physicians, more often they explicitly uphold the right of medical authorities to determine their children's care while simultaneously portraying their own actions as a form of passive resistance against medical professionals' authoritative, and often unreasonably restrictive, demands.

The Perfect Mother

That being a good mother involves both seeking out expert advice and intervention and resisting it should perhaps come as no surprise given the values that have historically been attributed to both motherhood and the domestic sphere. During the state socialist period, domestic space was characterized as apolitical, and motherhood was viewed as enabling women to live untainted by politics, at least while they were at home with their children (Heitlinger and Trnka 1998; Holy 1996; Šiklová 1997; Trnka and Busheikin 1993).

The notion that there can be a strict divide of social life into discrete public and private spheres has been rightly complicated by feminist scholars and scholars of postsocialism. Nonetheless, it has also been noted that the *perception* of an almost impermeable divide between public and private was highly valued in socialist contexts (Yurchak 2005). As Susan Gal and Gail Kligman (2000) write, even though where or what was characterized as "public" versus "private" was constantly shifting, this did not detract from the ideological force that was invested in this dichotomization. Living under state socialism, people engaged in what was popularly referred to as an "inner emigration," allowing them to "realize" themselves in private while keeping public personas intact (Wheaton and Kavan 1992: 9; see also Holy 1996). The most mundane facets of domestic life—such as home cooking, for example—were highly valued as "things that lay outside of the control of the state . . . and were often used as symbols of what was pure, real and 'ours'" (Haukanes and Pine 2003: 108). The domestic was thus defined as a "natural" apolitical space, characterized by maternal agency (although, as we shall see, the perception of motherhood as apolitical was also capitalized on by political groups such as the Prague Mothers as a way of enabling women to protest against the state socialist regime).

Immediately following the end of state socialism in 1989, the value of motherhood and domesticity intensified. In public discourse, the "return" of women to their "rightful" sphere of the home was hailed as a victory against the socialist state (Trnka and Busheikin 1993). For example, in interviews I conducted with young women in the early 1990s, many of them asserted that they felt most empowered by staying at home (Heitlinger and Trnka 1998). One stay-at-home mother, who was a former nurse, explained, "Both in the dental and the dermatology clinic [where I worked], I had to listen to someone else. I don't like listening to someone else. . . . [At home] I can set my own schedule. However I make it, so it is" (Heitlinger and Trnka 1998: 92). At the same time, however, changes in the economy have made it markedly more difficult for families to rely on a single income, leading to increasing numbers of women entering (or reentering) the paid labor force, despite the country's unusually liberal three-year maternity provisions (Heitlinger and Trnka 1998).

That said, motherhood remains a socially esteemed undertaking. In Czech discourse, the mother is the embodiment of love, often endowed with almost superhuman powers of protection. As Jekaterina Kalēja, Zane Linde, and Ilze Mileiko (2011) have noted, in many Central and East European societies, there is no model of a "good mother," much less of a "good enough mother," but only of the perfect mother who is able to do *everything* for her child and preempt all his or her needs. Even when women combine motherhood with paid labor outside of the home, they often emphasize their abilities to embody the elements of a stay-at-home mother. As forty-year-old part-time teacher Helena said, "I am a traditional mother [*tradiční matka*] even though I work, because I work only in the hours that my son is at school. When he comes home, he doesn't even know that I've been out. I am *always* here for him."

Not all mother–child relations can live up to this ideal, particularly given the historical shifts in both what mothering entails and what is economically and socially possible. It is, however, against this image of the perfect mother that many women, faced with children who are in need of ongoing health care, must construct their home lives. Many struggle to cope with not only the seemingly endless rounds of medical visits but also medical directives that are so specific and broad-ranging that they are difficult to realize in the space of domestic life. If motherhood is depicted as being about a mother's freedom and capacity for self-realization, the harsh reality is often one of balancing competing demands while attempting to do right by one's children and other family members.

In families of children with asthma, great maternal effort often goes into providing children with a socially appropriate home life while attending to the practical exigencies of asthma care. Three areas of concern that frequently emerge in managing children's home health care are reliable diagnoses (in particular, the use of spirometry), the efficacy and danger of steroids, and the difficulties of bolstering children's immune systems.

Diagnosis and the Need for Objective Technologies

Across the Czech Republic, the spirometer has become the primary means of providing objective diagnostic information about asthma.[1] In contrast to New Zealand, where the use of spirometry is much less frequent, without exception, every adult with asthma, every parent of a child with asthma, or even anyone who has been *suspected* by medical professionals of having asthma whom I spoke to in the Czech Republic recounted the first spirometry test as a defining moment in determining a diagnosis. Insurance policy guidelines recommend that asthma patients regularly have spirometry at three-, six-, or twelve-month intervals, and, for most patients, these tests are used to confirm and calibrate treatment.

In Czech clinics, spirometry is often administered by an allergy or respiratory specialist and is usually depicted as being simply *read*, rather than actively *interpreted*, by those who administer it. Indeed, it is rare for Czech doctors to mention any ambiguity with respect to spirometry results. Rather, the ease with which technologies such as spirometry are utilized is seen as affirming the expertise of medical professionals and further delineating the lay–professional divide (cf. Saunders 2008).

Most patients and parents of patients, including those who otherwise shy away from other forms of biomedical treatment, engage in what Mary-Jo DelVecchio Good (2001) has so aptly described as the "biotechnical embrace," welcoming the spirometer with great enthusiasm and hope, sure that it will provide objective evidence about one's respiratory health. Some parents even bemoan the fact that children under the age of three or four are usually not administered a spirometry test (as they would find performing the necessary controlled inhalations and exhalations too difficult). Helena and Radka, both mothers of two-year-old sons, are exceedingly pleased their doctors insist on doing spirometry with their boys despite their young ages. Both mothers told me that their sons "hate" and "fear" spirometry tests but that they are absolutely "necessary for evaluating their condition." Another mother explained to me that she is frustrated that her daughter cannot have spirometry tests because she collapsed the first time she tried and then a few years later, she similarly collapsed attempting to blow up a balloon. Being unable to exert her lungs as required means that "now there can be no spirometry for her, which makes it hard to know how she is progressing."

Nonetheless, there are rare occasions when parents raise questions about tricky or even faulty readings. Alena, who is both a mother and physician, was the most vocal about both her ambivalence about and reliance on spirometry readings. Her thirteen-year-old son has been using daily corticosteroids for the past ten and a half years. Twice a year he has spirometry tests that determine whether to adjust his current level of medication. Alena related that spirometry is a central feature of his care, as it constitutes "an objective measure and is therefore *very* important to figuring out what to do with his care.... Sometimes, once in a while, I wonder if he isn't using the drugs too much. But the spirometry shows me if and where there is a problem."

At the same time, however, Alena routinely disregards spirometry results that she thinks are inaccurate, explaining,

I know the autumn spirometry will be worse than the spring one—it always is due to the cold weather. But they take those numbers as if they represent the whole year and [set his medication according to them]. But I know as a mother (*jako matka*) that that's not right. So in the summer, when the weather is good, I lower the dose or cut it in half. . . . Usually I stop it completely for three weeks or up to a month . . . but I tell no one because his doctors don't agree. They don't think we should try [to occasionally stop using medication]. But [I think that] if it goes well all year, the doctor could lower the dose.

Significantly, her son's doctors are not the only ones who are not informed of Alena's alterations of drug dosages. I asked her what her husband thinks of taking their son off his medication every year, and she replied that he is unaware she does this. Then, a little bit defensively, she explained that "as a doctor," she feels competent to make this decision without discussing it with anyone. I then asked her what her *son* thinks about not using his medication over the summer, and she seemed surprised by the question, explaining that he is still young and unaware of what his dosage should be and therefore just follows her instructions.

Although it is likely that Alena's medical training gives her insights into how technologies such as spirometers can be interpreted in different ways, she portrayed her understanding of her son's physicians' use of the spirometry results as based not on her medical expertise but on another kind of knowledge—the *experiential* knowledge that she derives *as a mother*. Her account thus suggests that although physicians may be expert at reading spirometers, mothers know things about children's seasonal respiratory patterns that spirometers cannot. At other points, however, Alena justified her competency in determining her son's medication dosage precisely through her identity as a physician, suggesting a fluid and contextual use of both identities. Significantly, Alena was one of the very few people I spoke with who determines her family's use of medication in opposition to medical professionals' advice. Her sentiments, however, put her in good company, given the many mothers and fathers who wonder if their children aren't taking too many steroids for their own good.

Corticosteroids: The Power of the *Pharmakon*

Like Jaroslav, the librarian and lifelong asthmatic who narrated his life story by means of a journey through his own personal pharmacopeia, often when parents of asthmatic children first met me, they came armed with various packets of medication to show me exactly what their children are taking. They wanted to discuss both the specific medications and their concerted efforts to cut back on them, if and when possible.

Similar to some New Zealanders' concerns over the dangers of steroids, Czechs express widespread awareness of drugs as potentially having both positive and negative effects, of being a *pharmakon* in Derrida's (1981) use of the term. Numerous people's illness narratives center on drugs as panaceas, highlighting their almost instant ability to save lives. Michal repeatedly related to me how his son David had an extreme asthma attack at a local cinema, usually concluding the account by stating that once they got home and he gave David his prednisone "everything was OK." Similarly, my friend Jiří, whose sister was asthmatic as a child, recounted that "she would cough and cough until she choked and needed to use her inhaler. Then *puff puff puff*, and she would be OK."

At the same time there is also wariness over how easily doctors give out medication. Radim, an insurance salesman whose teenage son has asthma, told me, "Czechs take everything the doctor tells them to. They just take it, even if they don't know what it's for. People take medication to make their blood pressure go up or down *or both*. Everyone has loads of medicine. It's like people show off about all the drugs they take . . . [but] I don't trust drugs." Discussing her three-year-old daughter's asthma medication, Markéta, a thirty-year-old secretary, complained that "all the doctors give you higher doses than you need, just as a preventative." Her friend, who is the mother of a young boy with asthma, concurred, noting that "in the autumn the air is dirty [which makes you cough], but the allergy specialist just said [of my son], 'It's asthma.' And that's that [*a hotovo*]! And he gave him drugs for it! It's unbelievable!"

For some, concerns over the hasty diagnosis of asthma, as well as the eagerness of doctors to give out drugs, lead to diagnostic refusals, similar to those among New Zealanders. And yet, even those who refuse the diagnosis of asthma continue to give asthma medication to their children. Eva, for example, initially said there was no point in my speaking with her about asthma as her daughter does not have asthma any more, but then it becomes clear that her daughter uses a daily preventative inhaler, regularly sees a respiratory specialist, and undergoes spirometry every three months. Whatever Eva's thoughts about whether her daughter has asthma, she receives asthma care, including daily medication.

Similarly, Tomáš, the father of three-year-old Honza, who was diagnosed with asthma eight months earlier, suggested to me that his son might not be asthmatic given that he only had one bout of asthma about a year ago. His wife, however, quickly interjected that the boy's condition likely improved due to the change of seasons; come winter again, she thought he would be found to be asthmatic. Regardless of their divergent perspectives on young Honza's diagnosis, he is under the care of a respiratory specialist, receives daily allergy medication, and always has a Ventolin inhaler on hand, the necessity of which neither of his parents debate.

Unlike the many New Zealanders who view asthma as situational and therefore refuse daily medication, in Czech society medication is generally adhered to, albeit sometimes begrudgingly, even when patients or parents express concern over possibly premature diagnoses. For most parents, adjusting, much less experimenting, with pharmaceutical dosages is done only under the authority of a physician. With the exception of Alena, who holds the rather unique status of being both a mother and a physician, even those parents who were highly critical of their children's medication levels expressed trepidation over the idea of independently altering the dose. At most, they described "requesting" that their doctors stop or change the medicine. When I asked one mother if she ever considered cutting back on what she described as "useless" medication, regardless of what her doctor said, she looked shocked and retorted, "No, of course not."

Czechs are thus a long way away from embracing the "'democratic' character" of pharmaceuticals described by Sjaak Van der Geest and Susan Reynolds Whyte (1989: 346), who note that "anyone who gains access to [medicines] can apply their power." Instead, the notion of medicines as substances that can be disassociated from medical professionals is countered here with a deep appreciation of drugs as both powerful and dangerous substances that require specialist knowledge to be used efficaciously. Not surprisingly, overreliance on reliever medications in lieu of regular daily preventers, a concern that captivates so many New Zealand medical professionals, is not an issue raised by Czech doctors, as compliance rates for preventative medications are comparatively high. And even when uneasiness over asthma drugs leads some patients or parents to consider homeopathy as an alternative to corticosteroids, they often do so as a *supplement* to biomedical care.

Like lay people, many Czech medical professionals share the perspective that drugs are dangerous entities. Despite parents' complaints about doctors who are too quick to dispense drugs, many physicians go to great lengths to limit the amounts of corticosteroids dispensed to children, pointing out that, although children need to have their asthma symptoms under control, there is a danger in taking too many steroids.

Physicians therefore employ a range of strategies for boosting children's immune systems, from exercise to climate therapy, on the understanding that because steroids are both positive and negative, their power needs to be kept in check. To some extent, this is usual practice in most medical settings—no physician immediately reaches for the strongest possible medication, nor are corticosteroids generally available over the counter. What is unique, however, about a setting where medical professionals are giving out corticosteroids alongside prescribing facial massages or two-week visits to the Croatian seaside, is their reliance on a consortium of therapies, one of which is widely viewed as the most efficacious but also the most problematic. The *pharmakon* is thus tempered, not only in terms of being a restricted substance (available only via prescription) but also by being consciously restricted in terms of how often and how much is utilized through the promotion of supplementary therapeutics, many of which are taught to mothers to be carried out as part of home health care. Medical professionals are well aware that the success of this strategy requires mothers to cooperate and submit to their instructions. Their cooperation is, moreover, to be achieved through a process that does not require education in how or why a technique works, instead focusing on the transfer of practical know-how in terms of the laying down of habits and routines that will carry on outside of the hospital, clinic, or health spa.

Training Mothers

Visits to a pediatrician or physician in the Czech Republic often result in extremely detailed instructions for care alongside a prescription. Doctors are known to give specific instructions on topics such as the exact timing of a daily walk or two, the use of massage, and other procedures to boost the immune system. As one Scandinavian expat living in Prague related to me, when she first took her one-year-old son to the doctor with an ear infection, she was baffled by the list of instructions regarding not just medicine but a rigid schedule of walks and naps that she was expected to follow. In a similar vein, when my seven-year-old daughter had bronchitis, along with an antibiotic I was given detailed instructions on when we could and could not leave the house as well as the exact time of day I was supposed to administer the twice-daily respiratory massage that the doctor trained me to do.

But the most intensive form of training occurs over the course of six- or seven-week spa visits on which parents—usually mothers—accompany their young children. These mothers become the focus of concerted efforts to educate them in the proper techniques of respiratory massage, steam inhalations, and the use of alternating hot and cold showers. They learn how to clothe their children in cold weather as well as the necessity of remembering daily doses of medication and using correct inhaler techniques. The emphasis is on instilling rigorous routines in the mother and child alike. It is, however, ultimately the mother's responsibility to carry these activities over into their daily lives once they have left the spa.

At an open day for medical professionals that I went along to at Kynžvart Spa, some of the country's leading respiratory physicians, allergists, and respiratory nurses were shown how the spa's physiotherapists train mothers in the latest massage techniques. Dermatologists gave lectures discussing how to teach mothers to apply eczema cream. "We all know it won't work if the mother doesn't like the cream or doesn't know how to use it. You need to teach the mothers how to apply it properly," they explained.

But there is also a broader objective to teaching appropriate parental behavior, whether or not it is related to children's asthma. As I took a tour of another children's spa, a respiratory physician pointed out a row of about thirty pairs of shoes neatly lined up outside the door to a recreation room. "That's how perfectly we raise our mothers here [*tak vzorně maminky vychováváme*]," she said, referring to the Czech practice of removing your shoes on entering someone's home. The verb *vychovat* means to raise or to bring up and is usually used with respect to someone who needs to be trained or guided in his or her development, such as a child or pet. As this doctor's statement attests, spa personnel focus their attention on "training" not only asthmatic children but their mothers as well. This includes teaching them how to act like "civilized" or "educated" mothers as well as turning them into ersatz medical assistants who can mimic the actions of physiotherapists and other health professionals.

In recent years, the government index of state-supported services has become increasingly restrictive, and questions have been raised about whether the government should be subsidizing mothers to stay in health spas alongside their young children. I asked Mrs. Malinová of VZP, the insurance firm, about these subsidies, and she both explained the necessity of mothers' involvement and hinted at some of the criticism that has been voiced against it. As she put it, "The mother *needs* to be there to learn the exercises and rehabilitation procedures. But she needs to go only *one* year, not another two or three times, in which case she would just be there to meet up with her girlfriends and have a month's holiday." Mrs. Malinová's answer underscores the point she made with respect to the limits of *solidárnost* (solidarity)—namely that one of the purposes of health spas is to train their clients, in this case both children and their mothers, in appropriate health-care techniques and routines. There is a level of willingness to engage in self-care (or parental care) that is implicit in such programs. But this is a mode of self- or familial care that diverges radically from the responsibilization envisaged by neoliberal health policies, as well as from the dreams of compliance shared by New Zealand's asthma societies, given the degree of ongoing medical oversight. This is self-care in the sense of *complete compliance*—that is, submitting oneself to the expertise and knowledge of medical authorities and, to the best of one's ability, fulfilling their directives down to the letter. In such a schema, there is no need for patients to engage in decision making or judgment calls, as any recalibration of techniques or routines should be determined by medical professionals.

So how do these lessons actually translate into domestic practice?

The Work of Care

Many mothers highlight the huge amount of *work* they put into raising their children, including the various steps they take to mitigate their asthma. Most mothers view this work as a cooperative effort that dovetails with the efforts of their children's physicians. Instead of crafting themselves as parent-experts, they engage in actively seeking and implementing but also quietly critiquing and softening doctors' directives.

That said, many women struggle with complying with doctors' detailed regimes while managing the other demands of household life. They rely on doctors' advice but also diverge from it when they disagree with it or when the day-to-day practicalities of incorporating it into their domestic routines are beyond their capabilities. At the extreme, they engage in outright refusal, such as when Jitka removed her child from hospital. But usually, their resistance is much more subdued. Although Czech mothers share some of the same concerns as New Zealand parents about overmedication, most Czech parents rarely spoke of open negotiation, much less overt rejection, of doctors' instructions.

Indeed, most mothers diligently attempt to uphold the therapeutic regimes their children have been given. Such is the case of Miroslava, who has spent the past three years at home with her young son and two older daughters. A professional accountant in a government ministry, she credits not being laid off following the 2008 global financial crisis to the fact that she had been away on state-supported maternity leave and her job was thus effectively barred from being abolished for the three years of her absence. Miroslava's eldest daughter suffers from a spinal abnormality, her middle child Kateřina has asthma, and her youngest has developmental issues as well as bouts of acute eczema. Like many Czech mothers, Miroslava is deeply invested in the advice given to her by medical professionals and uses her and her husband's wide range of contacts to gain access to the best possible medical services, even if it requires concerted effort and expense.

When Miroslava invited me to spend the afternoon with her, she listed off what was on the schedule: we would have lunch together, go to the pool for her four-year-old son Pepík's aquatic therapy, pick up her two older girls from school, go home and have a snack, drop Kateřina off at her tennis class, and then return home by way of the supermarket, do homework with the girls, and make some dinner. It would be a day full of activity, much of it focused on sports and education. In addition to a regular regime of outdoor sports, which Miroslava considers imperative for dealing with Kateřina's asthma, Pepík takes part in aquatic therapy to stimulate his nervous system and, it is hoped, overcome some of his developmental delays. Miroslava and her mother-in-law, a physician, spent weeks drawing on various contacts and organizing approvals to enable funding for this therapy. Finally she found a physiotherapist who, despite telling her that she thinks this kind of therapy is a complete waste of time, was willing to sign the paperwork. Miroslava is proud of the lengths she went to to organize this for her son, if a little unsure of whether his recent gains in coordination are due to this latest intervention.

But, despite her detailed overview of their day, Miroslava and the children's routines didn't end after dinner. After we had our coffee, she set her eldest daughter up with some extra homework to prepare for her upcoming high-school entry exams and organized her two younger children's evening show-ers. Kateřina was just back from a health spa visit during which Miroslava was instructed to spray the top half of her body with cold water for one minute each morning and then spray her entire body for one minute each evening. Out of concern over what she described as Pepík's "weak" immune system, she applies the same "toughening" treatments to him as well.

"Do you give them a hot shower or bath afterward?" I asked, remembering the alternating cold and hot baths that I saw children being given at one of the health spas. "No, I am supposed to, but they just get dressed afterward as the water in our apartment is pretty bad," she explained; "It runs *either* hot or cold but never both at the same time." Pepík, however, finds even the cold shower to be too much. "He hates it," his mother explained. "He cries when you put him in it, but then cries when you turn the water off. It is really cold—I wouldn't have a shower in such cold water!"

Miroslava has successfully adopted the technique taught to her in the health spa and even extended it to her other child. At the same time, she has necessarily had to revise it to fit both her schedule and the resources available. Although she can explain the logic behind cold showers, she seems just as ambivalent about their efficacy as she is about the aquatic therapy, incorporating it as yet another technique that may or may not improve her children's health.

Finally, it was past 9 pm, the children were all off to bed, and Miroslava's husband was due home after another very late day at his legal office. In two months' time, Miroslava's maternity leave would be up. I asked her if she is looking forward to returning to work. She laughed and said, "I don't have *time* to go to work. I have so much to do, from taking the kids to their specialists to everything else in the day." Her plan, she explained, is to request a four-day work week, which given the budget crisis might be amenable to her boss, to keep her Fridays free for the children's health checkups.

Resisting Doctors' Directives

Although Miroslava strives to follow doctors' directives as much as possible, even she needs to make some amendments. As with any process of enskilment, to truly learn an activity requires not just imitation but also some element of improvisation (Ingold 2001: 141). Some women, however, adopt approaches radically different to those of Miroslava, embracing their role as providers of care while radically diverging from doctors' directives.

Jitka is on one extreme, launching herself into her children's care but in opposition to the biomedical establishment. Much like some of the parent-experts in New Zealand, she takes on the bulk of decision making for her daughter's care. She was the only Czech parent who, like many New Zealanders, described to me how she had independently learned to tell when her daughter is on the verge of an asthma attack and the steps that will ameliorate it: "A healthy child goes to bed and [then] at night you hear *ha—ha—ha*," she recounted, demonstrating the sound of her daughter's wheezing. "So now, when I recognize that her breathing is slightly off, I deal with it with natural remedies—so no more hospital. I give her potato and oil compresses, or honey with chopped onion, or herbs (*bylinky*) and vitamins to strengthen her. I also visited a Chinese doctor who adjusted her diet, and I took her to a natural healer who said she has weak lungs and gave her tea."

Jitka assumes others will find some of her actions a bit outlandish, but she explained that they are necessary: "As a mother, I pay a lot of attention so she doesn't catch a cold. You hear people say you are overreacting, but if you have already taken three trips to the hospital in an ambulance, you *do* overreact about dressing them warmly in winter or keeping them from getting wet in the rain." And indeed, as Jitka noted, there are many parents who take a decidedly opposite approach, believing in the need to "toughen" up their children and purposefully taking them out in the rain as part of the "exposure" methods taught in health spas.

At the other extreme are the parents who explicitly refrain from specific forms of caregiving, fearing the negative consequences of pandering to their child's condition. For some of these mothers and fathers, "toughening up" their child becomes an idiom for expressing the absence of otherwise socially valued acts of care and nurturance. Some parents, for example, related *not* wanting to remove allergic triggers from their homes to ensure that their children learn to cope. As one mother of a severely asthmatic child explained, "I've made very few changes [at home] . . . I have [kept the] curtains and carpets. We can't keep them [people with allergies] in a vacuum. . . . The body needs to adjust to these things." Others similarly agreed that there was no benefit to creating a completely sterile environment, suggesting that "children need to get used to dust mites."

These fears of overprotecting the body echo New Zealand parents' concerns that they not cotton-wool their children and thus impede their development. Here, however, developmental concerns are focused largely on children's physical capacities and do not dwell on the mental or emotional facets of growing up. Unlike New Zealand parents, most Czechs do not worry that being openly fearful of asthma will stunt their child's emotional development. Instead, their concerns form part of a larger discourse that characterizes those who suffer from allergies or asthma as physically "weak" and in need of "toughening."

Michal is in his mid-forties. Both his wife and his adult son have suffered from asthma since childhood. Michal was often flippant about his son's condition, commenting that David used to look like "Darth Vader" when he was on a nebulizer and joking about how difficult it is for his wife and son to accommodate to the local environment:

We tried a humidifier, a dehumidifier, and an ionizer as they are supposed to be good for these weaklings [*slabochy*]. We had special pillows, mattresses, bedding, and anti–dust mite spray. I would never buy this crap, but they did. It is a waste of money. But these two are weaklings. I grew up in a neighborhood dominated by the chemical industry where they made paint, gasoline, and explosives. There was a coal factory with a lot of smoke. I never had any allergies, breathing problems, or eczema. I have no problems—I am a mutant! And these guys can't eat an orange . . . without having an allergic reaction! And dust [is another thing they are allergic to]! I grew up next to a gas pump and woke up enjoying the smell of petrol.

In stark contrast to the very public concerns over the impact of pollution on children's respiratory health, Michal turned these fears around, jokingly suggesting that his son should grow up "enjoying the smell of petrol," as he did. Although he doesn't fret as much over his wife's condition, he expects his son to toughen up, hoping to compel him into adopting a more culturally appropriate form of manhood, characterized by physical robustness (cf. Šmídová 1999).

Michal's fear that his son is not manly enough is only one of the many fears that permeate his and other parents' accounts. The onset of asthma can radically disrupt familial visions of both children's futures and the power of the all-perfect mother to create a nurturing and healthy environment, forcing parents to face uncertainty, fear, and in some cases the threat of losing a child. These fears are shared by men and women alike and raise questions about accountability in terms of who is ultimately responsible for keeping a child safe, particularly when that child is growing into young adulthood.

Facing the Limits of Parental Care

Often when I met Michal, he asked how my research is going and then related some variation of the story of how when his son was a young boy, he started to choke at an outdoor cinema:

As soon as we pulled the seat down, David started to cough and then choke. We left the theater immediately, and luckily the car was parked just outside. As I drove home, he started turning a little blue. I got him into our building, and he was slumping over. I thought he might pass out and die on me. I got him into the apartment and gave him the pills he was supposed to take, and he was so much better. He said, "Can we go back and watch the movie?" When I said no, he was so disappointed and cried, "But I've been waiting for this movie all year!"

Like Dr. Veselá's dramatic accounts of children gasping for air when the pollution gets bad or mothers' accounts of the horror they feel when their children turn blue before their eyes, Michal's tales pivot on the plunge from normality into the life threatening. These narratives raise serious questions about the capacities of mothers and fathers to protect their children, as well as about the role of the state in children's lives. Some, like Dr. Veselá and environmental activists, turn their fears into political action, calling on the government to address what they see as the underlying issues that cause asthma in the first place. Others demand the state continue to heed its responsibilities to provide comprehensive health care to all its citizens.

But there is another player in these dynamics: the child. Although so much hinges on the role of the mother, perfect or otherwise, the child is generally left very little space to shape his or her own care.[2] Instead of being portrayed as an actor when it comes to health care (or other facets of domestic activity), the child is represented as the subject of training and reform—much as mothers are portrayed by medical professionals. In practice, in the same ways that mothers are often sidelined and silenced during medical exams, children are often sidelined when it comes to being informed about their treatments, as demonstrated by Alena's surprise when I asked how she explains to her thirteen-year-old son that she is taking him off medication for a month. (She doesn't.) This accords with a broader cultural perspective on child rearing in which children become the subjects of care without being encouraged to actively express their own perspectives or being informed of parental decision making.

Czechs are often quick to exemplify their culture as being particularly disciplinarian in terms of its approach to children. An underlying assumption of child care is that children need to be closely watched and assisted to conform to certain ideals, through physical punishment if necessary, as they cannot grow up *properly* on their own. There is general concern expressed over the need to raise children who are not "wild" by intensively training them to adopt particular bodily and social habits that are coded as "civilized" and necessary for being a cultivated human being (cf. Elias [1939] 2000; Bourdieu 1977). The assertive child who is not afraid to voice what she or he wants is both admired and seen as deeply problematic in terms of questioning the authority of their parents or other authorities, particularly institutional authorities such as teachers or doctors.

Violence and intimidation as tactics of familial control are not unfamiliar in Central and Eastern European households, as Mary Weismantel (2001) has noted for Germany and Lujza Koldeová (2012) for both Germany and Slovakia. Czechs openly speak of physically disciplining children, and it is not unusual to see parents hit, slap, or berate a child in public. In fact, fear is *both* derided and inculcated in children as a means of discipline. One incident I witnessed is emblematic: walking through a public park, I watched as a young child about two years old started to scream when a rather small, cute dog ran past him. "Stop it, stop it," his mother shouted at the boy, before reprimanding him and shouting, "You *must not* be frightened. The dog did *nothing*—it just ran past us. You *must* stop screaming, or I will beat you." When that threat proved ineffective and the child kept loudly sobbing, she added, "You must stop screaming or you *will* frighten the dog and it *will bite you.*" Such modes of disciplining children are not uncommon, and it is through such expressions of dominance and power that children come to learn, embody, and also *perpetuate* a rigid, hierarchical mode of social relations.

But there are also, and have been for a long time, social concerns over the need to move away from such dictatorial modes of child rearing. Sometimes even the therapeutic encounter is employed as a space in which to begin recalibrating parent–child relations. An interesting case is the work of Professor Václav Žilka, a musician and educationalist. From the late 1970s until 2003, Professor Žilka led an orchestra of asthmatic children playing recorders

(Makovská 2011). Reflecting back on this period, one of Professor Žilka's admirers, pediatric physiotherapist Dr. Libuše Smolíková, remembered how firmly he stressed the importance of including not only the children but also their parents, who were novices on the instruments, in the orchestra rehearsals so that "you are training them both. The parents can't already know how to play the recorder, or it defeats the purpose." The purpose, she clarified, is that instead of working to fulfill their parents' expectations, the children will relax and feel more able to give it a go if they see their parents struggling to complete the same tasks. "The most irritating thing is when a child cannot do something and the parents are upset at them about it," Dr. Smolíková said. "But [then you find out] their parents can't [do it] either! So instead we *all* do it together and make a joke out of it. If *both* of them need to learn it, then it isn't just another *demand* placed on the child." Even today, Dr. Smolíková uses the same technique in her children's physiotherapy sessions, deflecting parental demands by requiring them too to exercise and thus (momentarily) creating a level playing field between parent and child.

Such techniques reflect the tension between Czechs' emphasis on hierarchy as essential to duly recognizing knowledge and expertise versus the need to occasionally offset authoritarian demands. This tension is evident in ongoing interactions between not only parents and children but also doctors and parents, no matter how well they collaborate toward the common purpose of keeping children healthy.

For the most part, there is very little discussion among mothers or fathers about children having an agentive role in shaping their own care. Rather, even teenagers and young adults, especially males, are regularly derided for being unable to care for themselves. As Alena said of her thirteen-year-old son, "When he is on his own, he forgets [to use his inhaler], so I'm not sure if he really takes the full doses over the summer when he is off somewhere alone." Ironically, this is the same son she does not keep informed of his changing medication doses.

Michal similarly remains unhappy that his adult son, who lives in another city about forty-five miles away, is still unable to take responsibility for his asthma medication. But as his son grows more independent, Michal also worries about his own increasingly limited oversight: "When he was sixteen, David was away from home, had an asthma attack, and had to call the ambulance, and we had to pay for the ambulance because he had forgotten his inhaler. They said it was his responsibility to have the inhaler on him. And," he added, "he didn't even *tell* us about it. We didn't know about the attack until the medical bill arrived."

I asked, "So when did he start taking care of it himself?"

"When?" David's mother, Hana, replied, "Well, the truth is I still get the inhalers for him. And I say [to him], 'It's allergy season—how are you doing? Are you taking Zyrtec [an antihistamine]?' and he says, 'Oh, I should . . .'"

"That reminds me," Michal said to his wife: "Don't we need to check that his inhaler hasn't expired?"

Hana retorted, "Look, he is twenty-three years old. I told him to go to the [family] doctor about seven times, and he hasn't gone. I told him to go to the allergist; I *made* him an appointment, and he didn't go. He has *got* to take care of himself. He is twenty-three years old."

In contrast to the ambivalence expressed by many parents as they struggle to get their children involved in their own care, one parent spoke at length about her child's independence and ability to assess her own asthma. Veronika told me how she has instructed her twelve-year-old daughter Šárka to make her own decisions about doing fitness lessons at school: "It is up to *her* what she does or does not do. I told the teacher to trust her—if she doesn't feel like doing something it is because she is not up to it."

But Veronika is also extremely frustrated by the blurred boundary between the authority of parents and the self-assertion of children, more so than any other parent I met. I first met Veronika through a mutual friend when we visited her at the salt rooms, bar, and café where she works. School had just ended for the day, and, as we were introducing ourselves, Šárka and some of her school friends arrived and started settling down for the afternoon. Šárka was riffling through her bag, having trouble finding her homework, which sparked Veronika's anger. I was taken aback by the intensity of what followed as Veronika shouted at her daughter that she is "stupid" (*blbec*) and called her "the naughtiest (*nejzlobivější*) daughter in the world." For a few moments, the child sat at the table with her face hidden in her hands, but then she looked up at her mother with an expression of deep vehemence and calmly told her, "Up your ass" (*do prdele*), before starting to scream out further obscenities. Her mother shouted back at her, "Don't shout!" (*nekřič!*) Finally, the homework was found, and Šárka began working on it. Although there was a simmering tension in the air, things had quieted down, and Veronika asked me, "Do you want to talk about her asthma now?"

I was even more struck when a few minutes later, during our discussion about her daughter's health issues, Veronika related her opinion that any behavioral problems a child has are actually the fault of the parent as it is the parent who raises the child. "And that is why I am so hard on her," she explained. "I tell her she is naughty [*zlobivá*], but if anyone is to blame, it is *me*. I need to change—I need to be *firmer* with her." Underscoring the popular attitude that child rearing requires discipline and intensive training, Veronika, like so many other Czech parents, embraces strictness and hierarchy as the means of instilling good behavior and keeping children within the rules—in other words, *civilizing* them into appropriate personhood.

But if Veronika is encountering the limits of the myth of the perfect mother, she is also financially struggling in a capitalist economy that puts new requirements on parents. A single mother of three young children, she balances taking care of her family with her attempts to eke out a living by running an alternative therapy center, salt rooms, café, and bar. She was clear that money is tight, laughing when I asked her if she's ever taken Šárka, whose asthma is quite severe, to a health spa. Health spas, she explained, are out of the question as she cannot take any time off work to accompany her daughter. Tellingly, while clients stream in and out of the salt rooms and there are weekly bookings for yoga classes and school groups to spend an hour or two breathing in the salt air, Veronika's own children spend little time in them. "When Šárka went every day, her asthma really was better," Veronika attested. "I suppose I should her send there at least twice a week, but I don't really have the time."

Veronika also doesn't manage to carry out most of the health-care directives her doctor gives her. The detailed regimes given to her daughter by medical professionals need to be tempered against what is possible on any given day. The prospect of setting aside time to involve her child in her own alternative therapy center, much less seeking out other health-care activities, is far outside the realm of what is possible given constraints of both time and money. As she put it, "I just cannot live like that."

Although for mothers, fathers, and doctors alike, accountability for children's home health care is vested in the mother as the ideal provider of nurturance and care, in practice this role is impinged by a number of factors, including employment outside of the home and economic constraints. Though their familial, educational, and economic situations are worlds apart, much like Miroslava, Veronika is encountering the limits of a neoliberal work regime and a new kind of motherhood whose demands she finds at times overwhelming.

Parents' busy schedules and hectic lifestyles often mean they don't have as much time to spend on their children's health-care regimes as their doctors might like. Not everyone can work a four-day week to devote a whole day to her or his child's health-care needs. Although some parents are able to rely on extended family to pick up the slack, others find that their parents or in-laws are similarly engaged in full-time employment and cannot help out in the ways that grandmothers used to do, raising serious questions about the future viability of some of these modes of care.

Whatever the abilities of women to fulfill the high expectations of the "traditional mother," their caregiving takes place in a context where other forms of responsibility and care are viewed as just as vital. Indeed, to be *solely* responsible for one's child and his or her health would be seen as detrimental as it means that others, most notably medical experts, would no longer be invested in his or her child's care. The work of mothering thus involves careful maneuvering between encouraging physicians and other experts to feel responsible for the well-being of one's child and quietly asserting one's own abilities to make decisions regarding his or her health, all the while balancing up doctors' directives, the need for a manageable home life, and the absolute imperative of doing everything one can to prevent his or her child from turning blue.

Chapter 5

Body, Breath, and Mind

Subjugated Knowledge and Alternative Therapeutics

IN both New Zealand and the Czech Republic, a large part of medical professionals' and families' care strategies are directed at making the best possible
use of pharmaceuticals. But contemporary concerns over pharmaceuticals'
negative effects as well as shortfalls in how effective pharmaceuticals were in
the past—and, for a minority of people, still are today—drive some patients,
parents, and professionals to search out other means of coping. This chapter
and the following are about how people retrain their bodies to diminish the
impact of asthma on their everyday lives. Here I focus on how this carried out
in New Zealand through the twin activities of sports and Buteyko breathing retraining, whereas the following chapter considers Czechs' engagements in bolstering the immune system and "toughening" the body through climate therapy.
Each of these processes is about engaging in new modes of embodiment that
consist not just of different ways of treating one's body but also of being in one's
body and knowing one's body and mind. The bodily practices and therapeutic
regimes described in these two chapters are thus centrally concerned with reshaping subjectivity—that is, the making (and reinforcing) of certain kinds of
people through realignments of their bodies, their relationships to their bodies
(their being-in-the-body), and their minds

The wide-reaching effects of these therapeutic modes hinge on the ways
in which asthma is not only physically debilitating but also sometimes associated with mental or emotional distress. Up until the new pharmaceuticals of
the 1980s, members of the biomedical establishment argued that some forms
of asthma were best classified as a mental illness. Today, scientific and medical
consensus firmly locates asthma in the domain of respiratory rather than mental health. Phenomenological accounts of asthma indicate, however, that for a
significant number of sufferers, their asthma is interlinked with their mental
and emotional well-being. Taking seriously the range of mental and physical

facets that make up the experiential realities of asthma raises the question of whose responsibility it is to consider the impact asthma has on the whole person. It also encourages enlarging the therapeutic framing beyond the dominant pharmaceutical-focused self-management approach to consider alternative approaches to promoting healthy breathing.

In his "Two Lectures," Michel Foucault (1980) described the relationship between dominant epistemologies and "subjugated knowledge." According to Foucault, as scientific discourse systematizes itself and consolidates its dominance, two kinds of knowledge come to be marginalized. The first are formal, "meticulous [and] erudite" forms of knowledge that stand in the way of science's systematization—for example, perspectives within medicine that potentially block hegemonic framings and thus end up being subordinated. The second are "naïve," "popular," or "local" forms of knowledge that similarly speak back to hegemonic discourses; here Foucault gives the example of the knowledge "of the psychiatric patient, of the ill person, of the nurse, of the doctor—parallel and marginal as they are to the knowledge of medicine" (1980: 82). It is important to note that even members of the professional elite—such as doctors—can hold and act on subjugated knowledge, although to do so places them in tension with dominant practices and conceptions of health and medicine. Indeed, Foucault's point is that as medicine consolidates itself subjugated knowledge is not eradicated but remains in the margins, potentially available for acts of "insurrection" against dominant framings (1980: 81).

This chapter examines two different kinds of therapeutic practices—sports and Buteyko breathing retraining—that articulate subjugated perspectives of how to counteract breathlessness. Once lauded by family physicians as a route to coping with asthma, sports has largely fallen out of the register of the biomedical, acting today as a "local" or naïve" form of knowledge that is not systematized but nonetheless disrupts the hegemonic hold of pharmaceuticals while addressing both the physical and mental effects of asthma on sufferers. Buteyko, in contrast, is best described as a systematic "alternative" mode of respiratory therapeutics, invented under the auspices of (socialized state) biomedicine in Russia and now existing on (Western) biomedicine's fringes.

In referring to sports and Buteyko through Foucault's framing of subjugated knowledge, I do not intend to suggest that these therapeutic techniques are antithetical to the current emphasis on patient self-care. In fact, they often require patients to be *more* proactive than mainstream self-management programs do. Indeed, Buteyko, as well as some higher-end sporting activities, draws on self-auditing techniques that rival those of action plans and the charting of peak air flow. Nonetheless, these therapeutic modalities offer distinct counterpoints to standard self-management programs' predominant focus on pharmaceuticals. To understand how these therapeutic practices operate requires delving a bit more deeply into the experiential facets of breathing and respiratory disorders.

Breathing Matters

The disordered breathing caused by asthma affects more than one's lungs or respiratory system. Prior to the development of corticosteroid inhalers, asthmatics frequently suffered a variety of physical problems such as upper and lower back pain, shoulder pain, and foot misalignment. Attempts to prevent or mitigate these often fell to physiotherapists, who focused on correcting patients' postures and breathing patterns. With the development of more potent drug therapies, the frequency of such complications has waned over the past three decades. Nonetheless, some adults still have firsthand experience of a range of physical complications induced by asthma. Sybil, who is in her mid-twenties, attributes her chronic back pain to shallow breathing that overtaxes her upper body: "I have a bad back because I don't breathe properly, which is apparently common with asthmatics. . . . You breathe in the top of your chest instead of . . . breathing deeply, because it's so hard to pull in breath and so much energy."

The breathlessness associated with asthma can also supersede the categorization of asthma as a physical illness, as it may involve emotional components such as anxiety and panic. A significant number of sufferers experience asthma as having a negative impact on their mental well-being. Some of them also regard their mental or emotional state as capable of provoking an asthmatic response. The connection between the psychological component of asthma and therapies that focus on strengthening the body and retraining one's breathing patterns is one of the issues examined throughout this chapter.

Despite a very robust literature on embodied experiences of illness (for example, Csordas 1994; Good 1994; Jackson 2000) as well as a burgeoning anthropology of the senses (see Howes 2005; Stoller 1997; Trnka, Dureau, and Park 2013), as yet there have been relatively few phenomenological accounts of breathing and breathlessness, much less of how they are experienced as part of asthma, even though this is a central facet of living with the condition (see, however, Clarke 2002, as well as a cursory discussion in Benner 1994).

One exception is the work of sports sociologist Jacquelyn Allen-Collinson who, as part of her autoethnography of asthma, offers particularly detailed depictions of her own asthma attacks. Here is just one:

The heavy, pollen-thick air sticks to my throat, it feels as though only a third of my lungs can fill with air, even taking the air down my throat is difficult. Rib cage expands heavily with the effort of sucking in the humid air. . . . Chest heavy and laboring with the effort to breathe in, and even more with the effort to breathe out. . . . (as quoted in Allen-Collinson and Owton 2014: 600)

It is impossible, however, for the words of a single asthma sufferer, much less a single description of an asthma attack, to convey an experience that varies so widely. Despite the detailed lists of symptoms on action plans and health websites (for example: "wheezing when exercising," "wheezing at night or other times when not exercising," or "wheezing and breathlessness do not respond to the reliever"), the range of experiences and warning signs described by the asthma sufferers I spoke with far surpassed any medical descriptions I read. Many people, moreover, noted the variability of their own asthma, differentiating between their "usual" attacks and episodes that catch them off guard. For example, forty-year-old Charlotte, who grew up having asthma, was amazed when only a few years ago she first found herself needing a nebulizer ("Crikey! That can happen?" she remembered thinking).

Like Charlotte, Caroline similarly underscored the variable nature of her asthma, explaining that usually "it's a tightness of breath, though sometimes you can't quite tell what's being out of breath and what's asthma." She then recounted that her most recent attack

. . . came on really differently to all my others. Usually I'd be sleeping and I'd wake up in the night and be like *heeaagggghhhh, huuuurrrggghhhh, heeaagh*. And this one wasn't like that at all. It was very different. I just kept coughing and coughing and coughing and coughing. And I couldn't figure out why I was coughing, and I suddenly realized I couldn't breathe. . . . [So I said to my friend], "I can't breathe. You have to take me to the emergency room." And then I proceeded to collapse.

It is also not unusual for experiential accounts to highlight both the intensely physical and emotional experiences of breathlessness. As we've seen, fear is often part of what many parents experience when their child has an asthma attack. But sufferers themselves can also feel anxious, frightened, or panicked when an attack commences. A man in his forties described to Allen-Collinson and Owton a life-threatening attack he had as a moment when "you can't breathe either way in or out, for some time . . . It was . . . vigorous. Choked, glorifying panic . . . It was very, very scary. It was more scary than dangling off a cliff or, you know, being in a car accident . . . It's [a] scary, scary, scary thing and it's immediate and there's no time for your life to flash before you, you just think, how the fuck am I going to breathe?" (2014: 601). Although it is rare to hear directly from children, one particularly insightful account comes from fifteen-year-old Sasha Clarke, reflecting back on a series of asthma attacks she had between the ages of seven and eleven that required repeated hospitalization. She described sitting in the hospital waiting room "fighting for air and the pain of the ache in my chest. Sometimes I would get so scared I was *gonna* die. I sometimes even used to make out my will sitting there, waiting, and wondered if anyone would miss me" (Clarke 2002: 139).

How can we reconcile these experiences with the lists of warning symptoms that sufferers are asked to consult on websites or action plans? In his analysis of how asthma action plans can transform patients' relationships to their bodies, philosopher Dick Willems suggests that patients who rely on peak flow measurements to monitor their asthma must first learn to translate a bodily *feeling* into a way of *knowing* through the technology of the peak air flow meter (2000: 33). As Willems puts it, "Asthma patients need a device (not a psychological, but a material device) as a mediator between themselves and their bodies. Although feeling what goes on is not entirely useless, it only provides preliminary knowledge: feeling breathless is a reason for patients to start measuring their lung function" (2000: 35).

Willems does not develop this point, but there is another way of using action plans, namely by aligning one's bodily sensations with the symptoms outlined on the card's other half. But even patients who eschew technology and monitor their condition based solely on bodily symptoms would need to engage in a learned distancing from their bodies, training themselves to focus on the narrow range of bodily phenomena specified in the action plan and translating these sensations into color-coded levels of danger that determine when they are well ("green zone") versus when to increase their medication ("yellow zone") or visit their family physician or call an ambulance ("red zone").

To what extent have such practices of self-monitoring and the relationships to the body they entail permeated the experiences of asthma sufferers? Phenomenologically, many people's experiences of asthma are refracted through the kinds of self-monitoring practices that asthma action plans are intended to instill, as might be expected given the widespread uptake of self-surveillance practices in contemporary health care (Dumit 2012; Rose 2006). As we have seen, however, asthma sufferers generally engage in such self-monitoring based on their own individualized warning signs, derived through their ever-evolving experiences of coping with asthma or on terms codetermined with their health-care providers. A specific kind of "somatic mode of attention" (Csordas 1993) has indeed been created through the need to monitor the body, but it does not always accord with the warning signs laid out on action plans.

Moreover, although emotional facets of asthma attacks such as fear or anxiety are noted in the mainstream literature on asthma, they are not incorporated into standardized self-management therapies. Indeed, as Patricia Wilson, Sally Kendall, and Fiona Brooks note (2007), self-management programs tend to promote a division between the mind and body. The physical and emotional aspects of asthma, as well as its long-term effects on the body and mind, have, however, led to a range of alternative forms of therapeutics that attempt to do away with this division.

One method many New Zealanders turn to is sports. Youth from their teens up to their mid-twenties are particularly concerned with how their asthma may curtail their physical capabilities and therefore their relations with their peers. Many of them also view physical exercise as a means of counteracting, or at the very least mitigating, their asthma. Sports has been noted as a particularly important source of self- and peer esteem as well as national pride for New Zealand boys and men whose sense of masculinity is often tied to physical fitness and, more specifically, their success in playing rugby (Park 2000; see also Daley 2003). I suggest here that young girls similarly derive a sense of competency, capability, and acceptance based on their physical prowess. Together with their parents, both young women and men frequently describe sports as a way of not only coming to terms with their bodies but also of overcoming physical weakness. Their accounts, moreover, reflect a concomitant awareness of the ways that the focus and discipline required by sports can reshape one's mental capacities to cope with challenge and stress.

Sports as a Mode of Mental and Physical Therapeutics

Unlike in the Czech Republic, where doctors and parents alike note that children's asthma does *not* interfere with their participation in sports as it is generally very well controlled, a number of children and youths with asthma in New Zealand report having breathing problems related to exercise. These difficulties, moreover, may result in them being perceived as "weak" or "unfit" by others and thus sidelined in sports-related activities at school. Such perceptions resonate with portrayals of asthma sufferers in popular Western culture; as Cindy Dell Clark (2012) found in her review of English and American films and TV shows, characters with asthma are more often than not associated with physical weakness.

New Zealanders relate to these images and recount their own experiences of being unable to participate in sporting or school activities, imbuing them with deep social significance. James, who is in his mid-twenties, explained, "There definitely was something [negative] there for me as a young person with being on the seat at PE and being the last picked [for school sports games] . . . People would see you as being impaired physically—certainly your own peer group did anyway."

Samantha similarly remembers feeling ostracized when, as a ten-year-old, an acute asthma attack forced her to leave a school camp and go to hospital. She recounted the fear and distrust of her teachers both during the attack and when she returned: "I got really sick, and I was lying in some office somewhere, and my teacher was sitting there holding my hand and saying, '*Please*, keep breathing!' I would have really freaked them out because they weren't used to it. . . . [And when I came back] to camp the next morning, . . . the teacher was like, '*What* are you doing here!'"

Although it is understandable that teachers might be skittish about being left with a child who was hospitalized just the day before, the perception of asthmatics' bodies as dangerously poised on the precipice between life and death is something that the Asthma and Respiratory Foundation has spent years trying to combat. One strategy has been to promote images of asthma sufferers who *are* able to take part in sports at the highest levels, with public campaigns frequently fronted by well-known athletes such as swimmer Danyon Loader, Silver Ferns netball captain Casey Kopua, and rugby star Daniel Carter.

Many youths, however, experience difficulties in keeping their symptoms in check, resulting in having to seriously curtail their physical activities. Girls, in particular, describe being unable to partake in sports because of asthma. In her work with asthmatic teenagers in the UK, Clare Williams (2000) found that teenage boys are more likely than girls to keep fit, enabling many of them to mitigate their symptoms through exercise.[1] In comparison, the girls in Williams's study were not keen on exercise (but were much better at regularly using their inhalers). Williams doesn't indicate whether the girls felt they were missing out, but many of the teenage girls we spoke with in New Zealand expressed deep dismay over dropping out of sports. Some had been keen competitors and gave up dreams of one day becoming professional athletes. Twenty-year-old Courtney, for example, described asthma as the death knell of a promising running career. At fourteen she gave up cross-country running when it repeatedly caused her to pass out and wake up in the emergency room hooked up to oxygen. Although young Kiwi women are perhaps more willing to share their stories of sporting disappointments than young men, narratives such as Courtney's suggest that they share similar values of physical fitness and prowess.

Not everyone's stories have such sad endings. There are also a good number of teenage girls and boys who turn the tables on asthma, using sports to build up their lung capacity and overall physical fitness. Indeed, the ability to achieve athletic prowess *despite* one's asthma is idealized by both teenagers and adults and upheld as the ultimate marker of success. Like public portrayals of rugby stars who rise to fame on the back of their own determined efforts, images of kids with asthma turned into athletes spotlight highly valued qualities of personal drive, hard work, and intense perseverance—in other words, the responsibilized subject par excellence. Thus when Chris Trawley wanted to demonstrate the success of the Buteyko method in "curing" his son's asthma, he proudly related how the teenager who battled severe asthma metamorphosed into a thirty-two-year-old who "plays rugby, runs ten kilometers every second day, and rides mountain bikes."

Similarly, Jane recounted how, as a teenager, her son John benefited from having "an old-school doctor who doesn't like to wrap them up in cotton wool" and promoted the idea that all kids, including those with asthma, "have to get bigger and stronger, and the only way they'll do that is by exercising." It worked well for John, whom she described as having a very athletic and competitive personality, noting that "I think his obsession with sport was the driving force that resulted in asthma not affecting him in any kind of developmental way. Because he loved sports, and there was no way in the world that he was going to let the fact that he couldn't breathe very well stop him from going out and playing soccer."

Indeed, Jane posited sports as a turning point in John's life that enabled him to both overcome the physical effects of severe asthma and gain the confidence to become a successful young man. She explained,

Before that, when he was younger, he was reasonably delicate. He'd spend so much time vomiting from food [allergies] or general sickness that he'd just get his weight up to touching the line on the Plunket [infant weight] chart, and then all of a sudden he'd just go down and be skin and bones again. It looked like he'd been deprived or something. He always looked sickly with a little sunken chest, really concave because when you can't breathe properly your shoulders come forward, and it actually makes your lung capacity worse.

Being "sports mad," Jane explained, was in some ways

a curse, but, in other ways, it made him socially acceptable at school as I think sporting prowess at school is pretty highly regarded. He'd just take his inhaler wherever he was . . . and he had enough *mana* [social standing and influence] by that stage, being the kind of cool sportsman, that it wasn't something that anyone was going to say anything about— "Uh, no wonder you're such a wimp" or whatever. I think he had enough confidence in himself that nobody was going to make a mention of it.

Like John, thirteen-year-old Kavita derives dual mental and physical benefits from driving herself to build up her physical stamina despite her asthma. Her mother Nisha explained how preparing for any sort of physical exertion both requires Kavita to have mental stamina and reinforces and strengthens that stamina:

When she used to do gym, they had something called "the circuit." The first time she did it, she threw up and it sort of played on her mind. So every time she had to do a circuit, she'd say, "Oh my god, I don't want to have to do it, I'm going to get sick again." So there was a bit of mental preparation she required for that. I was always a bit wary that it would cause her to be breathless, but it never did. I think all the work she did in the gym, those six hours per week that she did and the swimming, I think it all just really helped her lungs get strong. We've always been wary that [a breathing problem] might occur, but the fact that we didn't sort of dwell on it too much helped.

Kavita seems to have embodied this advice. Despite encountering a number of physical challenges due to asthma, she related how she actively overcame them, describing, for example, a swimming test during which she had an asthma attack: "I stopped in the middle of the pool, and the coach was like, 'What're you doing!?' . . . I told her my asthma was acting up, and then she told me I could stop for a while if I need to. And I did. But then I started again. I realized that to be able to get further, you have to try to push yourself."

Not every young person has the same level of tenacity and individual motivation Kavita demonstrates. Nor does every child have a parent like Nisha who is willing to devote so much time and energy to promoting their child's fitness. For some children with asthma, physical fitness is more likely to be achieved through less demanding means. In the past, these have included externally organized activities such as state-sponsored swimming lessons for children with asthma and multiday overnight asthma camps that focused on sporting activities.

Twenty-six-year-old James was one of many children who took part in a popular group swimming program for children with asthma held in the Christchurch Hospital pool during the 1990s. Reflecting on what those three years of swimming lessons meant to him, he recounted, "I remember it vividly. . . . It was in an indoor heated pool, a really nice facility, [and] we had a lovely swimming teacher. We would go there twice a week, my sister and I. And it was challenging—it really was about increasing the strength of your diaphragm, confidence, and fitness." One of the things that made it such a good experience for James was the collective nature of the lessons. He explained, "If you read the fine print in terms of getting the opportunity, the lessons would have been for *my* asthma, but it . . . was also available for my sister who is younger but has never suffered asthma . . . That was a really positive thing for me."

Although still physically challenging, James's engagement in fitness is strikingly different from Kavita's determined and self-focused approach. Both describe acts of self-care but with a different valence. Kavita and her mother collaboratively cultivate Kavita's focus and self-determination. James described a much more relaxed manner of attending to the body, one that included little sisters who joined in just for the fun of it but that similarly pushed the body to extend itself—it was not only "lovely" but "challenging," he remembered. In each case, the child is not only learning to overcome the effects of his or her asthma but is developing a newfound confidence in his or her body and overall capabilities to succeed.

The sorts of free group swimming programs that James described are largely no longer available. Likewise the possibilities of engaging in extended sociality and sustained physical exercise in asthma camps have been discontinued. The few asthma camps that remain have narrowed their scope to daylong outings during which children learn how to take medication and avoid triggers and do a few sporting activities, rather than providing a sustained route to collectively strengthening the children's bodies and training their minds to overcome the challenges that asthma can throw in a child's way.

Buteyko: A Russian Method Comes to New Zealand

Swimming and other forms of exercise engage asthma sufferers in the pleasures of physical activity while strengthening their lung capacity, overall physical fitness, and in some cases mental well-being and perceptions of themselves as physically competent. Another route to a similar destination is that of breathing retraining. In New Zealand, breathing retraining methods are taught by Buteyko educators, respiratory physiotherapists, and sometimes asthma nurses, though many nurses we spoke with lamented that their skills in this area were far below what they would like them to be. All of these professionals focus on diaphragmatic breathing, that is, breathing using the diaphragm and lower muscles rather than the upper chest. Although some of the techniques they employ are intended as temporary stopgap measures for dealing with emergency situations when reliever medication is unavailable, most are focused on long-term recalibration of respiratory depth and rhythm. Though the primary aim of the techniques they instill is to alleviate respiratory distress, they are also described as improving emotional and mental well-being, particularly in terms of mitigating panic, anxiety, and overall stress.

Samantha first learned of the powerful effect of breathing techniques as a child in the hospital emergency room:

One time when I was having a really massive asthma attack, I was waiting to be seen, and the nurse, or maybe it was even the receptionist, said, "Look, breathe deeply and slowly." She sort of talked me through my breathing, and I felt so much better, so quickly. I had been panicking, and so I had been breathing *wrong*, and that had been making it worse. . . . Ever since then, when I start getting wheezy, I breathe differently—I open my chest, and I stretch my back.

Samantha employs breathing retraining on an as-needed basis for short-term relief. Buteyko, which is the most popular method of breathing retraining in New Zealand, however, focuses on *permanently* recalibrating respiration. First developed in Russia in the 1950s, the Buteyko program is the brainchild of Ukrainian doctor Konstantin Pavlovich Buteyko. While still a medical student, Buteyko monitored the breathing of patients with terminal illnesses and soon discovered respiratory patterns that he believed enabled predicting the timing of their deaths. Buteyko wondered if *changing* these patterns might mitigate or even cure illness, hypothesizing that a wide range of disorders, including asthma, is caused by breathing too deeply, resulting in hyperventilation and an excess buildup of carbon dioxide. After experimenting with his own breathing and mitigating his hypotension, Buteyko devoted his career to promoting a method for consciously recalibrating one's breathing, focusing on breathing through the nose (rather than the mouth), relaxation, and shallower inhalations and lengthier exhalations followed by a period of suspending one's breath, referred to as the "controlled pause."

During the 1960s and 1970s the Moscow medical establishment supported Dr. Buteyko's experiments and, by the 1980s, supported his findings. Despite its alliance with Soviet medicine, the Buteyko method was not, however, broadly picked up in the Eastern bloc. (Although I spent months interviewing asthma sufferers and respiratory specialists in the Czech Republic, I did not encounter a single person who recognized Buteyko.) Following the end of the Cold War, however, Buteyko's philosophy and methods became popular among alternative health practitioners in the West. Interest in New Zealand culminated in 2000 when the country hosted the first international Buteyko conference.

Today, alternative practitioners hail the Buteyko method as counteracting the "false belief" that asthma needs to be managed with pharmaceuticals. Linking asthma and other respiratory disorders to the stresses of "modern lifestyles," many promise their clients that not only will the method help them learn to *cope* better, it will likely *cure* their breathing disorders entirely.

Ironically, while Buteyko was developed as part of Soviet biomedicine, present-day Buteyko teachers have no medical training and must continually lobby for medical legitimacy. In New Zealand, the technique is taught by a tiny minority: in 2014 there were four full-time Buteyko educators. Training largely takes place in Auckland at a Buteyko institute run by Glenn White. In addition to training instructors, dealing with his own local clients, liaising with the Asthma and Respiratory Foundation, and opening his doors to the curious ethnographer, Glenn travels the world giving lectures and workshops.

Glenn's efforts to raise the method's profile seem to be effective as, despite the small numbers of educators, Buteyko garners notable attention. Not only sufferers but also a fair number of mainstream respiratory professionals, including GPs, nurses, and Asthma and Respiratory Foundation representatives, praise Buteyko, if only for drawing patients' attention to their breathing. As one hospital physiotherapist said, "It's about increasing awareness of your own body and knowing about breathing and relaxing—and anything that makes that happen for children must be good." In line with Shelley Adler's (2002) depiction of biomedicine's penchant for incorporating alternative therapies, Buteyko has become a form of therapeutics that remains outside of mainstream medicine but integrated into the sidelines of established practice.

Those who practice Buteyko as part of their own self-care generally credit it with enabling them to significantly cut back on, or even discontinue, steroid preventers and relievers. As one parent who saw a child through the program bluntly put it: "Buteyko means they can stop putting all that pharmaceutical shit into their body."

Another adherent was a bit more philosophical. James was taught Buteyko by his mother when he was young. He vividly remembers how she grew increasingly frustrated as "the drugs weren't really doing anything. They were just weakening my lungs, making me more dependent on them. So she started reading beyond what our GP was prescribing and found some Russian breathing exercises." Today a singer-songwriter, James explained that not only does he continue to use these methods in his own life, he also teaches them to his singing pupils.

James encapsulated many aspects of the Buteyko philosophy when he described pharmaceuticals as being largely unnecessary:

When you think about it, the human race was around long before these drugs came along, and breathing issues have too, and people got by, somehow. For the most part, people dealt with their asthma in other ways, without using drugs. . . . It's an absolute no-brainer that [alternative therapies] should be a commonly used remedy for asthmatics. Not entirely replacing drugs, but at least in conjunction with drugs and, in the long term, [a way of] getting completely off them.

In his own life, James struggles with his occasional use of emergency relievers, considering it a weakness to rely on them. He explained,

I think I've imbued Ventolin with negative energy. I have it with me for an absolute emergency situation, but I really never, ever, ever use it. I would see it as a real failure if I had to use it now, because it's about willpower. I *know* I can get through an asthma attack with the [breathing] exercises. So it would almost be lazy of me to take the blue inhaler. And if I have a puff, even though I get instant relief, it means that the next time I get an asthma attack, I'm not going to be able to deal with it so well.

Not everyone, however, finds Buteyko an easy solution. Coaching in Buteyko can take a bit of financial wherewithal: in 2014 the cost of taking a comprehensive course was NZ$500 to NZ$600 (approximately US$694 to US$833). Buteyko also requires not just desire but persistence, akin to the work Kavita puts into building up her physical stamina through sports. Buteyko teachers often give their students workbooks to fill in so they can chart their breathing retraining activities, engaging in levels of monitoring that often exceed those of mainstream asthma self-management. Many asthma sufferers thus find it simpler to rely on Ventolin. Jane, whose son John is about the same age as James, remarked, "John was a teenager when I first remember hearing about Buteyko. But I don't . . . think at that age that he would've been all that interested in hearing about it. He'd much rather suck on his Ventolin and be off." For James, however, Ventolin and other drugs proved ineffective, spurring his mother to explore other methods. Over time, Buteyko became James's ultimate self-management technique, used alongside his medications until it eliminated his need for them.

James is not the only one to suggest that Buteyko can lead to payoffs far beyond those offered by biomedicine. Chris Trawley is a Buteyko educator who helped the program gain a foothold in New Zealand in the 1990s. For Chris, Buteyko's main point of difference is its avoidance of pharmaceuticals. "Conventional treatment doesn't know what causes asthma, so they can't tell you," he asserted. "So they can only ever have *symptomatic* treatment," unlike Buteyko, which attempts to *solve* asthma by aiming to "normalize breathing" by lowering the intake of air. The actual causes of overbreathing can, according to Chris, be quite varied and are therefore difficult to address. "Asthma's caused by just about anything," he said. "It's emotions, illness, exercise. Anything where there's an increase in breathing causes asthma." The key is to know how to stop overbreathing before an attack sets in.

The ultimate—and most controversial—promise of Buteyko is that it will provide most people with an outright cure. Chris claimed that across New Zealand Buteyko "could reduce [the level of asthma] medication by 90 percent."

This, he stated, is much better than conventional approaches that do "nothing to eliminate asthma. It's all about, let's help asthmatics to stay asthmatics. A lot of people have been told, like I was, that you're going to have asthma for life and be on medication for life." In contrast, Chris described Buteyko as "a step-up, step-down program: as you're getting less asthma, you need less medication, until you've eliminated it and then you only have to go back on it if your asthma plays up again."

He admitted that his vision is not likely to be embraced by the pharmaceutical industry, which he sees as irresponsibly promoting drugs to the point of blindsiding other solutions. "There's this big myth that children die of asthma, but that's very rare, if ever. A lot of parents are *forced* to put their children on—well," he corrected himself, "they are not forced—but they *believe* they have to put their children on very strong medication because they think their child is in danger of dying of asthma." An ideal situation, according to Chris, would be if Buteyko were not only a remedy but a preventative strategy and "right from the word *go*, children [were] taught to breathe correctly. If that was done on a national level, if parents were taught in their prenatal classes that children must breathe through their noses and use their diaphragms—just the basics—you'd probably cut the amount of asthmatics diagnosed by 50 percent."

To promote greater uptake, many Buteyko instructors are keen to work with medical professionals and encourage the scientific validation of Buteyko, particularly through evidence-based research. One of Buteyko's most passionate scientific supporters is Dr. Patrick McHugh, a general practitioner who spent two decades working with asthma patients as a family physician and in the emergency room. He now runs a research trust that investigates complementary therapies.

Dr. McHugh doesn't find it difficult to reconcile Buteyko with mainstream biomedical approaches, explaining that

with Buteyko, when someone has symptoms of asthma, they're encouraged to take their attention to their breathing. Doing that would help change the way they feel, which will also influence their autonomic nervous system, which will impact what's going on in their body acutely and may well itself have a therapeutic effect. But whereas a biomedicalist may focus on inflammation in the airways, Buteyko people contend that the mechanism for action is within the CO_2 pathway . . . so how people breathe physically [matters].

But if how people breathe really matters, there is still the issue of how to best go about correcting the problems that result from poor breathing. Dr. McHugh, like so many others, is wary of the limitations of focusing only on pharmaceuticals, lamenting that compared to Europe "New Zealand seems to be caught by the pharmaceutical industry, so we tend to be selectively focused on medication-based interventions rather than being open-minded to other approaches."

Buteyko may have been developed within the biomedical establishment, but in the present-day context where pharmaceutical remedies dominate the therapeutic landscape, it offers a radically alternative approach to dealing with asthma. As yet, however, the scientific evidence on Buteyko is mixed. Some trials (for example, Cowie et al. 2008) report that as an adjunct to pharmaceutical therapy Buteyko can improve control of asthma, whereas others (Bruton and Lewith 2005) conclude there is insufficient evidence of efficacy.

Critics suggest that Buteyko offers *too much*. Proponents claim that Buteyko will mitigate or cure over a hundred different conditions, including not only asthma, anxiety, panic attacks, hyperventilation, sleep apnea, and snoring but also hypertension, allergies, hay fever, chronic bronchitis, diabetes, epileptic seizures, hypothyroidism, obesity, irritable bowel syndrome, and chronic fatigue syndrome. Sidelined by their lack of medical training, educators' sweeping promises and often passionate pronouncements, punctuated with statistics frequently used to make rhetorical points but not generated by scientific studies (for example, Chris's claims that Buteyko could reduce New Zealanders' medication levels "by 90 percent" or that teaching appropriate breathing techniques to children may "cut the amount of asthmatics diagnosed by 50 percent"), frequently elicit disbelief. As Anne Bruton and Mike Thomas have said more generally of breathing retraining programs (including Buteyko), "Extravagant claims have been made about the effectiveness of some techniques, resulting in skepticism from orthodox clinicians" (2011: 53).

From a critical medical anthropology perspective, another drawback is Buteyko's sole focus on the individual body. Like most alternative therapies, Buteyko foregrounds the individual's ability to regulate and monitor her- or himself, using self-discipline to bring about change. Collective issues of class, the environment, and rights to medical access are overshadowed by a gaze that looks inward (Baer 2004)—at the lungs, diaphragm, abdomen, shoulders—rather than at the larger structural or interpersonal features that may shape asthma.

There is, however, another important, but often overlooked, positive facet to Buteyko. Focusing on regulating how breath moves in and out of the body, Buteyko opens up a space in which the physical and the mental are conjoined. Indeed, the therapeutic strategies employed by Buteyko practitioners do not generally differentiate between a patient suffering from mental or emotional turmoil or a physical disorder. At, for example, the group training sessions I attended, all the participants were led through the same breathing exercises, regardless of whether they suffered anxiety, panic attacks, or asthma (see also Stark and Stark 2002). This approach may resonate with sufferers who experience asthma as simultaneously physically and emotionally fraught, offering a coping strategy without obliging them to distinguish between mental and physical distress.

In Body and Mind

Caroline, at twenty-four, has had asthma since she was five, but she is sometimes confused about whether she is actually having an asthma attack. She explained, "I often get tightness of breath, but it isn't so much an asthma attack. . . . Sometimes you can't quite tell what's being out of breath and what's asthma. So I tend to err on the side of caution and take some [Ventolin]." Encouraged to tell us about one of her recent asthma attacks, she recounted the following story: "I was leaving the bar [where I work] and I was with this guy . . . [who suddenly] ran off and left me in the dark . . . in a place I didn't know. I started panicking because my breathing had been really bad the day before, and suddenly now I couldn't breathe properly. . . . And so there I was in the corner just going *heeaaggghhh*, and that was scary." Asked if she was carrying her reliever, Caroline replied, "Yes [but it wasn't helping]. I think it was more the panic that exacerbated the situation." What started off as a story about asthma turned into an account of fright and panic, suggesting an experiential overlap between these states.

Fifty-two-year-old Mary told a similar story of her recent asthma attack:

What happened was that I was going up to Sky City [restaurant], and the elevator got stuck. I pressed the emergency button, and [the building operators] said, "We're going to send somebody but it might take two hours." I said, "No, I can't wait here for two hours," because what happens [is] the ventilation turns off . . . and you can feel that it's stuffy. Once that began to happen, I couldn't breathe. It triggered off a *massive*, scary asthma attack. And that brought about the panic. Because . . . it sort of works together like that. . . . You begin to hyperventilate, and there is a panic attack because you can't breathe.

Caroline and Mary's narratives portray asthma as both grounded in the body and intensely emotional and psychological. They are also indicative of how some sufferers struggle to reconcile their experiences of asthma alongside other common diagnostic categories, in particular anxiety disorders and panic attacks. Whereas both men and women relayed *fears* of having an acute asthma attack, and some men described attacks as inspiring a sense of panic, confusion over the overlaps between *medical diagnoses* of anxiety disorders or panic attacks and asthma are more frequently recounted by women. This is not surprising, given that figures from the United States suggest that women account for twice as many diagnoses of anxiety disorders as do men (Barlow 2004; Yonkers et al. 2003), raising the likelihood that women are more often faced with coming to terms with how gendered discourses of panic attacks and anxiety align with, or contradict, their experiences of asthma.

Even when other diagnoses aren't in question, the relationship between asthma and stress is controversial. It is well-established that asthma attacks can cause emotional and psychological stress, but the flip side of whether, and how, stress and emotional upheaval may exacerbate, much less *trigger*, asthma is much less understood. Experiential overlaps between asthma and emotional distress are not, however, antithetical to biomedical explanations, particularly if we step back a few decades.

From Parentectomies to Popsicles

Some forms of asthma were once treated by biomedical professionals as mental afflictions. In 1920s Britain, studies abounded of cases of "hysterical and emotional asthma" (Jackson 2009: 141). Similarly in the United States at this time, asthma was thought to be brought on by "strain, fatigues, depression and worry [over] caring for sick relatives, family arguments or marital problems" (ibid.). In the 1940s, American psychiatrist Helen Flanders Dunbar suggested that "there are certain specific emotions which seem to be linked especially to asthma and hay fever. A conflict about longing for mother love and mother care is one of them" (1947: 177). Dunbar considered psychotherapy the appropriate treatment, whereas, a decade later, American allergist M. Murray Peshkin recommended that for "intractable cases" of asthma, a *parentectomy* or removing the child from the family home's "asthmatogenic emotional climate" might be necessary

(1959: 94; see also Keirns 2004). The development of more potent pharmaceutical remedies as well as an outcry against such mother-blaming approaches by (not surprisingly) mothers of asthmatic children in the 1980s led to a shift away from considering emotions and mental distress as primary triggers of asthma, much less possible *causes* of this condition (Jackson 2009).

It would be inaccurate, however, to suggest that the emotional side of asthma has disappeared from biomedical understandings. Rather it remains, but without occupying the privileged position it once did. The Asthma and Respiratory Foundation NZ website, for instance, cites a number of different possible causes of asthma, including suggestions that asthma "may be related to 'modern living'—perhaps to changes to the environment, our diet, or different exposure to some infections" (Asthma Foundation n.d.[c]). A few pages further, some common asthma triggers are listed, categorized under the headings of animals, colds and flu, dust mites, molds, smoke, temperature, PMS/hormonal changes,[2] and exercise. Tucked away in the body of the text is the suggestion that "some people also find that their changing emotions, such as being worried, uptight, stressed, excited or happy, can make their asthma worse. At times you may need professional help to balance your emotions, and your doctor will be able to refer you to an appropriate professional" (Asthma Foundation n.d.[b]). In a similar vein, another New Zealand asthma website tells us that "common triggers include colds or 'flu, cigarette smoke, exercise and allergies to things like pollen, furry or feathery animals or house dustmites . . ." (Breathe Easy n.d.). The small print on a sidebar includes additional items like "perfume" and "stress" whereas an explanation on the website's Q&A page notes that "overexcitement and laughter are perhaps the two emotions most likely to bring on symptoms in children" (ibid.).

Strikingly, the primary guide for patients put out by the world's most influential asthma organization, the Global Initiative for Asthma, makes no mention of emotion, stress, or mental/psychological issues anywhere in its thirty-four pages (GINA 2007), despite the fact that GINA's guidelines for physicians and nurses list "strong emotional expressions" as "common risk factors" for asthma (GINA 2012b: 5, 7). A popular American reference book, *Asthma for Dummies*, initially ignores emotions in its initial list of "top ten triggers for asthma" (Berger 2004: front inside page), introducing them only later in the text, with the explanation that "although emotions aren't the direct triggers of asthma symptoms—and asthma isn't an 'emotional problem'—activities *associated with* emotions (happy or sad) can induce coughing or wheezing in people with pre-existing hyper reactive airways, as well as in individuals who don't have asthma but who may suffer from other respiratory disorders" (ibid.: 78, my emphasis).

That said, there are a number of techniques in mainstream respiratory health care that do target the emotional aspects of asthma. When I visited asthma societies across New Zealand, the nurses I met usually ended our conversations by opening up their file cabinets and giving me copies of the pamphlets they hand out to their patients. Typically there would be a half dozen or more with information on medications, minimizing household triggers, or how to use a spacer. Somewhere in the back of the drawer, though still clearly labeled and within easy reach, there was usually a homemade photocopied handout focusing on the interplay among asthma, hyperventilation, and panic attacks.

For many patients, the question of how emotions and breathlessness interact and, in particular, the issue of how to determine cause and effect, remains vexed. Whether their anxiety arises *alongside* their asthma or *precedes* it to trigger an attack is a question that troubles many asthma sufferers. Some felt particularly unsettled that being under *either* positive or negative stress seemed to cause an attack. Samantha, for example, related that as a young child special occasions were enough to trigger her asthma: "There was just the excitement and—*raaaaahh!*—something new [and it would trigger an attack]!" Even today, psychological distress can trigger her attacks: "If I don't have my inhaler with me at all, I sometimes get anxious, thinking '*What if something happens . . . ?*' Realizing I don't have an inhaler, I panic, and that triggers the asthma like a feedback," she explained.

Most of the sufferers who raised this issue wondered how to explain the possible connections between asthma and stress, querying if, how, and when stress has an impact on their asthma. Iris, whose daughter suffers from asthma, hesitantly put it, "When an asthmatic person is anxious, in some of them, the asthma can come on more severely. Whether anxiety about asthma makes the asthma come on worse or [whether asthma is due to] anxiety full stop, I'm not sure."

What is clear is that many parents of asthmatic children and adults with asthma feel they have to be aware of the ways that emotional stress interacts with asthma, regardless of whether it triggers it or exacerbates it once it is underway. Many have specific strategies in place, some of which are at odds with established medical practice. Mark, for example, insists on smoking when he feels an attack coming on and doesn't have his inhaler on hand. His friends described how "he'll sit down and have a cigarette, and that'll calm him down, and his asthma will go away. He *knows* that the asthma gets worse with the smoking, but the psychological thing of sitting down and *calming down* by smoking will make the asthma better." In fact, in the United States and Europe in the late nineteenth and early twentieth centuries, smoking was a popular technique for ameliorating asthma symptoms (Jackson 2010), though it is hardly advocated today.

James's emotional self-care consists of combining Buteyko with mental imagery. He explained,

When you're suffering an attack . . . it's very stressful and quite panicky. Physically your temperature goes up. You have to make a sort of conscious effort with every breath that you take to simply get through it. So it's a very dark and quite isolated place to be in, and imagery is something that is so helpful when you're going through it. The exercise that would particularly work for me with my mum [when I was a child] is that while I'd be lying down, I would imagine a small animal, I think it was a puppy, that would sit on my stomach, and my goal was to make the puppy go higher and higher by pushing out my stomach on the inhale. What you're physically doing is engaging your diaphragm to take the pressure off the constriction of your lungs and air pipe.

Others are amazed at how some medical practitioners are attuned to subtly alleviating their patients' stress. Kavita's father Ajay relates how a treat meant to deflect attention and soothe his teenage daughter almost instantly abated her asthma:

What I've found funny was that in the hospital, they would give her an ice block [Popsicle] before putting her on the nebulizer. And that would solve the problem. Just that ice block! It was to divert her attention—all children like ice cream. She was happy, because it was nice, sweet, and cold . . . It was like, "Wow! Ice block! Great!" And your mind is off, away [from the problem].

There are limits, however, to how far the link between asthma and emotional distress is usually taken. Whereas psychological stress is seen as exacerbating and perhaps even triggering individual asthma attacks, it is unusual today to suggest that someone's asthma *originates* from psychological or emotional upheaval. But this is indeed what Merata, a young Māori mother who lives in the relatively economically impoverished Northland district, told us.

Twenty years old when she got pregnant, Merata was in the midst of a difficult relationship, which soon ended. Merata's mother attributes Merata's daughter's asthma to the turmoil Merata's relationship caused. As Merata related,

Mum thinks that Ahorangi's asthma was emotional . . . it was mainly around the fact
that I was going through traumatic experiences with my relationship. . . . Mum always
thought that Ahorangi was a very intuitive child. She strongly believes in the connection
between a child and its mother, and with Ahorangi being my firstborn . . . Mum felt,
whenever I was stressed out or under some sort of emotional strain, that even though
Ahorangi was so young, that she was picking up on it, and that asthma was her way of
dealing with it and expressing that she was stressed out, too.

Accordingly, the child's grandmother was skeptical of inhalers as a remedy, instead suggesting to Merata that "I should get myself into a space that was . . . a
bit more conducive for Ahorangi's well-being."

Merata's account stands out for both its insistence on focusing on asthma as
emotionally induced and on highlighting sociality as the cause, and solution, of
her infant's respiratory distress. It provides a radical counterpoint to both mainstream biomedical perspectives and alternative self-care strategies such as individual sports activities and breathing retraining, which inculcate that it is up
to the individual, on his or her own, to take charge and overcome their illness.

*　*　*

For many asthma sufferers, asthma is more than a problem affecting their
lungs. Despite being sidelined by global hegemonic discourses of "what asthma
is" and the best-practice measures used to respond to it—most notably self-
management—broader physical, as well as emotional and mental facets,
remain a part of asthma care, often addressed by subjugated therapeutic practices that exist on the medical margins. The limited focus of self-management
policies has resulted in activities such as sports and breathing retraining being
largely up to patients to seek out and organize. Some medical authorities find
themselves torn between sticking to standardized models of care and their desire to help patients who may benefit from more "alternative" therapies, but
in a medical context dominated by pharmaceuticals, physicians don't have the
luxury of giving out prescriptions for free swimming lessons.

In contrast, the Czech state recently reinforced its physicians' *obligation* to
provide a broad array of therapies that not only extend far beyond pharmaceuticals but are often seen as vital for limiting drug use. Through the centuries-old

institution of the health spa, along with more recent practices such as children's asthma camps, Czech medical authorities remain responsible for overseeing comprehensive remedies. Although employing some of the same techniques that are popular in New Zealand, these approaches are not only much broader in scope but operate through a different dynamic of care focused on reconfiguring health through collective and highly regimented experiences of the body within the natural environment, discipline and pleasure, sociality and self-care.

Chapter 6

The Best Holiday Ever

The Pleasures and Pains of Spa Cures and Summer Camps

WHEN Dr. Veselá suggested that one solution to asthma was for all those families who could to move far away from the smoke stacks, she invoked a common Czech strategy for mitigating respiratory distress. But not everyone can permanently relocate away from industrial pollution. A much more widespread solution is to make temporary sojourns into the (ostensibly) healthier environs outside the city. Indeed, all across the republic, Czechs laud the benefits of spending time outdoors.

Many Czechs are intensely proud of the education and "high culture" (*vzdělaní*) enabled by urban living, but at the same time they passionately embrace spa cures and other forms of "therapeutic retreats" popular across Russia and Central and Eastern Europe (Caldwell 2011). Today, "tramping," or hiking and camping in rural areas, is a well-established youth activity (Trnka 2015); children often engage in scouting or outdoor sports; and picking wild mushrooms in the forest borders on being a cultural obsession, particularly among older Czechs. During the state socialist period, getting out into the countryside had added significance as visiting a *chata* or country cottage was viewed as a respite from the intensive oversight of socialist authorities and, more generally, the conventions of urban life (Franc and Knapík 2013).

Simply escaping the city for a day or a week or, better yet, a few months, to spend time in nature is seen as inherently therapeutic. There are, however, also more programmatic methods of leaving the city and achieving physical "toughening" by exposing oneself to the outdoor elements. The most popular programs for children with asthma take place in summer camps and health spas, both known for being entertaining as well as physically beneficial. Referred to as "climate therapy," these programs have been available for decades, initially subsidized directly by the state and now by state-supported insurance companies. Recent constrictions in the state health budget have, however, led a few

critics to suggest that summer camps and health spas may sometimes constitute nothing more than therapeutically useless "holidays." But to do so is to miss
the point of how pleasure itself can act as a therapeutic catalyst.

Pleasure promotes the adoption of new bodily techniques and, more
broadly, new ways of relating to the body. Even though not everyone who has
undertaken a spa cure will remember the specifics of how to use a massage
ball or how often to carry out steam inhalations, establishing a different understanding of their bodies can shape their health and well-being long after
they have returned home. Moreover, whether the impacts of these therapies
are long-term (and most medical authorities involved in summer camps and
health spas contend they are), even the short-term effect of removing participants from their homes and disrupting their daily routines sets the stage for
a comprehensive mind–body therapeutics, encouraging relaxation alongside
discipline and compelling participants to reframe their understandings of what
they and their bodies can do in spite of their illnesses.

Pleasure is an as yet under-theorized domain in anthropology, sociology,
and, more broadly, studies of the senses. Nonetheless, drawing on the work of
Darwin (1872) and Freud (1920–1922), a long line of biologists, psychologists,
and more recently neuroscientists have explored the role that pleasure may
play in motivating behavior, including the promotion of new behaviors (for
example, Cabanac 1979; Kringelbach and Berridge 2010). I argue here that like
pain, which is well known as being able to cause a cathartic shift in the body
(Daniel 1984; Turner 1964), pleasure can be employed to instill new attitudes,
relationships, and bodily practices, recasting one's routines and subtly recalibrating their sense of who they are.

Through their collective, highly institutionalized, and medically professionalized approaches, summer camps and health spas inculcate asthma sufferers
(and their accompanying parents) into new and rigorous self-care routines.
Combining discipline with pleasure, they redirect attention away from the
mundane responsibilities of everyday life and open up a space where novel
experiences of the body, social relations, and the great outdoors can come together and (it is hoped) create the foundations for health.

The Great Outdoors in Historical and
Cross-Cultural Perspective

Many Czechs consider asthma a "disease of civilization" (*civilizační nemoc*),
caused by the body's response to urban pollution. Despite widespread aware-

ness of the range of factors that can instigate or contribute to a child having asthma, much less trigger an asthma attack, removing asthma sufferers from the city and exposing them to the "clean" air of rural areas is widely taken to be a panacea for respiratory distress. As a site of freedom and escape, holding out the promise of returning to simpler, more "natural" ways of living (Knižák 2011), rural space has long been invested with deep cultural significance, one facet of which is its healing properties. Even short-term sojourns are thought to be beneficial. But the ideal treatments are annual multiweek stays that will strengthen children's bodies and allow them to "cleanse" their lungs.

In fact, the heterogeneity of asthma is such that asthma can be caused, much less exacerbated, by a multiplicity of factors (Brasier 2014; Pearce 2011). Air pollution is one, and there are demonstrable links between compromised respiration, small particles, and ground-level ozone caused by factory emissions, smoke, road dust, and car exhaust (Bertoldi et al. 2012; Laumbach and Kipen 2012). Even short-term exposure to respirable particulate matter up to 10 micrometers in size (PM_{10}) has been shown to increase hospitalization rates for asthma (Romieu et al. 1996).

Across the Czech Republic, urban areas are plagued by high levels of air pollution, with the worst air quality found in Prague, the industrial areas of the North, and eastern Ostrava (Jůn 2014). Under state socialism, many of these areas suffered decades of environmental devastation due to rampant industrialization (Vaněk 1996). Today they continue to suffer from the negative effects of industry, traffic congestion, and low-quality home heating. In Prague, the boom in personal car ownership has furthermore resulted in automobile emissions constituting a leading source of air pollution (Johnstone 2014). The capital also suffers from weather "inversions" during which a layer of cool air is overlain by a layer of warmer air, trapping in dust, smoke, and other pollutants and leaving the city covered in thick smog.

These conditions are both accepted and reviled as the obvious cause of a range of respiratory disorders. The link between air pollution and asthma is taken as such a truism that many parents, asthma sufferers, and respiratory specialists questioned me about New Zealand's asthma rates, unable to reconcile that a country with so little air pollution has such a high incidence. Some, including respiratory specialists, were adamant that I must have misunderstood the country's pollution levels and that, at least in Auckland, concentrations of heavy industry must result in high levels of airborne particulates. In fact, New

Zealand's rates of PM_{10} remain well below the OECD average and the World Health Organization's guidelines. Out of the cities worldwide that report on air quality, only 12 percent of urban residents live in areas that comply with the World Health Organization's limits, placing New Zealand's urban residents among a privileged minority (Morton 2014).[1] Indeed, recent efforts to capitalize on New Zealand's air quality have included the canning of "pure New Zealand air" for export to China (Cropp 2016).

Many Czechs are acutely aware of pollution statistics as far as their own country is concerned. Not only are they well informed about the differences in air pollution rates between rural and urban areas and between various cities, they can also tell you the breakdown of air pollution levels across different urban neighborhoods, sometimes distinguishing between specific streets. One area widely known for its poor air quality is the Prague 7 district around Veletržní ulice, a highway that ran through the center of the city. People who moved out of this area because of their children's asthma noted that their children's health markedly improved once they left. (In September 2015, after nearly a decade of construction, the city opened a tunnel to reroute traffic out of this area and alleviate the high levels of traffic pollution. The tunnel's impact on air pollution levels is yet to be ascertained).

But residents all around Prague tell similar stories of air pollution horrors. One mother recounted how a doctor told her to quit Prague entirely when her six-month-old child began to have serious respiratory difficulties, noting that after they left, her daughter's health radically improved. Another mother similarly concluded that anywhere in Prague is suspect: "You look at Prague, and you can *see* the smog. We live up on a hill [where the air is supposed to be cleaner], and Alex still has asthma. To live in the woods of Šumava would be better." So many people speak about the visibly positive effects of even short-term sojourns out of the city that the few who find that spending time in rural areas does *not* solve their respiratory issues are deeply dismayed. This is, however, widely considered to be the exception, to the point that one Czech physician told me she would "surprise and amaze me" by relating the case of one of her young asthma patients whose condition got worse when he moved out of the city.

But where one should go to escape the pollution is debatable. Clearly, pollution is worse in some parts of the country, but nowhere is untouched. When I visited the woods of Šumava, a mountain range in the southwest of Bohemia famed for its good climate, locals pointed out how the vegetation along the tops of the surrounding hills had gone black from air pollution, and doctors in Šumava told me they send children with allergies and asthma to faraway health spas to expose them to better climates.

Wherever one goes, the key thing is to get out of the city. Here, healthy breathing is not just a matter of *how* one breathes, but what *kind* of air one is breathing. And although individual excursions to the woods or mountains are seen as beneficial for asthma, the most effective routes to better health are more programmatic.[2]

Summer Camps as Asthma Therapy

Since the early 1970s, ČIPA (the Czech Initiative for Asthma) has run summer camps specifically catering to children with asthma and allergies. Funded by insurance companies and corporate and individual donors, along with small parental co-payments, camps are overseen by medical staff who ensure children use their medication and provide on-the-spot care in times of crisis. But the camps also have a much wider remit, exposing children to the outdoors, improving their physical fitness, and raising their self-esteem.

Although it is common today to involve children with asthma in sports and exercise, these activities were quite radical when they were initiated in the 1950s, overturning established views that children with asthma need to be protected from overtaxing their respiratory systems. The first Czechoslovak exercise and physiotherapy programs for children with asthma were begun by a group of physicians working under the guidance of pediatric specialist Dr. Josef Švejcar. One of Dr. Švejcar's original team, Dr. Miloš Maček, was a few months short of his ninetieth birthday when I interviewed him in 2010 in his office in Motol Hospital, where he still saw patients. Dr. Maček described to me how he and other medical professionals first realized they needed to stop thinking of asthmatic children as "helpless" and start building up their strength and lung capacity. "We wouldn't let them exercise in school as they had asthma," he recounted, "but they would go home and play soccer out in the street. So, we thought, what about if we actually get them to do exercises that can change their bodies and amend their [physical] defects?"

One of Dr. Maček's colleagues, Dr. Jiří Filsak, devised the exercises used for this physical conditioning. His first sessions with the children were held outside his office window in the hospital garden. In 1971, Dr. Filsak and his colleagues came up with the idea of taking the children away from the city for two weeks of concentrated exercise and exposure to the outdoors, modeled on the "nature camps" (*přírodní tábory*) that Czech primary schools run for their pupils. Much like American summer camps, Czech nature camps are the stuff of myth and legend, known for the pranks children play on one another as well as the novelty of being far away from home and parental oversight. But in the mid-twentieth century, many children with asthma were not allowed to attend nature camps due to concerns over their health. They thus found themselves left out of activities that are culturally enshrined as one of the highlights of childhood, until the efforts of doctors such as Dr. Filsak changed all of this.

Dr. Filsak's earliest publications on the summer camps are filled with pages of detailed diagrams of children's stretches and exercises, many of them marked with precisely positioned plus and minus signs indicating at what point during the exercise a child should inhale (+) or exhale (−). The result is a carefully laid out pattern of one inhalation followed by three exhalations (that is, each exhalation is three times as long as an inhalation, similar to the pattern advocated in Buteyko), matched to the movements of the body. Prior to the availability of corticosteroid inhalers in the 1980s, such techniques were considered essential for keeping asthmatic children alive. "Before the corticosteroids, we used to lose a lot of children," Dr. Maček noted. Though similar exercises still take place in contemporary summer camps, nowadays being physically active outdoors is viewed as much more important than the exact postures and timing of inhalations and exhalations that physicians spent so many years devising.

The central aim of today's summer camps is to extend children's physical abilities and their understandings of what their bodies are capable of. As the ČIPA camps' manager, Viktor Fraňk, explained,

Because parents coddle their children, they don't think they can do any exercise. But they come to the camp, and because the doctors are right there and can take care of them if they have complications, they find out that they can do all these things: they can run and exercise all day. And sometimes there is a kid there who doesn't have asthma, and the asthma kids are running around and beating him, and they see that. And then they go back home and start to exercise at school even though up until then they weren't exercising at all.

A physiotherapist who works in the summer camps and often brings her own children along described the camps as such intensive experiences that afterward "the children are so tired they sleep for days." Another doctor, who also has a son with asthma who has attended the camps, was a bit more dramatic in her assessment of the physical stress the children go through when she good-naturedly remarked, "It was really hard, physical work. Dr. Špičák almost killed those kids, but after my son went there five or six times, [he was so physically fit that] he really overcame the disability of his condition."

Programs such as the ČIPA summer camps focus their efforts directly on children, teaching them self-care and self-discipline without any direct involvement from their parents. Here, then, responsibility for learning new skills is not dispersed across the family; rather, the child is the sole subject of instruction. There is, however, a decidedly collectivist spirit to this form of knowledge acquisition.

A great deal of thought has gone into how to organize summer camps to emphasize not only physical achievement but also cooperative sociality. From the very beginning, the camps were structured to include elements of both interpersonal competitiveness and fun. In Dr. Filsak's first camp, children spent their two weeks organized into two teams—"cowboys" versus "Indians"—competing against one another to win feathers for their Indian headdresses (Filsak 1970). Professor Špičák described a similar ethos in today's camps but with teams based on different colored T-shirts, the red team vying against the blue for the most awards. Even though the focus of the summer camps is on exercises specifically designed for children with asthma, like the Christchurch swimming lessons, the camps are open to nonasthmatic children (mainly siblings), enabling possibilities for collaboration, competitiveness, and (hopefully) success.

Fraňk described the thinking behind this process:

Many of the children feel as if physically they can't achieve much. But you bring them to the camp, and you break them up into teams. Each team has physically strong and weak children, girls and boys, younger and older. They compete against each other for the fortnight. Yes, there are individual prizes, but the focus is on the group prizes, and the kids need to learn to work together. And so at the end of the fortnight you might have a kid who has never won anything sportswise whose team wins the top spot, and he gets a certificate and feels as if he is part of it. That is the idea of building cooperation between children. And you often find that the child who is not a leader at home, who is quiet and refrains from doing things, will suddenly be a leader at the camp. . . . And so the kids learn what they are capable of. And they go home and bring that energy back with them for the rest of the year.

When successful, discipline, pleasure, and a sense of accomplishment combine to transform the child from being reticent and physically unadventurous

Figure 6.1   Pavilion marking access to the "Richard Spring," a source of curative mineral waters at Kynžvart Spa.
Photo by Lubor Ferenc. Courtesy of Creative Commons.

to embracing both his or her own capabilities and the power of working collectively toward a common goal. Ideally, the child returns home with a new understanding of his or her physical strengths and a new sense of self.

From Summer Camps to Centers of Art and Culture: The Czech Health Spa

If asthma camps are about roughing it and getting close to nature, then a decidedly different form of climate therapy is offered through the institution of the *lázeňství* or health spas. Known throughout their history for their curative waters, healthy outdoor environments, and an array of intensive therapeutic "procedures" that range from drinking mineral waters to massage and, in more recent years, electrotherapy, health spas have provided Czechs with a unique mode of therapeutics for over 200 years (see Figure 6.1).

There are more than two dozen health spas in operation across the Czech Republic today. Significantly, spas are supervised by physicians and do not reject pharmaceutical remedies—indeed, like summer camps, one of their aims is to ensure better delivery and compliance with pharmaceutical regimes. But they are also vital sites for extending the scope of curative regimes far beyond medication, and spa personnel consider it their professional duty to provide patients with a panoply of curative remedies, of which pharmaceuticals are only one.

Many of the spas were founded in the late eighteenth or nineteenth century. At their height, they were international hubs of culture as well as sites for promoting good health. Originally associated with the elite of the Austro-Hungarian Empire, spa towns such as Františkovy Lázně—founded in 1793 in honor of the Emperor Franz I of Austria—list among their famous clientele Goethe, Beethoven, Strauss, Kafka, and, more recently, Václav Havel. During the state socialist period, however, the government opened up spa cures to any Czechoslovak who had a doctor's authorization for a fully or partly paid visit. For those with chronic conditions, visits were frequently organized on an annual basis.

Ask any Czech, and he or she will explain that the primary reason to stay in a health spa is to have time to recuperate and strengthen one's body while under the care and supervision of medical professionals. But there is something else that clients, especially those with chronic conditions, are often expected to walk away with: a reconfiguring of their understandings of themselves as physical beings. Spas pursue this by compelling patients to engage with their bodies in new and different ways and by inculcating them into new routines, some of which they are expected to bring home with them. As important as the medical assessments, immunity-boosting procedures, and exposure to clean climates may be, remolding patients through discipline and pleasure are inherent facets of the spa experience.

Citizens' Rights to Spa Care

Although the costs of spa stays vary widely, roughly speaking, a full six-week respiratory spa cure for a child with asthma under the age of seven costs approximately US$2,000, out of which the insurance company is billed approximately US$1,600 (and the child's parents are billed a daily co-payment of 100 crowns or approximately US$4.00, plus another 100 crowns per day for any accompanying adult). Some critics have suggested that rather than having the state subsidize such an expensive system, spa cures should be entirely privatized. But many Czechs fear that this will transform spa cures back into an elite system of care utilized primarily by foreigners.

In the early 2010s, government funding for health spas was increasingly under threat, with strict reductions in government subsidies leading to dwindling numbers of patient referrals. The immediate economic effects included a number of spas raising their prices and letting go of staff. Some spas were forced to close down, whereas others responded by broadening their scope by, for example, expanding their clientele to include both adults and children or putting on more "wellness and relaxation" packages to attract foreign tourists.

The financial controversy came to a head when a new (social democrat) government was elected in 2013 and twenty-one members of the Czech Senate pursued a legal case against the Ministry of Health, claiming that the more restrictive funding policy contravened Czech citizens' rights. The senators were successful, and the court's ruling, made in March 2014, upheld the state's responsibility to provide health care for its citizens, determining that until such a time as "democratic debate" results in a change in law, spa cures must remain an integral component of public health care. By late 2014 and 2015, some spas experienced a turn around, with rising numbers of patients and the reopening of services. Part of the so-called spa renewal is, however, due to the privatization of facilities, and currently controversies abound over how such privatization may in the future impinge on the average Czech's chances of accessing spa care.

Moreover, although spa visits may now be enshrined as part of citizens' democratic rights to health care, there are notable differences in quality as spas range from the very posh to the decidedly rundown. Kynžvart Spa (Lázně Kynžvart) is perhaps the most famous children's health spa in the Czech Republic. Kynžvart's director boasts that the spa, which is located in the far west of the country at 730 meters above sea level, enjoys the country's "healthiest air." It is also the site of curative waters whose beneficial properties have been noted since the mid-1400s. Providing therapeutic care for children aged two to fifteen suffering from respiratory illness, eczema, or obesity, Kynžvart is situated some five miles away from the internationally renowned Mariánské Lázně, an adult health spa and tourist site known for its picturesque surroundings, grand nineteenth-century architecture, and abundance of curative mineral waters. But unlike Mariánské Lázně (see Figure 6.2), Kynžvart caters mainly to Czechs and has little foreign clientele. Although its popularity has waxed and waned, the average annual intake is generally just over 1,000 children, accompanied by 600 or so parents (children under seven are accompanied throughout their stay by a parent or other adult family member). Most of the children stay for a full six-week course of care.

Figure 6.2   Spa clients on the promenade of the famous Mariánské Lázně.
Photo by Harke. Courtesy of Creative Commons.

In the North, there is a very different children's respiratory rehabilitation spa. Cvikov Children's Respiratory Hospital (*Dětská léčebna Cvikov*) was originally built over 100 years ago as a tuberculosis sanatorium. Cvikov similarly boasts a healthy mountain climate (400 meters above sea level) but offers no special curative waters.[3] It caters to a predominantly lower- and middle-class clientele and also takes in patients living on state support.

The differences between the two institutions are striking. Although Kynžvart has the lighthearted spirit of a holiday camp set in a lush and beautiful valley watched over by an imposing nineteenth-century castle, there is no escaping that Cvikov feels like an old, rundown hospital. Its buildings are gray, Soviet-style *paneláky* (state-funded prefabricated concrete housing). The surrounding landscape is unremarkable, and the facilities are shabby and uninviting. Doctors are well aware of the center's rundown appearance, with one remarking, "A lot of the times when the mothers first arrive, they say they are afraid of the place." I could see why the families might feel a bit skittish about staying there for six weeks, particularly when one of the support staff joked with me that "we always hope the mothers will leave here and take something new home with them—some kind of new knowledge or techniques—but last year the only new thing two of the mothers left with was a case of scabies!"

What families do get to partake in at both Cvikov and Kynžvart is a comprehensive array of respiratory therapies. Breathing in healthy air is only one aspect of what goes on during their stay. In each institution, patients receive daily assessments by on-site medical personnel who administer spirometry and other examinations and adjust and supervise their daily medication. They are also put through a rigorous daily program of exercise, outdoor activities, and respiratory and immunity-boosting therapies. As in adult spas, some of these activities are mandatory for all patients, but others are individually tailored, with physicians responsible for determining a specific assortment of therapies for each patient based on her or his particular needs. The therapies they draw from cover a range of techniques for respiratory care, immune support, and climate therapy.

Respiratory Therapy:
From Neti Pots to the Children's Recorder Orchestra

Respiratory therapy generally consists of three components: improving posture, removing excess phlegm from the nasal and other respiratory passages, and lessons in diaphragmatic breathing. Correct posture is taught by physiotherapists who train children how to stand up straight and hold their shoulders back. If necessary, they employ techniques such as taping their legs and feet into the right positions.

Phlegm removal, an activity considered vital for opening up the lungs and enabling healthy breathing, is mainly overseen by nurses. Techniques include nasal irrigation during which patients tip their head while pouring salt water or mineral water from a neti pot down one nostril so that it flushes out the sinuses and exits through the other nasal passage. Another popular technique is facial and upper body massage using either one's hands or a small rubber massage ball (*míček*), which is used to apply pressure against particular points, following similar meridians to those in Chinese acupuncture. Both forms of massage are taught to all the parents who accompany their children so they can incorporate them into their domestic health-care routines. Many I spoke with later remember leaving with a pack of different-sized balls and doing their best to reenact these techniques for the first few weeks after their return home.

A third set of techniques is breathing retraining. Applying the same principles as Buteyko, physiotherapists teach patients to change the tempo and depth
of their respiration, using the muscles of the diaphragm and extending their
exhalations. They employ a number of tools to slow down respiration, including respiratory machines that introduce resistance against the outbreath, forcing patients to exhale in a continuous, slow stream. Some of the technology is
cleverly designed to engage the interest of small children, such as a handheld
machine that features the figure of a little bird who flutters up and down when
children breathe into it correctly. Other technologies are more rudimentary but
seemingly effective: to teach children to breathe through their noses and not
their mouths, they are given small circles of paper to press between their lips as
they play, forcing them to keep their mouths firmly shut.

But one of the decidedly most popular methods of breathing therapy used
not only at Kynžvart and Cvikov but all across the country is playing music.
Wind instruments, especially recorders, have been utilized since the 1950s to
teach children how to control the rhythm and depth of respiration, strengthen
their lungs, and provide them with a source of relaxation and fun. Spearheaded
by Professor Václav Žilka, up until 2003 the music therapy program was best
known for its famous recorder orchestra made up of children with asthma.
Today a number of spas continue to teach children the basics of Professor
Žilka's program. Many parents also sign their children up for individual music
lessons with the same objective in mind, noting that as their children grow,
their musical tastes change, but playing the saxophone instead of the recorder
is just as efficacious.

Cvikov is particularly adventurous in its music therapy program and its staff
were keen to see if I, as a visitor from the Southern Hemisphere, could identify
the newest addition to their range of instruments. "It comes from Australia!"
they proudly exclaimed as they showed off their didgeridoo (a long pipe, usually about four feet in length, traditionally played by indigenous Australians).
The spa had the funds to buy only one didgeridoo, but the effect that playing on
the instrument had on the children's lung capacity was so impressive that they
set the children the task of building two more out of plastic tubing.

Music therapy and diaphragmatic breathing are just a few of the many techniques used by nurses and physiotherapists to improve children's breathing.
Some of the techniques they teach are useful for improving medication intake
as they help children open up their lungs and better inhale their medicine. But

in most cases, the primary reason for these lessons is to teach children how to self-regulate their breathing to become less reliant on pharmaceuticals. To drive this point home, physiotherapists proudly showed with me their emergency breathing procedure, the oral brake (*ústní brzda*), which consists of lengthening your exhalation while adding an element of resistance to it by shaping your mouth into a very small hole, as if you were trying to whistle. When it works correctly, the counter pressure required to force out an exhalation will open up the bronchial tubes, thus averting an asthma attack.

But, for such a technique to be successful, I was told that the child also needs to learn how to stay calm and not panic when he or she feels an attack commencing. This knowledge is imparted through the same technique, making the oral brake doubly useful: it enables patients to consciously change the pace and technique of their breathing (thus hopefully averting an asthma attack), while also providing them with the knowledge that they have the capability to halt an attack, thus allowing them to stay calm and focused and not succumb to feelings of panic that would further fuel their breathlessness. "The whole point," a physiotherapist explained, "is to learn that you *can* do this, instead of using Ventolin. We don't want them to always need to use an emergency reliever because it is so bad for the body."

Although such therapies could be seen as undermining the use of pharmaceutical remedies, they are usually presented by medical professionals as yet another useful measure for counteracting asthma symptoms. Indeed, pharmaceutical companies have even capitalized on the popularity of recorder therapy. In one doctor's office I picked up a coffee mug emblazoned with the cartoon image of an elephant playing on his trunk as if it were a recorder. Underneath the slogan "playing/blowing for health" (*pískání pro zdraví*) was the logo for the global pharmaceutical firm UCB, suggesting that it views such music therapy as complementary to its own focus on developing and promoting pharmaceuticals.

Boosting Immunity in the Great Outdoors

In addition to breathing retraining, health spas offer an array of techniques for boosting the immune system. These include balneotherapy, which may include whole-body baths in water or medicinal clays; the immersion of isolated limbs (the arms or the feet, for example) in alternating baths of hot and cold water; "Scottish sprays" (pressurized water sprays); and swimming or other organized exercise in thermal swimming pools. Also popular are saunas, steam rooms, and pressurized bubble baths (*perličková koupel*). Other possibilities include the oral consumption of mineral waters and steam inhalations of salt water or mineral waters. Less well-known therapies include infrared radiation, electrotherapy for electrical muscle stimulation, and phototherapy to alter melatonin levels. Also on the list of one children's respiratory health spa are weight lifting and psychotherapy. Whereas each of these techniques works on different aspects of the body or mind, taken together their aim is to raise children's immunity and protect them from succumbing to illnesses that will exacerbate their asthma symptoms.

But the most lauded method is perhaps the simplest one: going outside. It is not accidental that when Dr. Filsak first taught children how to exercise, he held his sessions on the hospital lawns outside of his office window as exposure to fresh air was seen to be as vital for their health as were the stretches. Summer camps and spas operate on the same underlying premise that one of the most beneficial therapies for respiratory ailments is exposure to the outside elements. Often referred to as toughening (*otužování*), exposure therapy assumes the body can be strengthened by being active in the outdoor environment and becoming acclimatized to all sorts of weather. Usually this involves walking or tramping daily for about an hour or more, but it can also include playing outdoor games, running, swimming, or even horse riding.

Toughening is about conditioning oneself into a state of physical robustness. When I asked one mother what the word meant to her, she gave the example of dumping a child into a cold bath or, as an adult, diving into an ice-cold river in the middle of winter to "shock" and toughen up one's physical constitution under controlled conditions. That way, she explained, if you later encounter those conditions accidentally, your body will be prepared to cope with them. The concept is not generally used to refer to emotional or mental fitness, though having a fit body is widely seen as vital for mental well-being.

Dr. Jindřich Němec, the head doctor at Cvikov, explained to me that among the array of immunity-boosting and breathing retraining therapies, spirometry readings, and careful calibrations of medication, toughening is a key component of asthma therapy. He also makes it clear that toughening takes a while to implement, that some parents are uncomfortable with it, and that it can have its short-term challenges. "To strengthen their immune system, children need to go out whatever the weather, even if it's raining," Dr. Němec asserted. "Their mothers do not like this, as they are used to coddling them and expect them to get sick. But outdoor exercise is so essential that at Cvikov it is on the daily program *no matter what the weather*."

It happened to be a particularly cold and rainy September day. "*Every* day?" I prodded him, pointing out the window at the pouring rain and thinking to myself that I had not seen any children going on walks that day.

"Well, not today," he admitted, "because today we have a brand new intake of patients and parents who are just starting their six-week visit. But after three or four weeks here, they would go out, even in *this* kind of cold and rain."

Dr. Němec also told me that often children get sick during their stays and need more medication and treatment. At other spas, physicians likewise recounted that although the overall long-term purpose of spa cures is to strengthen the body and reduce the amount of medication patients use on a regular basis, during their stay they need to remain on the same medication or sometimes even take more or different drugs, as their bodies are undergoing such intense changes. Parents concur that their children often get sick in spas, but they similarly view this as part of the process of strengthening their systems, usually judging the spa cure a success even if their child was sick for most of his or her stay.

Not surprisingly, the issue of efficacy is one on which many parents and medical practitioners have strong opinions. Most parents determine the efficacy of treatments based on their own experiences of their children's health. One parent after another related to me how the spa had had a tremendous impact on her or his child. Their accounts were, however, cast not in terms of diminished asthma symptoms or a decrease in their use of asthma medication but of boosting their child's abilities to fight off illness. Andrea, for example, explained that both her children have been to Kynžvart twice and each time "it did them very well—they didn't get sick the whole summer."

Strikingly, even parents whose children remained unwell made similar claims. Miroslava sends her son Pepík to Cvikov every year. This year his stay there wasn't as good as in the past as he was sick for half of his six-week visit. But in terms of the efficacy of the treatment, his illness is not seen as problematic. The staff at Cvikov, she said, explained to her that sometimes children are sick for the duration of their spa cure, but the rest of the year, their immunity is strengthened and they are very healthy. And if Pepík had not recently come down with yet another case of strep throat, she concluded, then indeed, "He would be very healthy right now." Miroslava's reasoning suggests a good deal of hopefulness and faith in a therapeutic practice into which she has invested a lot of time and a bit of her own money. It also, however, denotes the widely held view that the curative effects of spa treatments are often seen as not necessarily immediately tangible but as acting in more subtle and long-term ways to realign the body and increase health and well-being.

If climate therapy is upheld by both physicians and parents as central to spa cures' efficacy, it is also what parents and children highlight as being the most memorable and pleasurable element of all the spa activities. Time and time again, families described the outdoor walks and beautiful natural surroundings in glowing terms (cf. Speier 2008). They spoke passionately about their new understandings of how to enjoy the outdoors, with many parents noting that they have learned that their children really *can*, and in fact *should*, go out in all sorts of weather, just as long as, one mother told me, "you give them good rain jackets to keep them dry."

Although doctors are quick to hail climate therapy as pivotal to the efficacy of spas, they are also unwilling to compartmentalize the effects of the various treatments children undertake. Most of the doctors involved in climate therapy offered only rudimentary accounts of how the therapy works, citing that it improves circulation and blood flow. Generally, they suggested that climate therapy is best viewed as part of a package deal: from music therapy and massage to better inhaler techniques, patients must undergo the full array of treatments. And yet, the desire to disaggregate spa cures and delineate the effects of specific facets of care is growing, particularly among cash-strapped parents as well as the operators of alternative therapies who have stepped in to provide similar services for families who cannot undertake a full six-week therapeutic sojourn.

Alternative Treatments

Among the creative alternatives that have been developed to extend new and more flexible forms of climate therapy are therapeutic excursions to the Greek or Croatian seaside (referred to in Czech as a *mořský koník*, literally a "sea horse"). Predicated on the principle that air and water infused with sea salt have special curative properties and that intense exposure to them will enable children to mitigate their asthma, seaside excursions that involve disciplined exercise alongside games in the sea, snorkeling, and swimming became popular in the 1990s. Costing between 15,000 and 20,000 crowns (approximately US$600 to US$800) for a three-week visit, out of which parents pay approximately two-thirds and insurance companies cover the remainder, seaside excursions cost parents much more than a fully insurance-funded stay in a traditional health spa. Some of the excursions are led by renowned respiratory physicians, but nonetheless there is much controversy regarding whether these trips constitute actual therapeutic interventions or merely the aforementioned insurance-company-funded "holidays." Indeed, some medical professionals who have accompanied children on these trips complain that, although the principle of being exposed to salinized air and water is sound, "there is no regime—the children just hang out by the sea," and that, after the first few days, some of the children don't even bother to get into the water but just lie on the beach sunbathing.

Another, far cheaper alternative are salt rooms or "salt caves" (*solné jeskyně*), which have become popular over the last decade in the Czech Republic, the Ukraine, Germany, Israel, and, more recently, Australia. As the owner of one of these establishments in Prague told me, the purpose of salt rooms is to create an easily accessible space where people can breathe in "good, clean air" without having to leave the city. In her facility, as in a similar one that I visited in Sydney, the walls are made of bricks of salt imported from the Dead Sea. The rooms are equipped with comfortable chairs as well as toys and playground equipment including a "sandbox" lined with loose salt in which children sit and play. Some of the adults find the atmosphere particularly amenable for doing yoga or sitting under solar lamps and listening to relaxing music.

Yet another, shorter version of climate therapy is cave therapy (*speleoterapie*), which consists of spending several hours a day in some of Moravia's extensive cave systems, on the basis that the consistently cool, damp air is particularly cleansing. Proponents of this method explain that the cave air is so "pure" that climate therapy in caves can proceed in half the time of a typical spa visit. For parents like Alena, a physician and mother whose young son has severe asthma, an important feature of cave therapy is how much easier it is to arrange to take three weeks off work to accompany a child to a cave spa as opposed to the six weeks necessary for a regular health spa.

Alena isn't the only parent who struggles to sort out how to integrate climate therapy into her family's domestic and working life. Finances and the ability to take time off from work are significant factors in many families' therapeutic decision making as most forms of climate therapy demand commitment not only from children but also from their parents. Restricting the amount of time they can spend may, however, mean losing out on a crucial element of how spa cures operate.

Personhood, the Body, and Sociality

Health spas do not just provide a specific array of techniques and a beautiful environment in which to practice them. As "total institutions" (Goffman 1957) that immerse children and their accompanying parents into a novel and rigorous set of self-care routines, health spas aim to transform patients' and their parents' understandings of their bodies. Like most total institutions, spas create a unique and isolated environment—a space outside the usual demands of sociality and time—in which the imposition of new institutional regimes recrafts people's routines, behaviors, and perspectives. Some aspects of these new ways of being are, moreover, meant to travel back home with them, enabling them to better fulfill their social and familial roles. As Barbara Benedict points out in her analysis of eighteenth-century British spas, spas provide "a form of 'time out' of history and culture that, in fact, reinforced the values of 'time in'" (1995: 204). Such transformations (when they happen) are accomplished not only through discipline and routine but also through the transformative effects of pleasure.

The association of spas with relaxation and holiday leisure has deep historical roots. Amy Speier (2008: 145; see also Speier 2016) has noted that contemporary "Czech health spas are sites where the promotion of health and leisure are inextricably linked." Anthropologists and social historians have made similar points about contemporary Brazilian and Portuguese spas (Quintela 2011) as well as seventeenth-, eighteenth-, and nineteenth-century spas in Germany (Lempa 2002), France (Mackaman 1998), and Britain (Herbert 2009), often highlighting spas as sites of entertainment and intense sociality. In addition to the diversions of walks along the park and promenade, musical performances, casinos, and ballrooms, spas are described as infused with a liberatory ethos, associated with a break in daily routine and the many possibilities that arise from mixing with new people in a setting far from home, including romance and illicit liaisons.

But it is not incidental that such elements of pleasure and escape occur within, and not outside of, a highly regimented therapeutic space. The total institution of the spa produces a sense of pleasure and bodily mastery not only through its leisure activities but also through bodily discipline. As Christie Davies points out, from the tuberculosis sanatorium to the Buddhist monastery, the demands of total institutions are not always experienced as creating "a negative experience of self"; rather, organized discipline in and of itself can be experienced as positive and, in some cases, lead to a sense of transcendence (1989: 79). In Czech spas, the twinning of discipline and rigor with relaxation and leisure is not hard to understand if we think of spas as training grounds for the body and mind. Much like summer camps, which are considered to be fun but, as one parent noted, are also a space in which "Dr. Špičák almost killed those kids" due to the hard work demanded of them, spas similarly require discipline, rigor, and submission to a set regime that can, ideally, lead to a sense of success and inculcate a new sense of the body and the self.

The intensive therapeutics in health spas are coordinated through a rigorous daily regime that can often leave parents and children feeling a bit overwhelmed when first they arrive. At Cvikov, the day starts with a group exercise at 6:30 am. Following breakfast, children head off to the spa school which runs from 8 am to 12 pm. (As older children miss up to ten weeks of school to attend the spa, all school-age children are expected to carry on with their lessons, overseen by the spa's in-house teacher.) A second round of group exercise takes place after lunch at 12:30 pm, and then the afternoon is devoted to therapeutic activities such as the various respiratory and immunity-boosting procedures. The children also have daily sessions with physicians who measure their respiratory function, adjust their medication, and deal with any health crises. Every day the children must go on two outdoor walks, whatever the weather. Once a week they have a sauna and take part in music therapy. They also use the outdoor pool as frequently as possible.

The children are not only inculcated into a very strict regime in which every hour of their day is accounted for, but they are also expected to learn and be able to re-create the specific techniques taught to them in each of these sessions (such as, for example, the breathing and posture exercises). With younger children who attend health spas with their parents, the focus of training is not so much on the child but on the parent, who is expected to learn how to administer a number of the intensive treatments that the nurses and physiotherapists undertake.

It takes time to learn all these skills properly, and this is one of the reasons why spa stays are so long. Though four-week stays are possible, one of the physicians at Cvikov explained that "six weeks is the minimum [recommended time], as it takes this long to train mothers to know how to take care of their children." Unaccompanied children stay for up to ten weeks, as it is generally thought it takes young people longer to learn these skills themselves.

Mind and Body

As with summer camps, where part of the therapeutic process is immersing children in new social relations, the spa similarly encourages new forms of sociality that compel parents and children to work together differently, introducing them to new forms of bodily discipline, relaxation, and fun.

Dr. Lukáš Smetana is one of four respiratory physicians who work at Cvikov. When he took me on a tour of the establishment, he was very keen that I not only see how spirometry is undertaken and children are taught better inhaler techniques but also get an idea of the spa's music therapy program. Because there wasn't any music therapy scheduled that day, he showed me his homemade videos of one instead. "Look at the drumming we have them do," he said, excitedly pointing an image of a group of children sitting cross-legged in a circle on the floor, tapping on hand drums. "It teaches them two things," he explained. "The children learn to relax to the rhythm of the music, and we also teach them a different pattern of breathing, timing their inhalations and exhalations to the rhythm of the drumming."

"And now, look!" He pointed enthusiastically. "Look how the children are beating two sticks together, making another rhythm and breathing along with it!" He turned on a second video to show me how the children make rhythms using rattles they have created out of acorn tops.

The music therapy session concluded with the medical staff softly playing chimes while the children lay in a circle with their eyes closed. "Look how relaxed they are," Dr. Smetana sighed.

"You know, some kids do music therapy with their mothers in the room, but it is not as good," he added when the video was over. "They are not as spontaneous because they just do what they think their mothers expect from them. And sometimes their mothers actively hold them back, saying things like 'that's enough (*to je dost*)' if they get too loud."

I am struck by this comment as it comes from the same man who earlier in the day told me that one of the great benefits of spas is that they enable mothers to spend weeks of stress-free time with their children. He was also the person who explained to me that one of the merits of daily massage therapy is that "it requires mothers to touch their children. Not only is massage useful for stimulating pressure points, but the very fact that the child is being touched and stroked by someone can be a very enjoyable and positive experience. We shouldn't forget how important it is to be touched."

Dr. Smetana was particularly forthright in expressing his sentiments, but he is not alone in his point of view. Another of Cvikov's physicians, Dr. Jarmila Novotná, similarly stated that just as elemental as the various respiratory therapies she oversees at Cvikov is the fact that for six weeks mothers do not need to cook, clean, or organize their daily routines but instead can devote themselves to their children. "The children love the attention," she explained, "and the mothers love not having the stress."

Many of the mothers I spoke with concurred. Radka, who was initially hesitant to visit Kynžvart, ended up having an excellent time, describing it as "super" because "there was no stress—I could have a real break." Another woman explained that at first she felt under a lot of pressure in the spa, racing from one procedure to another. But after about ten days, she learned to relax and slow down her pace. "You can tell the people who are new as opposed to those who have been here for a while," she said, "because the expressions on their faces are not as relaxed."

It is tempting to think of these processes as the removal of responsibility, akin to Goffman's suggestion that "total institutions take over 'responsibility' for the inmate" (in this case the patient), ensuring that "everything that is defined as essential [is] 'layed on'" for them (1957: 47). However, life in a spa is more accurately depicted as a *shift* in responsibilities rather than a removal of them. Parents no longer need to worry about preparing the next meal or doing the dishes, so their attention is freed up to focus on other things, such as playing with their children, going on walks, and learning the techniques of self-care entailed in therapeutic regimes. But each of these is yet another kind of responsibility that is being inculcated through the spa regime. Once parents and children return home, the aim is that they will incorporate these practices into their daily routines. Thus, even though the spa may offer a momentary lull in domestic responsibilities, it is designed toward ultimately *expanding* mothers' and children's responsibilities rather than contracting them.

What is important here is that for Dr. Smetana and others helping children cope with asthma and other chronic respiratory ailments is a larger project than conducting spirometry tests or teaching better inhaler techniques. In addition to addressing the body of the child, there is a psychological facet to this care, focused on alleviating children's and mothers' stress, reinforcing the mother–child relationship, and giving children more space to express themselves. There are moments when these different objectives require a bit of juggling, as exemplified by the preference for keeping mothers out of the music therapy sessions, but, throughout their stay, mothers and children are taught new ways not only of organizing their daily routines but of thinking about and experiencing their bodies. Some of this instruction is explicitly conveyed through the spa's weekly health lessons or by the rigorous enforcement of daily schedules across patients' six-week stays. Other recalibrations are carried out more subtly through inhalations and exhalations timed with drumming or with eyes closed while lying on the floor, listening to chimes.

One could intimate from Dr. Smetana's comments that he advocates a return to the hypothesis that childhood asthma results from an incorrectly developed mother–child bond, but I would prefer to take his comments in the spirit of a physician who recognizes the complexities of getting to grips with the experiential side of asthma in the midst of twenty-first-century family life. The contemporary respiratory spa offers a space in which the body is acted on not just in terms of learning how to read symptoms or take peak flow measures and respond with appropriate pharmaceutical solutions—though that goes on there too—but through a full-body regime that spills over into the mental spaces and experiential realms of living with bouts of intense breathlessness.

What is essential here is that there is no attempt to differentiate the mental from the physical, to separate out people's experiences of stress or anxiety from the narrowing of their bronchial tubes—instead, all of these aspects are addressed through a comprehensive therapeutics that actively sidesteps such distinctions. In my reading of him, Dr. Smetana is not interested in whether stress causes asthma or asthma exacerbates stress as much as he is keen to create a space in which a range of physical, emotional, and interpersonal aspects of childhood illness that cannot be addressed in the daily routines of domesticity and schooling can come to the foreground and be collectively reshaped.

This is not always easy to do. As Cvikov's head doctor, Dr. Němec, complained to me, some of the mothers who accompany their children are upset when they arrive "because they think they are going on holiday and are going to give their children over to the staff while they enjoy themselves. . . . These kinds of mothers," he said, "have no intention of continuing on with what they learn here in terms of the therapeutic techniques. Instead, they come home from the spa and say to their own mothers, 'Here, Grandma—I've been stuck with him [my child] for six weeks, now you take care of him'—and *then* they go away on holiday!" Some of the parents who visited spas with their children made similar observations, remarking that at the beginning of the six-week cycle, they met mothers who seemed to think they were going to leave their children in the spa's care and "go down to the pub," raising the wrath of the spa's health-care team. Mrs. Malinová, the insurance specialist at VZP, is similarly scathing of mothers who attend spas and don't actively take part in learning the therapeutic techniques, stating that any mother who expected to sit back and not actively participate in her child's spa cure would not be subsidized to attend.

But not everyone, of course, can accommodate him- or herself to the spas' strict regimes. Even for parents who intend to engage with their children's care, taking part in the disciplined structure of the spa can be challenging, and, for some, downright alienating. Although the focus may be on inculcating routines of care and building stronger relationships between mothers and children, it occurs in a highly institutionalized context that presents its own challenges.

Many of the parents I spoke with reflected on the difficulties of living in such a milieu for a month and a half. One of these was my longtime friend Andrea, who had recently visited a spa with her six-year-old daughter. She described an atmosphere "full of tension," explaining that

as in any institution, when you have a group of strangers from different backgrounds living together for six weeks, you get a real mix of people, and they fight over the smallest things. For example, if there is a sandbox, some kids have shovels and buckets, and some parents didn't bring any. Sometimes their kids take the toys away from the others, and they don't say anything, and the other parents get angry. That's what happened when I was there. There was a very vulgar woman who got angry at another woman who was pregnant, and they started to fight. It got very physical, and the pregnant woman was thrown against the wall, and it looked as if she'd started to miscarry. The police came, and she was taken to the hospital. The pregnant woman's husband stopped by later and said that everything was OK, that she had just started bleeding but didn't lose the baby, but that she was badly injured. The other woman told us all that, if the police came back, we all had better keep our mouths shut or she would come after us.

Andrea concludes,

There were people like that there. You would bump into their chair by accident, and they would say, "What do you think you're doing! I'll punch you in the mouth if you do that!" When at first the staff warned all of us mothers not to (physically) fight each other, I laughed and thought, you don't need to worry about us. But then they told us that more than half the visits include one fight.

For others, the experience of being institutionalized proves too much. Dr. Novotná complained that many of the Roma or "gypsy" families who come to stay at Cvikov disappear within a week or two of their arrival. They can't stick to the regime, she said, and choose to leave, "though I can't see why anybody wouldn't like it here." I was not able to speak to any of these families, but given the extraordinary levels of ethnic prejudice against the Romany and their widespread mistreatment by the Czech state, most notably through the history of forced state medical care (Sokolová 2005), it is not surprising that many of them would find such institutions unpalatable.

Disciplined Pleasures

In contrast, those who get the most out of the spa visits are the clients who are not only inclined to submit to the disciplined rigors of spa routines but who also derive pleasure from the opportunity to take part in structured routines and enjoy the beautiful surroundings. Andrea encapsulated this dynamic when she described the initial difficulties she experienced fitting into the routine. "The only problem with the spa visit," she remembered, "was that it was so much work. You have to get up at 6:00 am to get [the children] to breakfast on time and then take them from one procedure to another or go on walks with them. When you aren't having a procedure, you are supposed to be outside in nature with them the whole time. I got sick with the flu. I took my kids to the pool and then had to run from the pool to get them to a procedure on time, and I was still wet, so I got sick. Another mother took them for a few days so I could rest."

Despite these difficulties, she summed up her overall experience as "fantastic. The nature was really great, and you had to go for walks all the time." When

I asked her what she meant by *"having* to go for walks," she explained that there is no option to do otherwise. "It is a required part of the program. The spa staff walk up and down the dormitories at a certain hour of the morning ensuring that everyone is out of their rooms and outside," she recounted. Then, without any irony, Andrea added that her six weeks in the health spa was "the best holiday I ever had." Other parents had similar, if briefer accounts, explaining simply, "The kids loved it, and they did all the breathing exercises, physical exercises, got fresh air, the place was beautiful!"

Although it is crucial to differentiate between the impacts of spas on patients who are under direct medical supervision and undergo the array of therapeutic procedures and the parents who accompany them, it is also, as doctors such as Dr. Smetana noted, important to recognize the far-reaching effects of changed environments and daily routines on both the children and adults. Weeks of clean air, daily walks, and having their meals and other needs catered for are often experienced as the best parts of the spa stay by both parents and children, revealing a shared experience of disciplined and pleasurable physical engagement.

Indeed, the twin dimension of pleasure and intense physical discipline are also highlighted in children's accounts. Frederik, who is eleven, loved the two trips he made to a spa, accompanied by his mother and younger sister. His most awful memory is of being wrapped up in hot towels and made to lie sweating on a table every day. "I had to read to him to keep him still," his mother remembered. But otherwise it was like a "tremendous holiday." Similarly, seven-year-old Kateřina, reflecting back on a recent stay in a spa with her mother, focused on the fun they had taking long walks together and seeing wonderful new sights. "Everything was nice, except for the very very hot baths, horribly hot baths!" she told me, referring to the hot baths with oil and oats in which she had to soak for twenty minutes a day. Her particular pleasure was "going for walks every day, even in the snow."

Although adult spas have long been associated with leisure and pleasure, this has not been the case for children's spas. Up to the early 1990s parents did not accompany their children. Many adults who had spent part of their childhoods in spas recalled horrible experiences. Květa is in her mid-thirties and spent every summer, from the age of two up until twelve or thirteen, at a respiratory spa in what is today Slovakia. "It was a miserable experience," she said. "In those days, you went without your mother, and I was terrified." Her descriptions suggest a profound sense of powerlessness in the face of harsh discipline. But every year she remembers her parents telling her the spa was good for her asthma and sending her off again. When her younger sister turned two, she too was sent away. Květa has a profoundly disturbing memory of her sister feeling so unhappy at the spa that she "tried to commit suicide by throwing herself under a moving car." After the 1989 revolution, Květa remembered subtle shifts in the spa ethos as "the nurses started being nicer to children, less disciplinarian." Jaroslav, who was sent to a respiratory spa in the early eighties when he was a young boy, likewise remembered horrific experiences of being at the mercy of "horrible nurses who beat the children and didn't care about us at all."

Today, while discipline is still key in spa stays, most children and parents described the experience as much more pleasurable, so much so that Andrea's depiction of the spa as "the best holiday I ever had" exemplifies the way many parents and children portrayed their visits. Indeed, a growing number of people with the financial means to do so have started to visit adult spas as an alternative way of taking a holiday. Instead of having a doctor recommend treatment, they simply sign themselves up. One couple explained that they take part in a range of therapeutic treatments in the morning, but otherwise, "It is like having a holiday—you have a place to stay and can spend the day walking through the mountains."

Many of the procedures offered by spas remain, however, antithetical to the "rest and relaxation" ideals that most Westerners associate with health spas (Speier 2008). And although spas are increasingly being chosen as holiday sites by non-Czechs, the results are not always what they expect. As Speier (2011) has found, after checking into their spa hotels, British tourists are often startled to be called down to the doctor's office to have their blood pressure checked and other health tests undertaken. Many spas are now waiving this requirement and allowing foreign visitors to come up with their own desired procedures (as opposed to having them medically prescribed by a physician), offered like a menu of options with prices listed per procedure. Some are also becoming more flexible about health regulations, such as serving only dietary meals, and are learning to cater to foreign tourists' culinary desires.

But with the state budget under increasing scrutiny, such measures are not necessarily helping spas retain their position as providers of vital health-care services. Some critics question not only how cost effective these institutions are but whether they are effective at all. The directors of various spas have responded by holding open days for visiting medical professionals and speaking out in other forums about the benefits of their services. But, as yet, there are few comprehensive scientific studies at their disposal, primarily because in the past there was much less need for them.

In response to such concerns, insurance companies such as VZP are trying to ensure that their clients do not use spas as an insurance-funded holiday by mandating certain levels of therapeutics. As of 2012, for example, VZP requires that spa patients receive at least three procedures a day, six days a week. In 2014, another leading insurance company told me that they would support patients' repeat visits to health spas only if they saw some visible, measurable change in their health status, such as a reduction in the amount of daily medication they take for chronic conditions.

Such attempts to measure and ensure the efficacy of health spas risk running counter to the philosophy that the therapeutics on offer act as a "package deal," in the sense that climate therapy works alongside massage, pharmaceutical oversight, music therapy, and swimming or horse riding lessons. Significantly, however, the Czech health-care system has not yet given in to the imperatives of evidence-based medicine (EBM), nor have pharmaceuticals diverted funding entirely away from health spas.

Nonetheless, globally the rise of EBM is refiguring medical practice, not only streamlining procedures but also radically changing the categories of value that are used in determining efficacy (Berg 1998). As Vincanne Adams (2013) has shown, the randomized control trial (RCT) has become the international baseline standard for assessing efficacy. "As a result," she argues, "it becomes increasingly the case that medical interventions that do not lend themselves to evaluations using RCT designs must be seen, from the EBM perspective, as being of *poor quality* and, by default, unreliable, and therefore of little use in determining policy, practice guidelines, or fiscal support" (Adams 2013: 57, italics in the original).

Things such as pleasure, discipline, and changes in daily responsibilities cannot, however, be measured through randomized control trials. According to EBM's system of values, they become irrelevant "side effects" rather than remaining part of the experiential realities that are integral to spas' therapeutic effects. These features are, however, often key to how participants engage in spa therapeutics and even what many of them actually look for when choosing a health spa.

In a study of how practitioners and adherents of complementary and alternative medicine (CAM) rate their efficacy, Christine Barry (2006: 2646) argues that many of those engaged in CAM are motivated by the desire to have a different kind of *experience* of their bodies, most notably "transcendent, transformational experiences; changing lived-body experience; and the gaining of meaning," none of which can be assessed through EBM criteria. Although spa therapies are not a part of alternative or complementary medicine in the Czech Republic but lie firmly within mainstream biomedicine, I have suggested here that their proponents and clients are similarly engaged in attempting to enable an *experiential shift* that is a fundamental aspect of the care provided. The very fact that spas (as yet) do not need to submit to EBM criteria as a mode of reckoning value is therefore something to be lauded.

* * *

Alongside summer camps, today's health spas must be considered, among other things, for their experiential dimensions, as sites in which discipline and pleasure, challenge and mastery, and the dramatic recasting of daily responsibilities play a pivotal role in how children and their families come to cope with chronic conditions. Physicians' refusals to delineate which of the spas' various "procedures" are the most central to their success may well be an acknowledgment of this.

In both summer camps and health spas, children have been brought together to learn new modes of self-care. They are taught not only what to do with their bodies but where to do it, exposing themselves to the outdoor elements while experientially learning new ways of being-in-the-body and of seeing themselves as physically and mentally competent. Relationships are central to this process, be they among children, between medical professionals and their patients, or between mothers, fathers (albeit less frequently), and their asthmatic children. Self-care is not jettisoned, but an asthma sufferer's relationship to his or her body constitutes just one of many relationships that are seen as being key for promoting, or hindering, therapeutic success.

Sometimes, however, even the most concerted individual or collective efforts at healing ailing bodies are insufficient. When temporarily escaping from the smokestacks proves not enough, the focus broadens to address the larger structural and contextual features that underpin disease. In the Czech Republic, efforts to galvanize public attention to high rates of respiratory illnesses, particularly in Prague and in the eastern Moravian city of Ostrava, enjoy a very high public profile. Defining asthma and other respiratory conditions as diseases of civilization, sufferers, scientists, and environmental activists address asthma not only on the therapeutic level but in terms of national politics. In the process, they stir up huge controversy over the appropriate roles of national and local government, citizens, and corporations in being held to account for children's health and well-being.

Chapter 7

Redistributing Responsibility among States, Companies, and Citizens

Struggles in the Steel Heart of the Republic

F EW visitors to Ostrava can escape the overwhelming sensation of being surrounded by a blanket of smog, particularly if they visit the Czech Republic's third largest city in winter. Located in the industrial center of Moravia near the borders of Poland and Slovakia, Ostrava's landscape has long been dominated by coal, iron, and smog, earning it the nicknames "black Ostrava" and "the steel heart of the republic." Today, Ostrava is famous for its residents' respiratory problems. Indeed, some Czech doctors and scientists have lobbied to have Ostrava recognized as having the highest rates of childhood asthma in the world.

It wasn't always so. Many of the air quality problems began after the establishment of the state-owned Nová Huť Klementa Gottwalda (NHKG) steel plant in 1951. As one local activist remembered, when his parents moved to the region in the 1940s, they specifically chose to settle in the Ostrava district of Radvanice and Bartovice as his mother suffered from respiratory problems. As the area housed a former tuberculosis sanatorium, they assumed the air would be healthy. He related that on the day the NHKG steel plant first started production, "it was sunny, and my father sat down to read the newspaper. Behind his back he could hear it start to rain. He kept on reading his paper until he realized it had been raining far too long. He turned around and looked out the window and saw it wasn't rain, but ash. And it never stopped falling."

The negative effects of such "rainfall" on residents' health were largely hidden from public view until the 1989 Velvet Revolution. Following the overthrow of the government, environmental conditions across the republic received intensive media coverage. New government policies promoting nationwide economic restructuring resulted in the widespread closure of the region's coal mines and the slowing down of steel production. Although mining did not recover, much of the steelworks industry did, having been bought and expanded

Figure 7.1   Mothers and children calling attention to the health effects of Ostrava's air pollution.

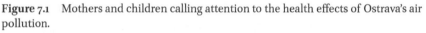

Photo by Pavel Sonnek. Reprinted courtesy of *Deník*/Pavel Sonnek.

by foreign companies. Luxembourg-based ArcelorMittal purchased the former NHKG, renamed it ArcelorMittal Ostrava, and refurbished it into what is today the largest steelworks in the Czech Republic, producing 3 million tons of crude steel per year. As a result, the air quality not only stopped improving but plummeted to the point that the district of Radvanice and Bartovice is widely considered to have the worst air quality in Europe due to high levels of PM_{10}, benzo(a) pyrene (BaP), benzene, and arsenic. Data collected in Radvanice and Bartovice in 2013, for example, reveal that levels of PM_{10}, which can lead to aggravated asthma, chronic bronchitis, and lung cancer, exceeded EU limits 129 days that year and levels of BaP, which causes cardiovascular diseases and damage to genetic material, exceeded EU directives by 900 percent (Czech Hydrometeorological Institute 2014). More recent research (for example, Vossler, Cernikovsky, Novak, et al. 2015) paints a similarly grim picture.

The plight of Ostrava's 300,000 residents and the half a million people living in the surrounding area has elicited widespread media interest in the Czech Republic and across Europe. In part, this is due to high-profile protests during which residents donned gas masks to highlight their concerns (see Figure 7.1).

Residents also wrote a petition, which garnered 19,000 signatures, demanding that steel companies and local and national government take action. A series of lawsuits against ArcelorMittal Ostrava and one by the local Ostrava government against the Czech state ensued. It is no wonder that, when I began researching children's asthma in the Czech Republic, one of the first questions I was asked was when would I be going to Ostrava.

The problems in Ostrava inspire public and legal debate over who is responsible for securing residents' health and well-being. Many locals, NGOs (nongovernmental organizations), physicians, and scientists look to the state—both local and national—as ultimately responsible for safeguarding Ostrava's inhabitants. At the same time, however, local and national politicians struggle to resolve the crisis of rising unemployment. Because there appears to be little scope for industry or commerce in the region *other than* through the steelworks industry, the unemployment rate sparks heated debate over how to best ensure residents' health and well-being. Splits between local and national government have exacerbated confusion over who exactly has fallen short of meeting their obligations to protect residents' interests.

In such a context, asthma and other respiratory illnesses emerge as a citizenship issue that provokes widespread and sustained interest. Indeed, despite ArcelorMittal's concerted efforts to suggest that respiratory health is a personal issue, activist efforts, along with lawsuits against both ArcelorMittal and the Czech state, have led to Ostrava's environmental conditions becoming a political rallying point for Czech politicians, scientists, and physicians. Respiratory illnesses get cast as a collective, national responsibility and taken up as a citizenship issue, inspiring nationwide debate over whether the state, corporations, or individuals are the ultimate guarantor of citizens' rights. Here, then, the question of personal responsibility for health has been turned into an explicitly political object, vociferously contested at community, national, and international levels and raising both support for and vehement opposition to neoliberal ideals of the self-responsible, self-reliant subject.

Reciprocal Obligations

Air pollution knows no boundaries, and to some extent everyone who lives in Ostrava suffers from the same overall environmental conditions. However, as Janice Harper (2004) and Phil Brown and his coauthors (2012) have pointed out, the links between environmental conditions and respiratory illnesses are often of central concern to lower-income communities based close to hubs of industry and transport. As Harper notes with respect to Texas, "All people living in the Houston area are breathing poisoned air, [but] the concentrations of ground-level ozone and air toxics are not equally shared by all" (2004: 308). This is also the case in Ostrava, where some parts of the city, most notably Radvanice and Bartovice, get more than their fair share of air pollution and respiratory illnesses. That said, air toxicity in Ostrava has received national attention, acting as a rallying point for politicians, scientists, and physicians far outside the region. Here, then, environmental politics is not ghettoized, but nationalized.

One reason for this prominence is that debate over Ostrava's air pollution evokes widespread concern over the appropriate roles of citizens, the state, and capitalist corporations in a fledgling democratic society. The story that makes the headlines is, furthermore, inflected with widely held traditional perspectives on (working-class) labor, gender roles, the needs of vulnerable children, and the ethnic constitution of local communities. All that is missing—and conspicuously so—is the state's role in protecting its citizenry.

In depicting the Ostrava situation as a struggle between citizens who are suffering and a state that is not living up to its obligations, Czech activists tap into deeply held convictions about the appropriate roles of states and citizens, epitomized through the ideal of the social contract. The idea that environmental health is a citizenship issue harkens back to struggles against the socialist regime. In the late 1980s, unrest over the impact of air pollution on respiratory health, particularly children's health, helped fuel protests that drew the era of state socialism to a close. Any revolution in state–citizen relations today would be of a lesser scale, but the implications of these demands remain significant.

As it is currently cast, the struggle in Ostrava evokes a *generational politics* of social contracts in which mothers and (male) workers contribute to the well-being of the nation-state through (female) reproduction and (masculine) labor. Their gifts are offered on the understanding that there will be a corresponding counteroffer, namely the state's protection. As in all gift exchanges, temporality is crucial (Bourdieu 1977) in that protection is particularly needed when citizens are still children (that is, mothers-to-be and workers-to-be) and unable to fend for themselves. When citizen–state reciprocities break down, children suffer more than others and become the focal point for struggles to reestablish order.

Didier Fassin (2013: 118) has recently pointed out the immense rhetorical power of children as iconic victims whose "innocence" and "vulnerability" cannot be questioned. When children's lives become the sites of political struggle, Fassin suggests, political debate shifts into a highly emotive register, in which questions of responsibility take on a different kind of valence. One could argue that young children represent the outer limits of notions of individualized personal responsibility as they simply *cannot* take care of themselves and thus represent the inherent need for collective interdependence. For many adults, moreover, the image of the child-in-pain is a highly affective trigger, eliciting concern and a desire to alleviate suffering in a way that is qualitatively different from other political objects, other than perhaps animals. The figure of the suffering child thus provides a powerful emotive focal point for debates over the obligations of the state.

As with all social contracts, this is a nationalist story, and the state's obligation to protect "its people" is heightened by the fact that the company is foreign owned. It is also an ethnic story, as citizenship is represented through the images of white families-in-pain. Not everyone can suffer, and Ostrava's Roma (gypsies) are left out of claims on the state, literally erased from scientific and medical discourse. The social contract is thus seen as encompassing only those thought to have appropriate relations with the state—who give enough and do not take too much—and excludes those deemed outside the reciprocal obligations of state and citizen.

And what about the role of the company? ArcelorMittal has taken major steps, both in Ostrava and internationally, to portray itself as a moral actor, but much of this has fallen flat in terms of its local and national reputation. Despite the early postsocialist period during which conservative rhetoric promoted free markets and unfettered capitalism as being both the most "natural" and the most "morally just" economic and political system, most of Czech society appears unwilling to consider the company as acting within a moral framework. Cognizant of what Peter Benson and Stuart Kirsch (2010: 459) have referred to as the "token accommodation" of many corporate social responsibility (CSR) programs, activists, scientists, and local pressure groups continue to turn to the state as the only source of (potential) justice.

This then is a case in which the social contract stands as a powerful ideal *even when it is constantly being undermined*. As Elisabeth Kirtsoglou (2010) has noted, modernization (locally glossed as "Westernization") is often embraced for its promise to deliver the ever-deferred ideal in citizen–state relations, even though it is also the mechanism through which multiple exclusions and loopholes in social contract ideals are constantly being (re-)created. In continuing to hold the state to account, Czech activists demand that the state act as it *should* rather than as it *does*. Despite deep-seated skepticism and wariness that the state has, historically, been the site of (Austro-Hungarian, German, and state socialist) oppression as well as concerns over current political corruption, the state emerges as the only force strong enough to protect those who cannot protect themselves. Calls on the state to protect the citizenry thus constitute a counterpoint to the "politics of resignation" that Benson and Kirsch have described as a component of global capitalism, "a symptom of the process through which corporate power normalizes and naturalizes risk and harm as inevitable conditions of modernity" (2010: 462). Rather, what emerges here is a "politics of last resort" in which protestors struggle to position the state as the ultimate moral agent that will protect "its people" in the face of rampant capitalist industry.

Environmental Politics: Past and Present

Public interest in environmental health can be traced back to the anti-Communist environmental movement that cast environmental damage as one of the quintessential issues determining citizens' relationships to the state. In 1987, two years before the dissolution of the socialist state, the first stirrings of a radical Czechoslovak environmental movement began to be felt. Initially, there was little government resistance as it was not seen to be a political threat (Vaněk 1996). However, alongside party-authorized environmental groups, a populist underground environmentalist movement was developing. Located in northern industrial centers such as Teplice, populist environmental activism quickly went from demanding environmental improvements to more radical calls for the government to step down. A week before the Velvet Revolution began, thousands of residents of northern industrial cities took the streets, demanding clean air as their human right.

Historian Miroslav Vaněk, who grew up in Teplice, has no trouble explaining how so many people were galvanized into action. "The pollution was so bad," he recounted. "So many children would get very sick every year. And everyone could see how sick they were. You would go to visit the doctor, and the waiting room was full of sick children with stuffed noses, coughs, their eyes red and so swollen that they could not shut them. . . . This was *not* an ideological struggle like the dissidents' arguments about human rights. It was something *everyone* in that area was living through."

A few months before the Teplice demonstration, another pivotal environmental group emerged. Based in Prague and thus closer to the cultural and political centers of power, the Prague Mothers stirred up antigovernment sentiment among members of the public who weren't usually predisposed toward political activism. One of their founders, Jarmila Johnová, was the mother of three young children in 1989. No stranger to politics, she was a member of a dissident circle that included Václav Havel. Her husband was a prominent activist who later served in Havel's government. During the late 1970s and 1980s, however, her husband spent long periods in prison. Johnová was also politically active but acutely aware of her role in holding her family together while her husband was incarcerated. When the secret police knocked on her door, one of her greatest fears was that, if she too were arrested, no one would be left to look after their children.

Nonetheless, Johnová and a group of Prague-based dissidents, all of whom were mothers of babies and young children, came together to raise public awareness about the effects of Prague's air pollution on children's health. Their primary complaint was the smog. "You could see it in the air," she explained, "and on the bad days, my son . . . went gray and had no energy. It was my own intuition that his listlessness was linked to the air quality, as we weren't doctors. But we knew there was dust in the air, and we couldn't bear to see our children like this. If it was made public, we imagined the government would need to start caring about the environment." In May 1989 Johnová organized a group of women who took their prams and parked them in the middle of the street, calling on the government to improve the air quality.

The inspiration to call their group "Prague Mothers" came from a male friend who convinced Johnová that a government that prided itself on "protecting mothers and children" wouldn't be able to brush them off. The name also proved an effective smokescreen, suggesting the protesters were not disgruntled dissidents, but "just mothers with prams." As Michael Kilburn and Vaněk (2004) note, "The parade of prams . . . left bystanders supportive and security forces completely disarmed."

By late 1989 the Prague Mothers' protests were influencing public attitudes about environmental destruction and its health impacts. Further buoyed by the activities of the Teplice protestors, these concerns were soon swept up into a much larger protest movement that in mid- November 1989 removed the state socialist government from power (Fagan 2004; Holy 1996). The public prominence of environmental concerns meant that the movement gained significant political traction in the new government. Across the nation, the air quality improved—until, in the country's southeast region of Moravia, it began to deteriorate again.

The Steel Heart of the Republic

Some 170 miles away from Prague, Ostrava is today the site of the republic's most intense air pollution and highest rates of respiratory problems. Since 2002, residents have been mobilizing to raise awareness of the health situation and demand redress from local and national government and from the steelworks company ArcelorMittal Ostrava.

Science and medicine have been at the forefront of their political struggle. One of the locals who spearheaded the citizens' movement is pediatrician Dr. Eva Schallerová, who became a media figure and candidate for political office in her effort to draw attention to local children's respiratory problems. Dr. Schallerová and others also won the attention of a team of scientists at the Prague-based Academy of Sciences. Led by Professor Radim Šrám, this team devoted several years attempting to conclusively demonstrate the health impact of air pollution on children. Professor Šrám found that the number of children in Radvanice and Bartovice with respiratory issues surpasses the national average by 15 percent, whereas the number of early deaths in the district exceeds the national average by 20 percent. He has also claimed that Ostrava's air pollution causes inheritable DNA damage. But Professor Šrám's most striking, and controversial, finding has been that the rate of childhood asthma in Radvanice and Bartovice is 37 percent (Šrám et al. 2013): the highest rate of childhood asthma in the world. (Most international rankings consider national rather than district-based statistics, according to which the world's highest rate of childhood asthma is in the United Kingdom and New Zealand at around 25 percent.)

According to Professor Šrám, the extremely high rates of asthma in Radvanice and Bartovice are explained by the fact that it is situated downwind of ArcelorMittal Ostrava and thus directly in the path of airborne dust particles released by the steelworks. He has carefully plotted the asthma statistics for each district on a large map of Ostrava and showed me how as you get closer to the wind stream that distributes the steelworks' emissions, children's respiratory problems increase. Most of the health issues, he said, are due to the Ostrava operations, though some of the pollutants are propelled across the border from ArcelorMittal's Polish plant.

Like Dr. Schallerová, Professor Šrám is eager to pit medicine against unchecked industrialism. For him, though the science is complex, the political story behind it is simple: the emissions coming out of ArcelorMittal Ostrava are much higher than EU policy recommendations, but if ArcelorMittal were pressured to actually uphold EU norms, the steelworks could easily close and shift production to the Polish plant, less than sixty miles away. Given the economic situation in Moravia, it is hard for anyone in the region to complain. It is thus, Professor Šrám contends, the duty of the nation's political leaders to stand up and protect the citizenry. Otherwise, he warned, the effects on Ostrava's population will be dire, as the pollution is causing damage not only to the health of current residents but also to their DNA, which will impact subsequent generations.

Some members of the government appear sympathetic to Professor Šrám's campaign, whereas others refer to his research as pointless. Ostrava's deputy mayor Dalibor Madej called Professor Šrám's team's research "a waste of money because they probe into things we all know—that we have pollution here" (quoted in Flemr 2011). The question for Madej and his supporters is not whether the pollution exists but how to proceed given fears of further economic difficulties in the Ostrava region.

Since the massive closures of its coal mines, Ostrava has suffered severe economic hardship. It has the nation's highest unemployment rate around 10 percent, as compared to the national average of 7.5 percent ("Czech Republic" 2013). The national government has announced numerous "rescue packages" for the region, none of which appear to be having much effect. Other than the steelworks, which are having economic difficulties of their own, there is little prospect for economic recovery.

Beaten by the Czech city of Pilsen in its bid for the 2015 title of European Capital of Culture, Ostrava also lost its recent attempt to garner European-wide attention to its admittedly sparse cultural scene. For many this was not so surprising, given that Ostrava is not well known as a cultural destination. As the "Ostrava" entry on Wikipedia gently put it, "Ostrava is usually not in the top ten list of tourist attractions of the Czech Republic" (*Wikipedia* 2014). The American

Figure 7.2   The lower section of Ostrava's Vítkovice Iron and Steelworks, now closed and turned into a museum.
Photo by the author.

magazine *Mother Jones* was not so kind, describing Ostrava as "not simply ugly. It is spectacularly, memorably ugly, the immense tombstone of an idea [of state socialist industrialization] carried to its illogical extreme" (Viviano 1994). In fact, to foreign tourists the area is best known for museums built out of defunct mines and an abandoned steelworks (see Figure 7.2).

Even among those who accept Professor Šrám's findings, many have trouble reaching the same political conclusions, suggesting that the actual lived impact of closing down the steelworks would be much worse than allowing them to continue to break emissions policies. As one ecologist pointed out to me, after the mining and steelworks closures in 1989, "The air certainly got better, and people's health improved, but how could people be delighted to be able to breathe again when they had no jobs? Clean air means to people improved health *and* lack of work."

In some respects, polluted air has not only been a part of the region's landscape for decades, it was also a signifier of prosperity from the very beginning. Ostrava first came to the fore with steel technology in the early 1800s. Following the discovery of black coal deposits, the Vítkovice steel and iron mill was established. The opening of its puddle furnace in 1830 was a highly ceremonial event, presided over by representatives of industry and trade, local politicians, and religious leaders. As recounted in a local text:

Invited to the ceremony were the most prominent figures in local society. . . . A special mass was said, and the new factory was blessed. The first puddle furnace in the entire Austro-Hungarian Empire was lit by the Ostrava priest Leopold Rada.[1] The main orator at the ceremony . . . Kašpar Hauke (representing the town of Moravian Ostrava) . . . stated that "the first blow of the hammer in this new works will awake the entire region from its sleep." (Ostrava město kultury 2013)

The "awakening" announced by Hauke did indeed see the area shift from a primarily agricultural base to a center of European industry as the number of mines and steelworks in the area proliferated. The state socialist period, in particular, fostered the massive expansion of both industry and the city itself, through projects such as the building of the NHKG steelworks in the early 1950s. NHKG was named in honor of the president, Klement Gottwald, who led the 1948 Communist Party coup that overthrew any pretense of a democratic government. Gottwald later increased his notoriety by overseeing the anti-Communist political purges of 1952 in which eleven politicians were found guilty of treason and executed. Following the 1989 revolution, NHKG quickly dropped its association with Gottwald and was put up for sale as part of the state's privatization scheme.

The plant was bought by the Indian-born, British-based steel magnate Lakshmi Mittal, who modernized and expanded its operations. In 2006, Mittal Steel acquired the world's second-largest steelmaking business, Arcelor; the resulting merger created the world's largest steel company, ArcelorMittal. The merger also gained Mr. Mittal a few new monikers, including "International Newsmaker of the Year 2006" from *Time* magazine.

Ostrava's steelworks have thus long been the focus of industrial growth, political symbolism, and, during certain periods, the expansion of personal wealth. But although mills such as Vítkovice and NHKG/ArcelorMittal Ostrava have provided the backbone of the local economy for close to 200 years and been used to reflect the success and largesse of their owners—be they the Austro-Hungarian Empire, the socialist state, or private, foreign ownership— they also raise profound questions about the social relations underpinning these enterprises.

Who Is Responsible?

The image of the steel mill's hammer swung by the united hands of religious authority, government, industry, and tradespeople to "awaken" a long dormant region into industrial activity has today given way to intense struggles over how to ensure the health of the nation, in both economic and bodily terms. Religious authorities have long exited the scene and are no longer viewed as central to industry, but three of the original participants in the founding of Ostrava's steel industry—government, industry, and trade—remain pivotal in contemporary debates over how to respond to air pollution. How should tradespeople and other ordinary citizens of Ostrava engage with a mill that both provides them with much-needed employment and poisons their environment? What is the responsibility of government for ensuring economic prosperity (keeping the region "awake") and for protecting its citizenry against rampant profiteering? Has the state stopped caring for its people? Can industry play a more active role in community protection? Or have multinational companies taken over the role of the socialist state in privileging the economy over health?

Since 2006, a series of public demonstrations, petitions, legal cases, and media announcements by NGOs, scientists, and company representatives has created a battleground over the question of culpability. One of the first points of contention was the origin of the air pollution. When activists initially called on ArcelorMittal to improve Ostrava's air quality, the company denied being the source of the problem. Instead it pointed a finger at other local steel plants and at a large local heating plant as well as at individuals' automobile and home heating emissions. Scientists and NGOs stepped in to quantify the role each contributor plays in creating the city's air pollution. A study undertaken by the Technical University of Ostrava determined that emissions from the Arcelor-Mittal Ostrava steelworks contribute approximately 60 percent of airborne dust and almost 92 percent of arsenic and BaP found in the air around Radvanice and Bartovice (Peek et al. 2009). These findings, along with growing pressure by activist groups, led ArcelorMittal Ostrava's spokesman, Sanjay Samaddar, to admit, "We know that our company has a significant influence on the quality of the air in Radvanice and Bartovice. Of course we do not renounce our shared responsibility for the air quality, and we will invest billions [of crowns] into its improvement" (quoted in Pleva 2008).

Samaddar's statement, made in October 2008, was considered a milestone by many in the environmental movement as the company had finally accepted responsibility for its role in damaging the air quality. But it was not the turning point that many hoped for, as the company continued in its plans to build new and larger facilities. These facilities would be more environmentally friendly, but, given their increased production levels, residents were concerned that the bigger facilities would in fact result in similar levels of pollution. The question of taking responsibility therefore remained and as the situation intensified, so did demands that the company, the local government, and the state recognize their obligations and rectify Ostrava's air quality.

With the support of the civic organization Vzduch (Air) and the environmental legal group Ekologický právní servis (EPS), local residents wrote a petition calling on the company to halt its polluting practices and on various branches of the government to stop capitulating to industry. A series of court cases followed, the most high profile of which was filed by the city of Ostrava against the Czech state, the ramifications of which are discussed below.

In response to rising pressure, primarily from citizens' groups but also from local political bodies, ArcelorMittal promised to continue reforming its production processes to lower its emissions. In 2014 the company opened a new dedusting plant worth a billion crowns (approximately US$40 million). Although activist groups have welcomed these steps, many see them as not going far enough and as a continued reflection of ArcelorMittal's primary commitment to ensuring profit over the health of local residents.

The national government also responded to the increasing pressure put on it by announcing a series of new policies focused on addressing the air pollution problems. These include a 220 million crown (nearly US$9 million) boiler exchange program, through which households with old environmentally unfriendly boilers can replace them with new ones, and a 90 million crown (approximately US$3.6 million) scheme for building ecologically sound homes. The national government also promised to lend support to local government to put in place low-emission zones (akin to those in the United Kingdom and Germany) to cut down on vehicle emissions. Even so, news reports suggest that Ostrava's future continues to look bleak. Despite various antipollution measures, the air quality ratings for Ostrava in 2013 were worse than in preceding years (Baroch 2014). As this decade unfolds, Ostrava's air pollution continues to cause serious health concerns and inspire both political activism and heated debate over how to rectify the ongoing environmental damage (Čisté Nebe 2016; Velinger 2015).

For many activists and scientists the most viable solution is increased public pressure, which—they point out—requires citizens to take responsibility
themselves.

Personal Responsibility: Combating Civic Apathy

In the midst of their many calls on government to rein in capital, activists are
also occupied with exhorting the citizenry to stand up and pressure government
to bend to their collective will. Indeed, some activist efforts focus as much, if
not more, on educating and engaging the citizenry as they do on political lobbying. For example, in 2009, Vzduch listed among its primary strategic priorities
keeping citizens engaged and combating civic apathy (Skýbová 2009).

A politics of personal responsibility is thus inherent in these debates. In this
context, however, responsibility and self-empowerment are understood not in
terms of *self-reliance* as in Western neoliberal discourses of responsibilization
(Rose 1996) but rather in terms of the need to stand up for oneself to make collective political demands on the state. Self-responsibility thus becomes political
responsibility as promoted in the writings of Václav Havel (for example, Havel
[1978] 1986), drawing on decades of debate over the role of individuals in civil
society, both during and after state socialism.

Those involved in the frontlines of environmental health efforts frequently
complain about high levels of public apathy. For an outsider, this comes as a
surprise as Czechs appear to be comparatively more involved in environmental health activism than members of other European states. Indeed, ecologist
Miroslav Šuta notes that the uproar against environmental damage is much
more significant in the Czech Republic than in neighboring Slovakia and Poland, where environmental conditions are similar if not worse. Yet, in my multiple conversations with a range of environmental activists and environmental
scientists, the issue of civic apathy was repeatedly highlighted.

For example, although speaking very highly of the "ordinary mothers" who
made up the 1989 Teplice environmental movement and the early activities of
the Prague Mothers, Professor Šrám complained that such a sense of initiative
has been lost. As he put it, "In the Ostrava region, people say that around elec-
tion time, environmental degradation motivates their voting—it is their first or
second priority [in choosing candidates]. But . . . at other times, no one cares."

Other activists expressed similar attitudes, with some of them specifically
tailoring their data collection to engage citizens, especially children, in hands-
on activities that will *compel them to care.* Many of the projects on environmen-

tal pollution organized by the Prague Mothers thus involve children recording air pollution and undertaking rudimentary analysis of this material. This way, Johnová explained, the children learn that it is every citizen's responsibility to personally ensure a healthy environment.

Public health specialist Dr. Veselá advocated a similar point of view. For her, the answer of how to deal with health problems like the rising rates of child-hood asthma is to engage in focused collective mobilization. She was scathing about individual solutions, suggesting that the asthma problem is due to "lack of education. People prioritize their finances over their health, because they are not educated. They don't form groups and get active. Instead they go play foot-ball and don't worry about the environment. [The result is that] babies get put on inhalers, people get put on corticosteroids, and everyone is passive."

Civic apathy is often described as a two-pronged problem: not only are people not educated or cultured (*vzdělané*) enough to be able to adequately understand what is happening and why, they are also afraid to voice an opin-ion. As one environmentalist colorfully put it, we call this the problem of being "a person who shits by the wall" (*přizdisráč*). She explained this expression: "If there is a big field that you could go shit in the middle of and you shit by the wall, it's because you're refusing to expose yourself." It is, I later realized, the Czech equivalent of the American term "chicken shit."

Environmental health discourse thus firmly focuses on promoting personal responsibility, but this is a markedly different kind of responsibility from that envisioned by the "responsibilization" discourses that vest individuals with the power and burden of determining their own lives. Personal responsibility here entails *political responsibility* for ensuring a collective future, whose protection begins—but does not end—in one's personal actions (cf. Havel [1978] 1986). What is crucial in this vision is that people's sense of personal responsibility results in increased civic engagement and collective action, rather than preoc-cupation with their own individual, or familial, conditions.

Some activists worry, however, that the focus on personal responsibil-ity can lead to blaming individuals and shifting attention away from industry. The Arnika Association is a national NGO that focuses on galvanizing support for improving environmental conditions. Explaining how their own research revealed that home heating contributes a significant proportion of Ostrava's air pollution, Arnika's spokesperson expressed concern that such findings do not result in a backlash against the city's residents. Many of Ostrava's residents have no choice over how to heat their homes, she said, and it is poverty, rather than apathy, that leads locals to make the infamous "Ostravian comets": empty plastic drink bottles filled with sawdust and oil that are burned in domestic coal heaters, resulting in a blast of heat along with a variety of chemicals released into the air. Arnika and other groups thus embrace government programs like the boiler exchange and eco-friendly homes grants as long as they constitute supplements to larger structural changes rather than solutions in themselves.

The Company as a (Non)moral Actor
In all of this talk of citizens and government, one aspect left out of many activists' sweeping visions is corporate responsibility. Although they may call on industry to change its practices, many activists work on the assumption that there is little to be gained by appealing to a corporate conscience as industry is "beyond reason." Corporate social responsibility is new to the Czech Republic. Although the CSR activities of some corporations, most notably Vodafone, are embraced by consumers (Trnka 2013), these tend to target young and globally savvy consumers. Most of the public appears more comfortable relying on the state to act as the intermediary for mediating relations with business.

International companies such as ArcelorMittal are, however, keen to publicize their CSR programs. In Ostrava, ArcelorMittal has reinforced its image as one of the region's primary employers, running a youth training program to prepare young people for various jobs at the steel mill. The company also engages in activities that situate it more broadly as a local benefactor, donating to build parks, support children's reading programs, and promote the beekeeping industry. The company's employees are photographed donating blood at the local hospital, and the steelworks has contributed an incubator to the neonatal unit.

Perhaps the most widely publicized and controversial CSR program was ArcelorMittal Ostrava's donation of asthma inhalers to children (*Intolerance* 2010). Many locals viewed this as the height of hypocrisy and yet another indication of ArcelorMittal's unwillingness to put health before profit. One parent whose son suffers from acute asthma related, "If ArcelorMittal has made a profit, I'd ask them not to spend it on inhalers but on improving the environment" (ibid.).

Given the experiences of labor over the past twenty-five years of capitalist development as well as the enduring legacies of socialist perspectives on unrestricted capital, privately owned corporations cannot be easily recast as protectors of the interests of common, working people. For most Czechs, the issue at hand is decidedly *not* how to improve relations between industry and employees, much less between industry and the community, but rather how to ensure that the state does its duty of protecting Czechs against the activities of industry balanced with the need for employment.

There is an added nationalist element to this demand as ecologists, scientists, and activists frequently compare the Czech situation with Poland's, suggesting that although the Polish state may be content with even laxer emissions regulations, the *Czech* state must do what it can to protect its citizenry. The fact that ArcelorMittal's headquarters is in Luxembourg whereas its owner is originally from India but now lives in Britain further fuels nationalist sentiments in calling on the Czech state to protect its "own people."

But does the state care? Is it willing to protect its citizens?

The Nonreciprocating State

Many activists and scientists involved in these political debates focus on restoring the role of government in providing for and protecting its citizenry. In our conversations, Professor Šrám situated the Ostrava situation in the context of a country where free health care is being stripped away and medical standards are slipping. Add to this a government that capitulates to industry, and you have a situation in which it becomes increasingly difficult for those who are sick to survive, much less thrive, he suggested.

Although the national government has implemented a series of initiatives to deal with some aspects of Ostrava's pollution, the boiler exchange program and the eco-friendly home initiative have been widely criticized as being ineffective. Nor has there been much traction from the EU's involvement. The EU's guidelines for emissions limits are described by activists as having "no teeth," as they are up to the Czech government to administer. Similarly, EU funding to help alleviate Ostrava's pollution has been handed over to the Czech government. In 2010 the EU went a step further by threatening to sue the Czech government if it did not rectify the pollution problem, but still concrete results have not been forthcoming.

The most controversial attempt to leverage the government into action has been the city of Ostrava's suit against the national government and the transport and environment ministries. The unprecedented nature of a lawsuit brought by one level of government against another led many commentators to shrug it off as mere "political comedy." Nonetheless, the case, which was heard in 2013, raised serious allegations about the state's unwillingness to defend its citizens, with the city claiming that the state is responsible for ensuring a "favorable environment" for its citizens and that in not enforcing emissions limits it was shirking its obligations to fully and effectively protect Ostrava's atmosphere. In the end, the case was settled in favor of the state. The head of the court, Ludmila Sandnerová, explained that while the court was convinced that "the limits of polluted substances have been breached and that some illegal activity has clearly led to this," the city had not proven "that inaction or passivity on the part of the [state] is what led to this illegal outcome" (TV Nova News 2013). Sandnerová then turned the tables by adding that the city of Ostrava had not shown that *it* was doing all it could to improve the air quality, referring to the city's reluctance to establish no-emission zones.

Ostrava's mayor, Petr Kajnar, publicly responded, "We have done all we can, but the question is, what *can* we do? What is the point of having a no-emission zone of ten square kilometers if it's within a 2,500 square kilometer zone darkened by an [atmospheric] inversion [that holds in the smog]?" According to Kajnar, the court did not have the "courage" to decide in the city's favor as to do so would have meant taking on the government (TV Nova News 2013). The fact that the judiciary would not stand up to the state did not, however, in Kajnar's mind, alleviate the state's responsibility toward its citizenry. "The essential issue," Kajnar declared, "is that people are dying here because the state is not acting" (ibid.).

For Kajnar and many others, the situation comes down to the state's legal and moral obligation to act. Although many would agree that citizens *should* act in the interests of the wider collectivity, they may *choose* whether to do so. The state, on the other hand, *must* do so, or its legitimacy is under threat. That the state may not always uphold its side of the bargain is well known, and thus it must be held legally liable for not acting on behalf of the citizenry.

But in addition to the power of the legal courts, there is also the court of public opinion. Another way of attempting to force the state to take up its role is by shaming it, as Kajnar tried to do in his public statement. Activist groups who stage public demonstrations engage in similar efforts. In both cases, the figure of suffering citizenry, and in particular, of suffering children, becomes a central trope in the political struggle.

Who Gets to Suffer? Labor, Gender, and Citizenship

The social contract requires that contributions be made by each side, as the state and the people engage in a reciprocal relationship with one another. Some citizens are, however, deemed more able to give than others. Historically, the most valuable gifts given in Moravia have been the bodies and labor power of men, primarily those of miners and steelworkers.

There is widespread acknowledgment that the working conditions in mines and steel mills can be profoundly debilitating. ArcelorMittal's own publications note that some workers have particularly physically and psychologically arduous jobs and are therefore entitled to more generous health benefits, including medical rehabilitation and fitness programs such as the use of a "sauna in the Company premises, outpatient rehab programs, [and visits to a] salt cave for respiratory . . . treatments" (ArcelorMittal Ostrava 2008).

Both mining and steelworks are culturally coded as masculine jobs and are premised on the understanding that social well-being is reliant on such forms of masculine sacrifice. In Ostrava, everyone is well aware that the lives of men who mine or work in the steel mills will be characterized by intense bodily labor that takes place in the midst of physically demanding conditions, be it the loud, hot, and cramped spaces of the coal mines or the equally physically onerous sites of steel production. During the state socialist period, miners were held up as symbols of national progress. As intimated by the widely known saying "I am a miner, who is more than that" (*Já jsem horník, kdo je víc*), the Communist Party proclaimed that nothing was more respectable than mining. The miner or steelworker was honored for shouldering the burden of regional and national development. It was his suffering that enabled Moravia to prosper following the first blows of the steelworks' hammer.

During my visit to the ArcelorMittal Ostrava steelworks facility, the company's HR people proudly spoke of the measures taken to make the industry as safe as possible. However, when wearing the standard-issue blue jumpsuit, hard hat, gloves, and visor, I found myself struggling with the heat, noise, and overall intensity on the steelworks floor, nearby workers laughed and told me of the extremes they encounter as the heat sometimes reaches as high as 130 degrees Fahrenheit. My suggestion that some of the novice steel workers might find the physical conditions arduous was only met with more laughter and the proclamation that "we are men!" (*my jsme hoši*).

In contrast, there is the widely held view that children are not supposed to suffer for the state but rather should be protected from harm. As Fassin argues, the image of the suffering child is one of the strongest emotive symbols of twentieth- and twenty-first-century humanitarian discourse (2013: 113). Its political power rests on two assertions regarding children: "first, that they were innocent creatures who could not be held responsible for what happened to them, and second, that they were vulnerable beings and needed protection against the hazards of life" (ibid.: 118).

Another important feature of the potential to politicize children is their ambiguous position in social contracts, in the sense that the child receives protection without being required to reciprocate (yet). Reflecting the outer limit of individualization discourses, the young child *cannot* be asked to take care of him- or herself. Families, however, are not always able to provide for children. As Fassin argues with respect to the AIDS epidemic in South Africa, families thought to be falling apart generate even more community or national concern over vulnerable children's fates.

In the Czech Republic, the specter is not of families falling apart but of families unable to protect their children in the face of rampant foreign industry, with the result being that the state must step in. The privileged role of the Czech state in protecting children is nothing new. For decades in state-socialist Czechoslovakia, the child, whether part of a family or not, was under the guardianship of the state. Regardless of parental consent, the state regularly enacted a range of interventions, from enforcing childhood immunizations to removing children from their parents if they held politically undesirable opinions (Rehak 2012). Unlike in New Zealand, where the child ultimately indexes familial responsibility, here the final onus of responsibility rests with the state.

It is thus not surprising that some of the most stirring images and pronouncements about the need for the state to curtail Ostrava's air pollution have involved children. One example is the widely reproduced photographs of children and their mothers wearing gas masks (see Figure 7.3). Another is activists' claims that children, and not adults, are the ones who really matter in this dispute. For example, a father speaking on a television program characterized his family's struggle against ArcelorMittal by noting, referring to himself and his wife, "It is not about us. We will stick it out in our lives. It is about our kids." He then added that the only one who can put a stop to their suffering is the government (*Intolerance* 2010).

If children are posited as innocent victims and labor is clearly coded as masculine, where are the women in this story? Despite the fact that many Czech women work outside the home, as we have seen, widespread, self-consciously

Figure 7.3   Girl removing gas mask during demonstrations against air pollution in Ostrava.

Photo by Pavel Sonnek. Reprinted courtesy of *Deník*/Pavel Sonnek.

"traditional" gender ideals promote the perspective that women's primary roles lie in reproduction and nurturance of children. Usually, these activities are thought to be confined to the domestic sphere (Heitlinger and Trnka 1998), making mothers' entries onto the political stage even more noteworthy. Many of the photographic images that focus on Ostrava's women and children are indeed reminiscent of the early protests by the Prague Mothers or the "ordinary mothers" of Teplice who were seen as having *no choice* but to publicize their very private domestic struggles to keep their children healthy to get the state's attention.

But politicking over children's asthma can also result in intensely emotive denunciations of the political mileage derived out of the figure of the suffering child. When I mentioned that my research would consider the question of asthma and air pollution in Ostrava, one asthma sufferer who lives in Prague angrily declared, "Don't overemphasize the air quality issue—it is not so important . . . We do *not* have such unusually high asthma rates in the Czech Republic. Those people who claim it is so high are . . . generating these statistics for political purposes."

Certainly there have been some notable controversies with respect to Professor Šrám's studies and the role his political commitments to the people of Radvanice and Bartovice might play in shaping his findings. Much of the scientific controversy has focused on issues of diagnosis. Professor Šrám's asthma rate of 37 percent was derived from a study of children under the care of Dr. Shallerová. This was then expanded through a larger study involving close to 2,000 children under the care of ten different pediatricians: 37 percent of them were found to suffer from wheezing, which may or may not be due to asthma (Dostál et al. 2013). Critics suggest that some of the children in the original sample may similarly suffer from other respiratory conditions and were misdiagnosed, thus inflating the figure of asthmatic children and gaining international attention through the claim that Radvanice and Bartovice has the highest rate of childhood asthma in the world.

One of the scientists on Professor Šrám's team related to me, "I gave these results as part of a presentation and a well-known respiratory specialist tore them apart. . . . He said, 'You cannot tell if these children suffer from asthma or obstructive bronchitis because you cannot do spirometry on kids under the age of four and skin prick tests [for allergies] will turn up negative for kids under the age of two, so how can you know what is going on?'" He assured me that Dr. Schallerová had carried out "a very intensive check on these children" and then waived the controversy away in light of the larger political issues it threatens to overshadow. "When people told *her* not all the children have asthma," he went on, "she retorted, 'My children [that is, my patients] are *choking*, whether it is due to asthma or not.'" As these statements suggest, if the underlying issue is that air pollution causes respiratory illness, then the differentiation among asthma, chronic bronchitis, and other respiratory conditions may be irrelevant. However, in the domain of scientific practice, ensuring reliable diagnoses remains a central concern without which the epidemiological results regarding rates of childhood asthma are meaningless.

Possibly a more troubling question that has been raised is how central a role air pollution plays in determining Ostrava's asthma levels. The team's own findings uphold the now increasingly accepted perspective that there may be no "single" asthma but rather a variety of them, some due to air pollution and others to viral illnesses or other factors (Pearce 2011). Multicausal models furthermore indicate that some asthma is associated with multiple factors, suggesting that industrial air pollution *alongside* other factors may be at play in Ostrava.

Indeed, Professor Šrám's colleagues have made similar findings, implying that the steelworks may not be as singularly responsible for local rates of asthma as activists contend.

One team member, for example, determined that the high asthma rates are related to exposure to secondhand smoke and to children's own smoking habits. Publication of this part of the study was, however, held up due to statistical complications, its lead author explained, before adding that a research center devoted to demonstrating the causal links between industrial pollution and respiratory illness will hardly welcome findings that demonstrate the significant role that "individual habits" such as smoking may play. All of this complicates the rather simple story of the industrial giant that makes children ill and the political mileage that the figure of the suffering child has been made to carry.

Erasing the Roma

Smoking isn't the only thing that can disqualify children from being seen as innocent victims. In both activist and scientific discourses the innocent party is always Czech, necessitating the erasure of yet another group of families and children who are breathing polluted air, namely the Roma.

Given the reluctance of many Roma to publicly identify themselves, it is difficult to get reliable statistics on the number of Roma currently in the Czech Republic. Although the European Roma Rights Centre estimates they compose 2 to 3 percent of the overall population, it is generally agreed that the Ostrava region has a higher percentage, with Roma constituting roughly 3 to 10 percent of the city's population (Sudetic 2013). Roma tend to be concentrated in the lower economic classes and are thus likely to live in areas most affected by air pollution.

Originally a nomadic people who spoke the Romany language and today hold a range of distinctive cultural traditions, the Roma are widely scapegoated in Czech society for acting outside of Czech social norms. There are frequent descriptions of Roma as unproductive malingerers who are happy to consume state handouts while making little effort to contribute back to the state or to society. For many Czechs, such depictions culminate in the sentiment that Roma are irrevocably "other."

There is no specific research that I am aware of on Czech Roma's respiratory health, and in part this appears to be due to ethnic prejudices that pervade some of the medical and scientific establishment. A Czech public health specialist, for example, explained to me that Roma don't get asthma (or diabetes) because "they are completely different from us." Referring to them with the derogatory but widely used name of *cikáni* or gypsies, she told me that "gypsies don't work. They receive state support for their children, so they might have five children just so they can get more state support. They steal and move from one place to another to get away from the laws they have broken."

A Czech scientist and member of Professor Šrám's research team similarly asserted that the Roma don't get asthma or allergies and explained how he removed them from his statistical computations. "In Ostrava there are a lot of Roma kids, but they never get asthma, so you need to take them out of the sample so they don't confuse the statistics," he recounted. "Once you remove them, then you get the figure of over 30 percent [of children in Radvanice and Bartovice suffering from asthma]. Before [they are removed], the statistics are lower." When I queried how he could be so certain the Roma never suffer from asthma or allergies, he explained that the Roma don't use medical services for these conditions and that at least one local allergy specialist he knew in Ostrava had confirmed to him that he doesn't have any Romany patients. "I don't know why they don't have asthma, but they don't," he assured me.

This kind of prejudice, as well as the fact that state statistics do not differentiate health conditions based on ethnic groups, makes it difficult to get information on the rates of asthma (or other health conditions) among the Roma. However, a medical anthropologist who worked with Roma in Slovakia disputed such suggestions, asserting that her fieldwork experiences suggest the Roma suffer from high rates of respiratory conditions but refrain from seeking care from medical authorities due to racism.

Asthma is thus defined as a citizenship issue, but with citizenship restrictively defined. Although Czech Roma technically hold Czech citizenship, the wider Czech public reserves "true membership" in the nation-state to ethnic Czechs, Moravians, and Slovaks, who are collectively viewed as upholding their end of state–citizen exchanges.

The Limits of Responsibility

Although few would suggest that the nation is on the verge of another political upheaval the size and significance of the 1989 Velvet Revolution, childhood asthma and the suffering of Radvanice and Bartovice's children are held up as a banner of protest and a widespread call for realigning relationships between citizens and the state. What is at stake here is twofold as the Ostrava crisis raises profound questions about what happens to the citizenry if the state does not hold up its end of the bargain, as appears to be the case, as well as what happens to the future of the state if the citizenry's fate has been irrevocably poisoned. On the local and national level, the struggle over structural issues such as environmental degradation, poverty, unemployment, and the cost of medical care has been crystallized through the historically familiar battles among trade, industry, and the state but with growing concerns that, this time, the state might have already divested itself of the responsibilities entrusted to it. In this respect, the situation in Ostrava has become a litmus test of the relations among the state, the EU, citizens, and industry during twenty-first-century capitalism.

It is also a litmus test for how far the discourse of personal responsibility can be extended, as the company attempts to blame individuals while individuals, in turn, call on a larger power than themselves (that is, the state) to be held accountable for their and their children's plight. What is significant in activist conceptualizations of responsibility is the breakdown of the dichotomy of personal versus collective responsibility. Instead, there is an active intertwining of different scales of responsibility as citizens are exhorted to take on more personal responsibility to force the state to recognize its obligations in solving what is envisioned as a collective national problem. Companies are cast as outside the sphere of moral life, not out of some inherent *lack* of ethical obligation but from a pragmatic recognition that labor will find little traction in calling on the moral responsibilities of management. Instead, the state is constantly reminded of its role as the final guarantor of citizens' rights and as the site where responsibility for social well-being must ultimately lie. Asthma becomes a contested political object in terms of both how causation is attributed (is it emissions by ArcelorMittal or something else that is making so many children in Ostrava sick?) and the ways in which different forms of personal and collective responsibility for mitigating respiratory distress are articulated. Far from the question of how to best implement policies promoting self-managed care, childhood asthma emerges as the fulcrum of public debates and contestations over some of the most fundamental principles that govern relations among citizens, states, and corporations in twenty-first-century capitalism.

Conclusion
Problematizing Asthma

W HEN I first started to interview doctors and scientists, many of the New Zealand professionals I spoke with seemed very surprised that anyone would want to discuss government policies on asthma. Asthma *isn't* a problem anymore, they emphatically asserted. A few suggested that, although New Zealand's approach to asthma was fiercely debated in the 1980s during the tragic days of fenoterol-induced deaths, surely there is nothing debatable, much less "political," about asthma today. Two or three even complained about how *unproblematic* asthma is, pointing out that respiratory health is a decidedly "unsexy" profession in which to work. "Cancer, diabetes, cardiac diseases—now *those* are sexy conditions," one leading respiratory health researcher told me. "*Those* researchers get the grant money, not the people working on asthma." Indeed, the removal of fenoterol from the government drug tariff alongside the development of a new line of medications in the 1980s resulted in asthma losing its status as a grand medical drama. But for a number of New Zealanders, asthma continues to constitute a problem, be it a problem as simple as knowing how much—or, more often, how little—medication to take.

To speak, however, of asthma as *a problem* in the singular is to risk compounding the challenges of finding adequate solutions. Both in New Zealand and in the Czech Republic, *the problem of asthma* is multiple. Its different facets, moreover, involve distinct constituencies. There are the problems faced by physicians weighing how to compel patients to take more responsibility for their health while also convincing them to take their medication. For sufferers and their families, there are the problems of when and how to take control, or not, of their own lives and health. There is the challenge of determining the respective obligations of physicians, pharmaceutical companies, and government in ensuring the safety of drug use, and the question of how crucial free health care as well as healthy homes, clean air, and other forms of "environmental compliance" might be. And there is the task of understanding aspects of asthma that lie far beyond the influence of pharmaceuticals on respiration, such as how to cope with anxiety and panic, help children achieve (culturally determined) "normal" emotional and physical development, or assess the utility of breathing retraining. Some of these problems are thought of as belonging to the domain of "asthma" whereas others bear related but distinct identities—problems of air pollution or child poverty, for example.

Scientific and medical problems do not exist in and of themselves as objective entities waiting to be researched or to become the focus of policy initiatives. Rather, as David Hess has suggested, "Controversy over what the important problems should be, what the best methods are, and how the problems should be defined are part of 'normal' science" (2004: 701). There is, moreover, often convergence between public and scientific concerns with respect to producing both scientific and medical problems and solutions to them. As anthropologists, sociologists, philosophers, and scholars of science and technology studies (STS) have demonstrated, the construction of medical problems and scientific facts tends to cross the ostensible divide between "scientists" and the "general public," with science and medicine often determined by the interests of multiple constituencies (Canguilhem [1966] 1989; Epstein 1995; Hacking 1995; Rabeharisoa and Callon 2004). One factor in how medical and scientific problems are constituted in Western advanced liberal democracies is public dissatisfaction with the current status quo—what Sheila Jasanoff (1997) has referred to as "civic dislocation." Some members of the general public, however, have more sway in creating a sense of civic dislocation than others. Not surprisingly, as STS scholars note, "Because elites set agendas for both public and private funding sources, and because scientific research is increasingly complex, technology-laden, and expensive, there is a systematic tendency for knowledge production to rest on the cultural assumptions and material interests of privileged groups" (Frickel et al. 2010: 3). In addition, there is often the need for complementary scientific dissatisfaction on the part of scientists in response to civic pressure (Rabeharisoa and Callon 2004) or as part of scholarly competition and collaboration with colleagues in similar fields (Frickel et al. 2010; Hess 2004; Latour 1987) before a scientific problem is recognized as in need of solutions.

When and how asthma constitutes a problem—or not—and under what categories and names this problem is presented are highly political questions.

Moreover, how we define a problem helps determine not only where and how we look for solutions but also *whose* problem we think it is. The recognition of a particular problem, what lies within it, and what is in effect "a different problem" or simply irrelevant to the problem at hand are inherently a means of determining responsibility and apportioning blame.

Throughout this book I have delineated a number of different kinds of scientific, medical, social, legal, and governmental problems that have been produced with respect to asthma and the kinds of responsibilities, obligations, and duties they are understood to entail. My intention in doing so is not to detract from their validity. To say that these problems have been produced (or coproduced) by science and society does not make them less *real*. Patients feel, or felt, a dehumanizing lack of control and authority over their bodies and their health care in the Czech Republic today and in New Zealand during the 1960s and 1970s; New Zealanders were dying from fenoterol in the late 1970s and 1980s; children in Ostrava suffer from respiratory distress because of air pollution; asthma sufferers around the world rely on pharmaceuticals to save their lives while questioning the benefits and detriments of regularly using drugs for a condition that they don't currently feel the effects of. My aim has been to raise questions about how such problems are determined, where their boundaries are seen to lie, and who is given the task of being responsible for addressing them. By doing so, I endeavor to show how often hidden assumptions about what the problem of childhood asthma actually entails come to frame our decisions about health and health care.

In New Zealand, tensions between promoting patient autonomy and ensuring patient compliance largely deflect public and policy makers' attention away from the possibilities of constituting asthma in terms of the dangers of using too many pharmaceuticals, the need for minimum housing standards, or the alleviation of poverty. In the Czech Republic, the challenge of patient education focuses on training patients rather than assisting with their "empowerment," but serious tensions emerge out of desires to ensure solidarity while promoting individual accountability for health and the need to both enable economic advancement and protect citizens' rights.

Each of these problems and the debates they generate raise a number of fundamental questions about the relationships between the state and society. Each also requires the weighing up of a variety of competing responsibilities and obligations that draw on culturally and historically specific values and practices of health, government, and family life. In New Zealand, the "can-do" model is upheld as something both to aspire to and to judge others against. Personal independence and autonomy have become emblematic of the Kiwi ethos. In the Czech Republic, activists and government officials alike exhort citizens to take more personal responsibility for their health and well-being. There is, however, wide variability in their understandings of what such personal responsibility should lead to.

Critics of neoliberalism(s) have painstakingly delineated the new kinds of people and of health that the era of advanced liberal reform requires of us. But there are a variety of ways of cultivating personal responsibility and becoming a new kind of person within the parameters of twenty-first-century societies. As Czech activists argue, self-cultivation does not need to result in exiting civic life but can act as an entrée into deeper, more meaningful modes of collective political engagement (cf. Foucault 1997; Havel [1978] 1986). Cultivating personal responsibility while combating the blinders of advanced liberalism's overriding emphasis on individual autonomy is a difficult but necessary task.

Although self-management may have once been viewed as a leap forward, giving patients and families the tools they need to assert their perspectives and capabilities against those of "patronizing" doctors, to stop here and suggest that this is empowerment is to fall short of truly enabling patients to cope with their conditions. Fostering patient autonomy must go hand-in-hand with an acknowledgment of different parties' distinct roles in promoting health and well-being. Self-managed care must be consistently guided and overseen by professional experts whose depth and breadth of medical knowledge surpass the practical know-how of patients. Indeed, the rising prevalence of chronic diseases that require increasing numbers of us to provide sustained, home-based health care makes it even more critical to ensure that appropriate, professional support is routinely available for those engaging in self- or familial management of illness.

Recrafting self-management to support and guide patients while not overlooking the importance of domains of health and illness that lie beyond pharmaceutical management requires taking into account the following four principles:

1. There is a need for more patient involvement in determining the shape of care. The strength of self-management should lie in involving patients in not only partaking in their care but *actually coauthoring it*. As a first step, self-

management programs should be implemented in health-care settings that do not already enable them. Wherever they are used, action plans should be employed not as another tool for enforcing compliance but as an avenue for patients and doctors to collaboratively determine therapeutic strategies. One simple step in this direction would be for patients and physicians to discuss patients' perspectives on various pharmaceuticals as well as the possibilities of nonpharmaceutical remedies as part of determining what kinds of information and care strategies are recorded on patient-doctor action plans.

2. There are serious limitations and dangers in self-management programs as currently practiced. In particular, it is vital that the overuse of pharmaceuticals in self-management contexts be addressed, ideally through *increased interaction between patients and medical professionals*. Research has shown that resources and technologies of care such as written action plans or online technologies for monitoring medication use are not enough. Patients do better when they have individualized one-on-one care and responses from trained medical professionals. Self-management needs to be guided through interactive professional supervision that includes regular face-to-face medical checkups and consultations over medication use.

3. There is an ever-increasing need to *address the broader, structural factors that affect respiratory health* including access to readily available health care, improved home environments, and pollution control measures. Moves to implement policy in these areas are hampered not only by lack of political will but also by the fact that asthma itself poses a complicated set of problems to which there is no easy one-size-fits-all solution: fixing damp homes or mitigating air pollution will undoubtedly help but will not end the asthma epidemic. However, without more comprehensive measures, health services are in danger of creating barriers alongside solutions as increasing numbers of individuals and their families flounder to bring together the strategies and resources necessary to keep themselves well.

4. More awareness needs to be drawn to the significant numbers of asthma sufferers who experience overlaps between asthma and anxiety, panic attacks, or other forms of emotional distress. *Therapies that focus on breathing patterns and address both emotional and physical aspects of asthma* need to be integrated alongside pharmaceutical remedies. Precautions should be

taken to ensure that international protocols, evidence-based medicine, and the drive to keep abreast of the latest pharmaceuticals and technologies do not overshadow the desirability of some older forms of therapeutics, if and when they are still available. Whether the remedies in question are the total institutions of Czech health spas or more short-term therapeutic incursions such as asthma camps, breathing retraining programs, or sports activities, these sites constitute vital spaces for enabling more comprehensive approaches to promoting both physical and mental or emotional well-being and need to be protected.

In the course of this book, we have encountered a number of children who turned blue during an acute asthma attack, from Dr. Veselá's portrayal of the emblematic "one blue child" overlooked by government and industry to the more intimate personalized accounts of Geoff turning blue as a baby in his crib, Pamela watching her daughter Samantha struggling for air despite being hooked up to a nebulizer, or Michal's son David nearly choking to death on their way home from the outdoor cinema. Whatever the country or context, the image of a child whose respiratory distress is so acute as to make them literally go blue in the face or fingers elicits a widespread sense of horror. To ensure that someone in addition to the child her- or himself or that child's parents takes responsibility for responding to the blue child's distress requires looking beyond the implementation of current international asthma protocols to consider more widely what asthma *care* entails in its broadest sense.

Using a methodological approach that "follows a policy" (Shore and Wright 2011: 12) through multiple domains—from ministries of health to homes and medical clinics, from steelworks to activist NGOs and the debating chambers of Parliament—enables us to move far beyond the questions that occupy many public health professionals of how to improve the health outcomes of "self-managing patients" to consider more broadly who in fact might be responsible for childhood asthma and how they might be held to account. This requires stepping away from authoritative instrumentalist approaches promoted by traditional policy studies, which consider policies as the outcomes of neutral problem-solving exercises that address empirically determined problems (that is, problems that have an independent existence in the "real world") (Colebatch, Hoppe, and Noordegraaf 2010). Instead, as anthropologists of policy have demonstrated, there is much to be gained by undertaking more open-ended examinations of how problems emerge as social and political entities, the multiple and sometimes contested processes that result in the formulation of policies addressing these problems, and the ways that these policies are taken up, reshaped, resisted, and sometimes completely ignored by the actual people whose lives they are intended to affect (Greenhalgh 2008; Shore and Wright 2011). Doing so, moreover, casts our attention to, as Emily Martin (1997) suggests, not only "Policy" in terms of formal statements or written texts but also the "policies" or culturally acknowledged "guides to action" that underpin them. As demonstrated by Martin's own work (1997, 2009) on mental illness in the United States, which traverses examinations of media representations of mania, corporate training programs instilling employee flexibility, advertisements for Netscape, and personal narratives of the recipients of psychiatric care, undertaking such an endeavor often requires taking a very broad view of the variety of sites in which both "Policy" and "policies" are made meaningful. Aiming to come to grips with how self-management has structured certain ways of thinking and responding to asthma and has itself been reshaped and countered by other ways of conceptualizing responsibility and care, I have utilized the model of broadly focused, deeply ethnographic research but with the added element of cross-cultural comparison. As our understandings of health and medicine are increasingly framed by global health markets and initiatives—including global health policies—it becomes even more vital to investigate how health and medicine are carried out in distinct historical and cultural settings. By comparing childhood asthma in two very disparate, neoliberalizing states, we can shed light on the multiple ways that responsibility for health is enacted in practice and vividly illustrate the variety of possible dynamics among patients, medical professionals, families of sick children, and the state. As a result, we can see the benefits and shortcomings of different approaches to care, recognizing self-management as but one of a number of ways of envisioning responsibility for asthma.

The challenges that asthma poses are growing rather than receding: asthma is currently thought to affect approximately 334 million people worldwide, and this number is expected to rise to over 400 million over the next decade (Bousquet and Khaltaev 2007; Global Asthma Network 2014). Policies governing asthma care pose a far-reaching and potentially radical site for promoting health-care programs that draw on the strengths of patient-centered, self-managed care without eroding the knowledge and expertise that biomedicine and its alternatives have to offer. There is no better time for a reassessment of how to further incorporate democratic principles into medical care such that patients have more authority over their health, physicians are enabled to use their expertise to provide quality care, and structural solutions and non-pharmaceutical therapies are not overshadowed by the imperatives of market-driven medicine.

Reference Matter

Notes

Introducton

1. GINA is an international organization founded in 1993 through the collaboration of the (American) National Institute of Health; the (British) National Heart, Lung and Blood Institute; and the (global) World Health Organization. For over two decades, GINA has been issuing international guidelines on asthma diagnosis and treatment. As of 2007, their policies highlight patient-doctor co-partnership and self-management as platforms for best-practice asthma care (see Kroegel and Wirtz 2009). Similar self-management approaches are promoted in the joint American Thoracic Society/European Respiratory Society asthma guidelines, the British Thoracic Society's BTS/SIGN Asthma Guideline, the pan-European Brussels Declaration on Asthma (2007), and both Australia and New Zealand's national asthma guidelines.

2. The names of all the parents and children and most of the medical professionals and activists I spoke with have been changed to pseudonyms, with the exception of well-known individuals who reflect on their own scientific, medical, or political achievements.

3. Much of the recent health social science literature on asthma focuses on assessing the viability of self-management programs (for example, Aroni et al. 2003; Pohlman and Becker 2006; Smith et al. 2007; Trollvik and Severinsson 2004). A particularly revealing project led by Michael Rich uses visual technologies to highlight discrepancies between what patients say to their doctors and their actual behavior at home (Chalfen and Rich 2004; Rich, Lamola, and Woods 2006). A less developed line of analysis has been the impact of self-management on family dynamics (but see Prout, Hayes, and Gelder 1999; Trnka and McLaughlan 2012). New lines of scholarship have recently begun to address a broader range of issues including patients' fears of drug dependency (Gabe, Bury, and Ramsey 2002; Rose and Manderson 2000; Van Sickle 2009), the sociopolitical contexts of asthma research (Langstrup and Winthereik 2008; Whitmarsh 2008a), and the environmental dimensions of asthma, most notably in Mexico (Schwartz 2004; Schwartz et al. 2015) and the United States (Brown 2007; Brown, Morello-Frosch, and Zavestoski 2012; Fortun et al. 2014a, 2014b; Harper 2004).

4. A similar finding appears in a 2004 survey that revealed that 70 percent of physicians and pediatricians stated that they do not hand out action plans to families of asthmatic children (McNally et al. 2004).

Chapter 1

1. According to popular speech conventions in New Zealand, it would be common to refer to both doctors and patients by their first names—that is, as "Julian" rather than "Dr. Crane." The informality of such nomenclature is not coincidental but is a facet of New Zealanders' perspectives of medical professionals as "just like us." In the Czech Republic, in contrast, it would be rude to refer to physicians by their first names and without their titles. In this book, I have chosen to refer to all physicians as "Dr. So-and-so" both to clarify who my various interlocutors are and to maintain consistency.

Chapter 2

A portion of this chapter is adapted from "Domestic Experiments: Familial Regimes of Coping with Childhood Asthma in New Zealand." *Medical Anthropology: Cross-Cultural Studies in Health and Illness*, 33(6, 2014): 546–560.

1. Bricanyl is a terbutaline-based bronchodilator, whereas Ventolin is based on salbutamol. Both are used as emergency reliever medications.

Chapter 3

1. Text in italics is not a direct quotation but a paraphrase that has been translated into English.

2. The director of one company furthermore told me that the various insurance companies pool their earnings, redistributing funds among themselves to ensure that all patients are adequately covered, no matter which company they are actually insured with. I was unable, however, to corroborate this with other sources.

Chapter 4

1. Newer eNO (exhaled nitric oxide) tests are available but much less utilized.

2. Unfortunately, as all of my discussions with Czech children occurred in familial contexts in which they deferred to the opinions of adults, I was unable to elicit their own perspectives on their care and have therefore had to refrain from including their voices here.

Chapter 5

1. This strategy worked best for boys with mild or moderate asthma; boys with severe asthma were more likely to end up hospitalized (Williams 2000).

2. The inclusion of PMS and other hormonal changes in women is the only gender-specific trigger listed. Put alongside gendered diagnoses of panic and anxiety, it suggests the need for further analysis of possible overlaps among the emotional, hormonal, and physical aspects of breathlessness.

Chapter 6

1. According to the latest OECD figures, the average level of PM_{10} across New Zealand is 11.7 micrograms per cubic meter (mcg/m^3), significantly lower than the OECD average

of 20.9 mcg/m^3 and well within the World Health Organization's guideline of 20 mcg/m^3. Although PM$_{10}$ rates in Auckland are higher than in many other parts of the country and escalated to 15 mcg/m^3 in 2012, they remain well below levels considered dangerous (Morton 2014).

2. The cultural and historical specificity of climate therapy may best be revealed through comparison as Czechs' attitudes are both strikingly similar to and different from New Zealanders'. Many of the same images of the great outdoors as a site of naturalness, health, and freedom reverberate through Kiwi thinking. Like the promises of escape offered by the chata and the forest, New Zealanders similarly embrace the "simple," "no-fuss" lifestyles typified by spending one's leisure time in private baches (cottages) that dot the country's coastlines (Daley 2003). There was, moreover, a time when New Zealanders looked to the country's natural hot springs as a source of healing. In the early 1900s, the appointment of the first government balneologist initiated the building of the Rotorua bathhouse and sanatorium, completed in 1908. Although the bathhouse was to accommodate up to a thousand bathers a day, treating conditions ranging from skin diseases to asthma, architectural problems and the fact that New Zealand was too remote for most Europeans seeking spa cures led to the bathhouse formally closing its doors in 1948 (Foley, Wheeler, and Kearns 2011; Johnson 1990).

The twentieth century also saw the rise of another widely popular "outdoor cure" in New Zealand. Initiated by Dr. Elizabeth Gunn in 1919, health camps for children identified as suffering from a range of physical conditions, from malnutrition to "nervousness," were popular up through the 1960s (Tennant 1994). Based on the principle that outdoor living would invigorate children's physical health, health camps emphasized the healing properties of clean air, sunlight, and fresh food. However, since the 1970s and 1980s, the shift away from collective institutional-based care toward inculcating personal responsibility has resulted in health camps losing both government support and public popularity (Kearns and Collins 2000; Tennant 1994).

Although their histories are not so distant, outdoor cures very rarely feature in contemporary New Zealand health discourses. No one with asthma mentioned going to a health camp, much less remembered the days of balneotherapy. And certainly, no one ever suggested going outdoors as a way of coping with respiratory distress.

3. Despite not having a local source of curative waters, the institution is listed as a spa and is widely referred to as such.

Chapter 7

Portions of this chapter are adapted from "Reciprocal Responsibilities: Struggles over (New and Old) Social Contracts, Environmental Pollution, and Childhood Asthma in the Czech Republic." In *Competing Responsibilities: The Ethics and Politics of Contemporary Life*, eds. Susanna Trnka and Catherine Trundle (Durham, NC: Duke University Press, 2017).

1. Puddling allowed for mass production of high-grade wrought iron, enabling the construction of architectural emblems of the Industrial Revolution such as the Eiffel Tower and England's Victorian-era bridges.

Bibliography

Abraham, John, and Graham Lewis. 2002. "Citizenship, Medical Expertise and the Capitalist Regulatory State in Europe." *Sociology* 36(1): 67–88.

Adams, Vincanne. 2013. "Evidence-Based Global Public Health: Subjects, Profits, Erasures." In *When People Come First: Critical Studies in Global Health*, edited by João Biehl and Adriana Petryna, 54–90. Princeton, NJ: Princeton University Press.

Adler, Shelley R. 2002. "Integrative Medicine and Culture: Toward an Anthropology of CAM." *Medical Anthropology Quarterly* 16(4): 412–414.

Allen-Collinson, Jacquelyn, and Helen Owton. 2014. "Take a Deep Breath: Asthma, Sporting Embodiment, the Senses and 'Auditory Work.'" *International Review for the Sociology of Sport* 49(5): 592–608.

Applbaum, Kalman, and Michael Oldani. 2010. "Towards an Era of Bureaucratically Controlled Medical Compliance?" *Anthropology & Medicine* 17(2): 113–127.

ArcelorMittal Ostrava. 2008. "2008 Corporate Responsibility Report." Retrieved on March 14, 2014, from www.arcelormittal.com/ostrava/pdf/report_Mittal_en.pdf.

Aroni, R. A., S. M. Sawyer, M. J. Abramson, K. Stewart, F. C. K. Thien, D. P. Gocman, and J. A. Douglass. 2003. "Asthma Self-Management: What Do We Really Mean?" *Australian Journal of Primary Health* 9(2&3): 10–17.

Asher, M. I, S. Montefort, B. Björkstén, C. K. W. Lai, D. P. Strachan, S. K. Weiland, H. Williams, and the ISAAC Phase Three Study Group. 2006. "Worldwide Time Trends in the Prevalence of Symptoms of Asthma, Allergic Rhinoconjunctivitis, and Eczema in Childhood: ISAAC Phases One and Three Repeat Multicountry Cross-Sectional Surveys." *Lancet* 368(9537): 733–743.

Ashton, Toni, Nicholas Mays, and Nancy Devlin. 2005. "Continuity through Change: The Rhetoric and Reality of Health Reform in New Zealand." *Social Science & Medicine* 61(2): 253–262.

Asthma Foundation. n.d.(a). "Asthma Medication." Retrieved on March 15, 2015, from www.asthmafoundation.org.nz/your-health/living-with-asthma/asthma-medication#Preventer%20medication/.

———. n.d.(b). "Common Asthma Triggers." Retrieved on March 15, 2015, from https://www.asthmafoundation.org.nz/your-health/living-with-asthma/common-asthma-triggers.RLs have changed. As your quoted text is still on their site, I have updated the URL. What to do with the access date?ext. sho.

———. n.d.(c). "Living with Asthma." Retrieved on March 23, 2015, from www.asthma-foundation.org.nz/your-health/living-with-asthma.

Baer, Hans. 2004. *Toward an Integrative Medicine: Merging Alternative Therapies with Biomedicine.* Walnut Creek, CA: Altamira Press.

Bandura, Albert. 1977. "Self-efficacy: Toward a Unifying Theory of Behavioral Change." *Psychological Review* 84(2): 191–215.

Barlow, David H. 2004. *Anxiety and Its Disorders: The Nature and Treatment of Anxiety and Panic.* New York: Guilford Press.

Barnes, Peter J., and Sören Pedersen. 1993. "Efficacy and Safety of Inhaled Corticosteroids in Asthma." *American Review of Respiratory Disease* 148(4 pt 2): S1–S26.

Barnett, J. R. 2000. "Rationalising Hospital Services: Reflections on Hospital Restructuring and Its Impacts in New Zealand." *New Zealand Geographer* 56(1): 5–21.

Baroch, Pavel. 2014. "Miliardy nestačily, smog na Ostravsku loni opět zhoustl." *Aktuálně.cz* (online news site), January 21. Retrieved on March 19, 2014, from http://zpravy.aktualne .cz/domaci/miliardy-nestacily-smog-na-ostravsku-loni-opet-zhoustl/r~12844d048288 11e39d22002590604f2e/.

Barry, Christine Ann. 2006. "The Role of Evidence in Alternative Medicine: Contrasting Biomedical and Anthropological Approaches." *Social Science & Medicine* 62: 2646–2657.

Beasley R., N. Pearce, J. Crane, C. Burgess, and the National Library of Medicine. 1995. "Withdrawal of Fenoterol and the End of the New Zealand Asthma Mortality Epidemic." *International Archives of Allergy and Immunology* 107(1–3): 325–327.

Benedict, Barbara M. 1995. "Consumptive Communities: Commodifying Nature in Spa Society." *The Eighteenth Century* 36(3): 203–219.

Benner, Patricia, ed. 1994. *Interpretive Phenomenology: Embodiment, Caring, and Ethics in Health and Illness.* Thousand Oaks, CA: Sage.

Benoit, Cecilia, and Alena Heitlinger. 1998. "Women's Health Care Work in Comparative Perspective: Canada, Sweden and Czechoslovakia/Czech Republic as Case Examples." *Social Science & Medicine* 47(8): 1101–1111.

Benson, Peter, and Stuart Kirsch. 2010. "Capitalism and the Politics of Resignation." *Current Anthropology* 51(4): 459–486.

Berg, Marc. 1998. "Order(s) and Disorder(s): Of Protocols and Medical Practices." In *Differences in Medicine: Unraveling Practices, Techniques, and Bodies*, edited by Marc Berg and Annemarie Mol, 226–246. Durham, NC: Duke University Press.

Berger, William E. 2004. *Asthma for Dummies.* Hoboken, NJ: Wiley.

Bertoldi, Martina, Alessandro Borgini, Andrea Tittarelli, Elena Fattore, Alessandro Cau, Roberto Fanelli, and Paolo Crosignani. 2012. "Health Effects for the Population Living Near a Cement Plant: An Epidemiological Assessment." *Environment International* 41: 1–7.

Biebricher, Thomas. 2011. "(Ir-)Responsibilization, Genetics and Neuroscience." *European Journal of Social Theory* 14(4): 469–488.

Biehl, João. 2010. "Human Pharmakon: Symptoms, Technologies, Subjectivities." In *A Reader in Medical Anthropology: Theoretical Trajectories, Emergent Realities*, edited by Byron J. Good, Michael M. J. Fischer, Sarah S. Willen, and Mary-Jo DelVecchio Good, 213–231. Malden, MA: Wiley-Blackwell.

———. 2013. *Vita: Life in a Zone of Social Abandonment*. 2nd ed. Berkeley: University of California Press.

Biehl, João, and Adriana Petryna. 2013. "Legal Remedies: Therapeutic Markets and the Judicialization of the Right to Health." In *When People Come First: Critical Studies in Global Health*, edited by João Biehl and Adriana Petryna, 325–346. Princeton, NJ: Princeton University Press.

Bourdieu, Pierre. 1977. *Outline of a Theory of Practice*. Translated by Richard Nice. Cambridge, UK: Cambridge University Press.

Bousquet, Jean, and Nikolai Khaltaev, eds. 2007. *Global Surveillance, Prevention and Control of Chronic Respiratory Diseases: A Comprehensive Approach*. Geneva: World Health Organization.

Brasier, Allan R., ed. 2014. *Heterogeneity in Asthma*. New York: Springer.

Breathe Easy, Asthma New Zealand—The Lung Association. n. d. "All about Asthma" and "Frequently Asked Questions." Retrieved on March 23, 2015, from www.asthma-nz .org.nz/All+About+Asthma.html and http://www.asthma-ginnz.org.nz/All+About+ Asthma/Asthma+Questions.html.

British Thoracic Society. 2014. "BTS/SIGN Asthma Guideline 2014." Retrieved on August 10, 2015, from www.brit-thoracic.org.uk/guidelines-and-quality-standards/asthma-guideline/.

Brotherton, P. Sean. 2012. *Revolutionary Medicine: Health and the Body in Post-Soviet Cuba*. Durham, NC: Duke University Press.

Brown, Phil. 2007. *Toxic Exposures: Contested Illnesses and the Environmental Health Movement*. New York: Columbia University Press.

Brown, Phil, Rachel Morello-Frosch, Stephen Zavestoski, and The Contested Illnesses Research Group, eds. 2012. *Contested Illnesses: Citizens, Science, and Health Social Movements*. Berkeley: University of California Press.

Brussels Declaration on Asthma. 2007. Retrieved on May 3, 2011, from www.theipcrg .org/download/attachments/190115/newslaunchbrusselsdecasthma.pdf?version=1& modificationDate=1335259470000.

Bruton, Anne, and George T. Lewith. 2005. "The Buteyko Breathing Technique for Asthma: A Review." *Complementary Therapies in Medicine* 13(1): 41–46.

Bruton, Anne, and Mike Thomas. 2011. "The Role of Breathing Training in Asthma Management." *Current Opinion in Allergy and Clinical Immunology* 11(1): 53–57.

Bryant, Joanne, Maree Porter, Sally K. Tracy, and Elizabeth A. Sullivan. 2007. "Caesarean Birth: Consumption, Safety, Order, and Good Mothering." *Social Science & Medicine* 65(6): 1192–1201.

Buford, Terry A. 2004. "Transfer of Asthma Management Responsibility from Parents to Their School-Age Children." *Journal of Pediatric Nursing* 19(1): 3–12.

Cabanac, Michel. 1979. "Sensory Pleasure." *The Quarterly Review of Biology*, 54(1): 1–29.

Čada, Karel. n.d. "Reforms of the Health Policy in the Czech Republic." PhD thesis, Department of Sociology, Charles University, Prague.

———. 2014. "Category Making in Discourses of Health Policy Reforms: The Case Study of the Czech Republic." *Asia Europe Journal* 12(4): 431–443.

Caldwell, Melissa L. 2011. *Dacha Idylls: Living Organically in Russia's Countryside*. Berkeley: University of California Press.

Canguilhem, Georges. [1966] 1989. *The Normal and the Pathological*. New York: Zone Books.

Carr, E. Summerson. 2010. "Enactments of Expertise." *Annual Review of Anthropology* 39: 17–32.

Červinková, Hana. 2009. "The Phantom of the Good Soldier Švejk in the Czech Army Accession to NATO (2001–2002)." *International Journal of Politics, Culture, and Society* 22(3): 359–371.

Chalfen, Richard, and Michael Rich. 2004. "Applying Visual Research Patients Teaching Physicians through Visual Illness Narratives." *Visual Anthropology Review* 20(1): 17–30.

Charlton, Ian, Gillian Charlton, Judy Broomfield, and Mark A. Mullee. 1990. "Evaluation of Peak Flow and Symptoms Only Self Management Plans for Control of Asthma in General Practice." *British Medical Journal* 301(6765): 1355–1359.

ČIPA (Česká iniciativa pro astma). 2008. *Diagnostika, léčba a prevence průduškového astmatu v České republice*. Prague: Author.

Čisté Nebe. 2016. "Poběž s maskou za Čisté nebe." July 18. Retrieved on July 20, 2016, from www.cistenebe.cz/.

Clark, Cindy Dell. 2012. "Asthma Episodes: Stigma, Children, and Hollywood Films." *Medical Anthropology Quarterly* 26(1): 92–115.

Clarke, Monica. 2002. "Ineffable Experiences: Memories of Breathing." In *Writing in the Dark: Phenomenological Studies in Interpretive Inquiry*, edited by Max van Manen, 137–155. London, Ontario: Althouse Press.

Colebatch, Hal, Robert Hoppe, and Mirko Noordegraaf, eds. 2010. *Working for Policy*. Amsterdam: Amsterdam University Press.

Conrad, Peter. 1985. "The Meaning of Medications: Another Look at Compliance." *Social Science & Medicine* 20(1): 29–37.

———. 2007. *The Medicalization of Society: On the Transformation of Human Conditions into Treatable Disorders*. Baltimore: Johns Hopkins University Press.

Cowie, Robert L., Diane P. Conley, Margot F. Underwood, and Patricia G. Reader. 2008. "A Randomised Controlled Trial of the Buteyko Technique as an Adjunct to Conventional Management of Asthma." *Respiratory Medicine* 102(5): 726–732.

Creer, Thomas L., and Walter P. Christian. 1976. *Chronically Ill and Handicapped Children: Their Management and Rehabilitation*. Champaign, IL: Research Press Company.

Crengle, Suzanne Marie. 2008. "The Management of Children's Asthma in Primary Care: Are There Ethnic Differences in Care?" PhD thesis, University of Auckland.

Crengle, Sue, Ramon Pink, and Suzanne Pitama. 2007. "Respiratory Disease." In *Hauora: Māori Standards of Health IV: A Study of the Years 2000–2005*, edited by B. Robson and

R. Harris, Chapter 10. Wellington, NZ: Te Rōpū Rangahau Hauora a Eru Pōmare. Available at www.otago.ac.nz/wellington/otago067749.pdf.

Cropp, Amanda. 2016. "Canned South Island Air for Chinese Tourists and Polluted Asian Cities." *Stuff* (online news site), May 20. Retrieved on June 28, 2016, from www .stuff.co.nz/business/80206772/Canned-South-Island-air-for-Chinese-tourists-and-polluted-Asian-cities.

Csordas, Thomas J. 1993. "Somatic Modes of Attention." *Cultural Anthropology* 8(2): 135–156.

———. 1994. *Embodiment and Experience: The Existential Ground of Culture and Self.* Cambridge, UK: Cambridge University Press.

Czech Hydrometeorological Institute. 2014. *Graphic Yearbook 2013.* Retrieved on July 20, 2016, from www.portal.chmi.cz/files/portal/docs/uoco/isko/grafroc/13groc/gr13e/ Obsah_GB.html.

"Czech Republic: 'Rescue plan for Ostrava.'" 2013. *VoxEurop* (online news site), September 13. Summary of article published in *Mladá Fronta Dnes* (newspaper), September 13. Retrieved on March 9, 2014, from www.presseurop.eu/en/content/news-brief/ 4141721-rescue-plan-ostrava.

Dahl, Ronald. 2006. "Systemic Side Effects of Inhaled Corticosteroids in Patients with Asthma." *Respiratory Medicine* 100(8): 1307–1317.

Daley, Caroline. 2003. *Leisure and Pleasure: Reshaping and Revealing the New Zealand Body 1900–1960.* Auckland: Auckland University Press.

Daniel, E. Valentine. 1984. *Fluid Signs: Being a Person the Tamil Way.* Berkeley: University of California Press.

Darwin, Charles. 1872. *The Expression of the Emotions in Man and Animals.* London: John Murray.

Davies, Christie. 1989. "Goffman's Concept of the Total Institution: Criticisms and Revisions." *Human Studies* 12(1/2): 77–95.

Davis, Elizabeth Anne. 2012. *Bad Souls: Madness and Responsibility in Modern Greece.* Durham, NC: Duke University Press.

DelVecchio Good, Mary-Jo. 2001. "The Biotechnical Embrace." *Culture, Medicine, and Psychiatry* 25(4): 395–410.

Derrida, Jacques. 1981. "Plato's Pharmacy." In *Dissemination,* translated by Barbara Johnson, 61–171. Chicago: University of Chicago Press.

Donovan, Jenny L., and David R. Blake. 1992. "Patient Non-compliance: Deviance or Reasoned Decision-Making?" *Social Science & Medicine* 34(5): 507–513.

Dostál, Miroslav, Anna Pastorková, Stepan Rychlik, Eva Rychlíková, Vlasta Švecová, Eva Schallerová and Radim J. Šrám. 2013. "Comparison of Child Morbidity in Regions of Ostrava, Czech Republic, with Different Degrees of Pollution: A Retrospective Cohort Study." *Environmental Health* 12(74): 1–11.

D'Souza, W., J. Crane, C. Burgess, H. Te Karu, C. Fox, M. Harper, B. Robson, P. Howden-Chapman, L. Crossland, K. Woodman, N. Pearce, E. Pomare, and R. Beasley. 1994. "Community-Based Asthma Care: Trial of a 'Credit Card' Asthma Self-Management Plan." *European Respiratory Journal* 7(7): 1260–1265.

Dumit, Joseph. 2006. "Illnesses You Have to Fight to Get: Facts as Forces in Uncertain, Emergent Illnesses." *Social Science & Medicine* 62(3): 577–590.

———. 2010. "Inter-pill-ation and the Instrumentalization of Compliance." *Anthropology & Medicine* 17(2): 245–247.

———. 2012. *Drugs for Life: How Pharmaceutical Companies Define Our Health*. Durham, NC: Duke University Press.

Dunbar, Helen Flanders. 1947. *Mind and Body: Psychosomatic Medicine*. New York: Random House.

Eaton, Tam, Steve Withy, Jeffrey E. Garrett, Jill Mercer, Robert M. L. Whitlock, and Harry H. Rea. 1999. "Spirometry in Primary Care Practice: The Importance of Quality Assurance and the Impact of Spirometry Workshops." *Chest* 116(2): 416–423.

Elias, Norbert. [1939] 2000. *The Civilizing Process*. Translated by Edmund Jephcott. Edited by Eric Dunning, Johan Goudsblom, and Stephen Mennell. Malden, MA: Blackwell.

Ellison-Loschmann, Lis, and Neil Pearce. 2006. "Improving Access to Health Care among New Zealand's Maori Population." *American Journal of Public Health* 96(4): 612–617.

Epstein, Steven. 1995. "The Construction of Lay Expertise: AIDS Activism and the Forging of Credibility in the Reform of Clinical Trials." *Science, Technology, & Human Values* 20(4): 408–437.

Fagan, Adam. 2004. *Environment and Democracy in the Czech Republic: The Environmental Movement in the Transition Process*. Cheltenham, UK: Edward Elgar.

Fassin, Didier. 2013. "Children as Victims: The Moral Economy of Childhood in the Times of AIDS." In *When People Come First: Critical Studies in Global Health*, edited by João Biehl and Adriana Petryna, 109–132. Princeton, NJ: Princeton University Press.

Feldman, C., D. Evans, W. Davis, B. Feldman, and N. Clark. 1982. "Establishment and Evaluation of an Asthma Self-Management Program." *Journal of Allergy and Clinical Immunology* 69(1 pt. 2): 144.

Ferzacca, Steve. 2000. "'Actually, I Don't Feel That Bad': Managing Diabetes and the Clinical Encounter." *Medical Anthropology Quarterly*. 14(1): 28–50.

Filsak, Jiři. 1970. *Rehabilitace Sportem a Hrou Respiračně Oslabených Dětí*. Prague: Olympia.

Fitzgerald, Ruth. 2004. "The New Zealand Health Reforms: Dividing the Labour of Care." *Social Science & Medicine* 58(2): 331–341.

———. 2012. "Occupational Therapists, Care and Managerialism." In *Clinical Reasoning in Occupational Therapy: Controversies in Practice*, edited by Linda Robinson, 45–62. Sussex, UK: Wiley-Blackwell.

Flemr, Jan. 2011. "Smoke from Czech Steel Hub Is Harming Kids." AFP News, December 1. Retrieved on March 9, 2014, from https://sg.news.yahoo.com/no-breath-relief-kids-dirty-czech-steel-hub-071154914.html.

Foley, Ronan, Abbey Wheeler, and Robin Kearns. 2011. "Selling the Colonial Spa Town: The Contested Therapeutic Landscapes of Lisdoonvarna and Te Aroha." *Irish Geography* 44(2–3): 151–172.

Fortun, Kim, Mike Fortun, Erik Bigras, Tahereh Saheb, Brandon Costelloe-Kuehn, Jerome Crowder, Daniel Price, and Alison Kenner. 2014a. "Experimental Ethnography Online." *Cultural Studies* 28(4): 632–642.

Fortun, Mike, Kim Fortun, Brandon Costelloe-Kuehn, Tahereh Saheb, Daniel Price, Alison Kenner , and Jerome Crowder. 2014b. "Asthma, Culture, and Cultural Analysis: Continuing Challenges." In *Heterogeneity in Asthma*, edited by Allan R. Brasier, 321–32. New York: Springer.

Foucault, Michel. 1980. "Two Lectures." *Power/Knowledge: Selected Interviews and Other Writings, 1972–1977*, 78–108. Edited by Colin Gordon. New York: Pantheon.

———. 1997. *Ethics: Subjectivity and Truth*. Edited by Paul Rabinow; translated by Robert Hurley and others. New York: The New Press.

Franc, Martin, and Jiří Knapík. 2013. *Volný čas v českých zemích 1957–1967*. Prague: Academia.

Freidson, Elliot. 1970. *Professional Dominance: The Social Structure of Medical Care*. Chicago: Aldine.

———. 1986. *Professional Powers: A Study of the Institutionalization of Formal Knowledge*. Chicago: University of Chicago Press.

Freud, Sigmund. 1920–1922. *Beyond the Pleasure Principle*. Translated by James Strachey. London: Hogarth Press.

Frickel, Scott, Sahra Gibbon, Jeff Howard, Joanna Kempner, Gwen Ottinger, and David J. Hess. 2010. "Undone Science: Charting Social Movement and Civil Society Challenges to Research Agenda Setting." *Science, Technology, & Human Values* 35(4): 444–473.

Gabe, Jonathan, Michael Bury, and Rosemary Ramsay. 2002. "Living with Asthma: The Experiences of Young People at Home and at School." *Social Science & Medicine* 55(9): 1619–1633.

Gal, Susan, and Gail Kligman. 2000. *The Politics of Gender after Socialism: A Comparative-Historical Essay*. Princeton, NJ: Princeton University Press.

GINA (Global Initiative for Asthma). 2007. *GINA Patient Guideline*. Retrieved on March 9, 2014, from www.ginasthma.org/Patient-Guide.

———. 2012a. Pocket Guide for Asthma Management and Prevention. Retrieved on March 9, 2014, from www.ginasthma.org/local/uploads/files/GINA_Pocket_Guide_2012_wms .pdf.

———, 2012b. *Pocket Guide for Asthma Management and Prevention: A Guide for Physicians and Nurses*. Updated 2012. Retrieved on March 9, 2014, from www.ginasthma.org/ local/uploads/files/GINA_Pocket2013_May15.pdf.

———. 2014. *Global Strategy for Asthma Management and Prevention*. Retrieved on March 9, 2014, from www.ginasthma.org/local/uploads/files/GINA_Report_2014_Aug12.pdf.

Global Asthma Network. 2014. *The Global Asthma Report 2014*. Auckland, New Zealand.

Goffman, Erving. 1957. "On the Characteristics of Total Institutions." In *Symposium on Preventive and Social Psychiatry, 15–17 April 1957*, sponsored by the Walter Reed Army Institute of Research, the Walter Reed Army Medical Centre, and the National Research Council, 43–84. Washington, DC: Government Printing Office.

Good, Byron J. 1994. *Medicine, Rationality, and Experience: An Anthropological Perspective*. Cambridge, UK: Cambridge University Press.

Gramsci, Antonio. 1971. *Selections from the Prison Notebooks of Antonio Gramsci*. Edited and translated by Quintin Hoare and Geoffrey Nowell-Smith. London: Lawrence & Wishart.

Grasseni, Cristina. 2004. "Skilled Vision. An Apprenticeship in Breeding Aesthetics." *Social Anthropology* 12(1): 41–55.

Greene, Jeremy, and David Herzberg. 2010. "Hidden in Plain Sight: Marketing Prescription Drugs to Consumers in the Twentieth Century." *American Journal of Public Health* 100(5): 793–803.

Greenhalgh, Susan. 2008. *Just One Child: Science and Policy in Deng's China*. Berkeley: University of California Press.

Hacking, Ian. 1995. *Rewriting the Soul: Multiple Personality and the Sciences of Memory*. Princeton, NJ: Princeton University Press.

Hardey, Michael. 1999. "Doctor in the House: The Internet as a Source of Lay Health Knowledge and the Challenge to Expertise." *Sociology of Health & Illness* 21(6): 820–835.

Harper, Janice. 2004. "Breathless in Houston: A Political Ecology of Health Approach to Understanding Environmental Health Concerns." *Medical Anthropology* 23(4): 295–326.

Hartert, Tina V., Hugh H. Windom, R. Stokes Peebles Jr., Linda R. Freidhoff, and Alkis Togias. 1996. "Inadequate Outpatient Medical Therapy for Patients with Asthma Admitted to Two Urban Hospitals." *American Journal of Medicine* 100(4): 386–394.

Haukanes, Haldis, and Frances Pine. 2003. "Ritual and Everyday Consumption Practices in the Czech and Polish Countryside: Conceiving Modernity through Changing Food Regimes." *Anthropological Journal on European Cultures* 12: 103–130.

Heitlinger, Alena. 1987. *Reproduction, Medicine & the Socialist State*. London: Palgrave Macmillan.

Heitlinger, Alena, and Susanna Trnka. 1998. *Young Women of Prague*. London: Macmillan.

Herbert, Amanda E. 2009. "Gender and the Spa: Space, Sociability and Self at British Health Spas, 1640–1714." *Journal of Social History* 43(2): 361–383.

Hess, David. 2004. "Medical Modernisation, Scientific Research Fields and the Epistemic Politics of Health Social Movements." *Sociology of Health & Illness* 26(6): 695–709.

Hilgers, Mathieu. 2012. "The Historicity of the Neoliberal State." *Social Anthropology* 20(1): 80–94.

Hoffman, Lily M. 1997. "Professional Autonomy Reconsidered: The Case of Czech Medicine under State Socialism." *Comparative Studies in Society and History* 39(2): 346–372.

Holt, Shaun, and Richard Beasley. 2002. *The Burden of Asthma in New Zealand*. Wellington: Asthma and Respiratory Foundation of New Zealand.

Holy, Ladislav. 1996. *The Little Czech and the Great Czech Nation: National Identity and the Post-Communist Social Transformation*. Cambridge, UK, and New York: Cambridge University Press.

Howden-Chapman, Philippa, Anna Matheson, Julian Crane, Helen Viggers, Malcolm Cunningham, Tony Blakely, Chris Cunningham, Alistair Woodward, Kay Saville-Smith, Des

O'Dea, Martin Kennedy, Michael Baker, Nick Waipara, Ralph Chapman, and Gabrielle Davie. 2007. "Effect of Insulating Existing Houses on Health Inequality: Cluster Randomised Study in the Community." *British Medical Journal* 334: 460.

Howes, David, ed. 2005. *Empire of the Senses: The Sensual Culture Reader*. Oxford, UK, and New York: Berg.

Hrešanová, Ema. 2010. "The Moralities of Medicine and Birth Care in the Czech Republic: The Case of the Arrested Mother." *Durham Anthropology Journal* 17(1): 65–86.

———. 2014 "'Nobody in a Maternity Hospital Really Talks to You': Socialist Legacies and Consumerism in Czech Women's Childbirth Narratives." *Czech Sociological Review* 50(6): 961–986.

Ingold, Tim. 2001. "From the Transmission of Representations to the Education of Attention." In *The Debated Mind: Evolutionary Psychology Versus Ethnography*, edited by Harvey Whitehouse, 113–153. Oxford, UK: Berg.

Intolerance: Když vzduch zabíjí [Intolerance: When Air Kills]. 2010. Documentary film. Directed by P. Všelichová. As shown on Česká televize (Czech TV). Retrieved on March 4, 2014, from www.ceskatelevize.cz/porady/10275866938-intolerance/410235100141006-kdyz-vzduch-zabiji/.

Jackson, Jean E. 2000. *"Camp Pain": Talking with Chronic Pain Patients*. Philadelphia: University of Pennsylvania Press.

Jackson, Mark. 2009. *Asthma: The Biography*. Oxford, UK: Oxford University Press.

———. 2010. "'Divine Stramonium': The Rise and Fall of Smoking for Asthma." *Medical History* 54(2): 171–194.

Jasanoff, Sheila. 1997. "Civilization and Madness: The Great BSE Scare of 1996." *Public Understanding of Science* 6(3): 221–232.

Johnson, Ralph H. 1990. "Arthur Stanley Wohlmann, the First Government Balneologist in New Zealand." *Medical History* 34(S10): 114–126.

Johnstone, Chris. 2014. "Prague Advances Low Emission Zone Plan for City Centre." Český Rozhlas (Czech Radio). July 15. Retrieved on March 28, 2015, from www.radio.cz/en/section/in-focus/prague-advances-low-emission-zone-plan-for-city-centre.

Jůn, Dominic. 2014. "Tackling the Czech Republic's Poor Air Quality." Český Rozhlas (Czech Radio). November 20. Retrieved on March 28, 2015, from www.radio.cz/en/section/panorama/tackling-the-czech-republics-poor-air-quality.

Jutel, Annemarie Goldstein. 2011. *Putting a Name to It: Diagnosis in Contemporary Society*. Baltimore: Johns Hopkins University Press.

Kalēja, Jekaterina, Zane Linde, and Ilze Mileiko. 2011. "Exploring Medical Biotechnologies in Post-Soviet Latvia." Paper presented at the Health in Transition: (Bio)Medicine as Culture in Post-socialist Europe conference, Charles University, Prague, June 10–11.

Kaufman, Sharon R. 2005. *. . . And a Time to Die: How American Hospitals Shape the End of Life*. Chicago: University of Chicago Press.

Kearns, Robin A., and Damian C. A. Collins. 2000. "New Zealand Children's Health Camps: Therapeutic Landscapes Meet the Contract State." *Social Science & Medicine* 51(7): 1047–1059.

Keirns, Carla. 2004. "Short of Breath: A Social and Intellectual History of Asthma in the United States." PhD dissertation, University of Pennsylvania.

Kelsey, Jane. 1995. *The New Zealand Experiment: A World Model for Structural Adjustment?* Wellington: Bridget Williams Books.

Kilburn, Michael, and Miroslav Vaněk. 2004. "The Ecological Roots of a Democracy Movement." *Human Rights Dialogue* 2(11): Environmental Rights, April 21. Carnegie Council for Ethics in International Affairs. Available at www.carnegiecouncil.org/publications/archive/dialogue/2_11/section_1/4443.html.

Kirtsoglou, Elisabeth. 2010. "Introduction: Rhetoric and the Workings of Power: The Social Contract in Crisis." *Social Analysis* 54(1): 1–14.

Knižák, Milan. 2011. "Weekendová utopie: Fenomén trampingu v Čechách [The weekend utopia: The phenomenon of the tramping movement in Bohemia]." In *Volný čas: Utopie na hranicích všednosti* [Spare Time: Utopias on the Verge of Commonness], 25–28. Prague: Národní Galerie [National Gallery].

Koch, Erin. 2013a. *Free Market Tuberculosis: Managing Epidemics in Post-Soviet Georgia.* Nashville, TN: Vanderbilt University Press.

———. 2013b. "Tuberculosis Is a Threshold: The Making of a Social Disease in Post-Soviet Georgia." *Medical Anthropology* 32(4): 309–324.

Koldeová, Lujza. 2012. "Systém odmien a trestov v kontexte rodinnej výchovy v Slovenskej republike a Nemeckej spolkovej republike" [Rewards and Punishments System in the Context of Family Education in the Slovak Republic and the Federal Republic of Germany]. *Kultura i Wychowanie* 3(1): 85–97.

Kringelbach, Morten L., and Kent C. Berridge, eds. 2010. *Pleasures of the Brain.* Oxford, UK: Oxford University Press.

Kroegel, Claus, and Hubert Wirtz. 2009. "History of Guidelines for the Diagnosis and Management of Asthma: From Opinion to Control." *Drugs* 69(9): 1189–1204.

Langstrup, Henriette, and Brit Ross Winthereik. 2008. "The Making of Self-Monitoring Asthma Patients: Mending a Split Reality with Comparative Ethnography." *Comparative Sociology* 7(3): 362–386.

Lass, Andrew. 1994. "From Memory to History: The Events of November 17 Dis/membered." In *Memory, History and Opposition under State Socialism*, edited by Rubie S. Watson, 87–104. Santa Fe, NM: School of American Research Press.

Latour, Bruno. 1987. *Science in Action: How to Follow Scientists and Engineers through Society.* English translation. Cambridge, MA: Harvard University Press.

Latour, Bruno, and Steven Woolgar. 1979. *Laboratory Life: The Construction of Scientific Facts.* Beverly Hills, CA: Sage Publications.

Laumbach, Robert J., and Howard M. Kipen. 2012. "Respiratory Health Effects of Air Pollution: Update on Biomass Smoke and Traffic Pollution." *Journal of Allergy and Clinical Immunology* 129(1): 3–11.

Lawson, Colin, and Juraj Nemec. 2003. "The Political Economy of Slovak and Czech Health Policy, 1989–2000." *International Political Science Review* 24(2): 219–235.

Lempa, Heikki. 2002. "The Spa: Emotional Economy and Social Classes in Nineteenth-Century Pyrmont." *Central European History* 35(1): 37–73.

Lerner, Barron H. 1997. "From Careless Consumptives to Recalcitrant Patients: The Historical Construction of Noncompliance." *Social Science & Medicine* 45(9): 1423–1431.

Lewis, Nick. 2004. "Geographies of 'The New Zealand Experiment.'" *GeoJournal* 59(2): 161–166.

Lorig, Kate R., and Halsted R. Holman. 2003. "Self-Management Education: History, Definition, Outcomes, and Mechanisms." *Annals of Behavioral Medicine* 26(1): 1–7.

Luhrmann, Tanya M. 2000. *Of Two Minds: The Growing Disorder in American Psychiatry*. New York: Alfred A. Knopf.

Mackaman, Douglas Peter. 1998. *Leisure Settings: Bourgeois Culture, Medicine, and the Spa in Modern France*. Chicago: University of Chicago Press.

Mahoney, Michael J., and Carl E. Thoresen. 1974. *Self-Control: Power to the Person*. Monterey, CA: Brooks/Cole Publishing Company.

Makovská, Dana. 2011. "Využití zobcové flétny v muzikoterapii: Žilkova metoda [Use of the Recorder in Music Therapy: Žilka's Method]." MA thesis, Department of Music, Charles University, Prague.

Maříková, Hana. 2008. "Caring Fathers and Gender (In)Equality?" *Polish Sociological Review* (162): 135–152.

Mariskind, Clare. 2014. "Good Mothers and Responsible Citizens: Analysis of Public Support for the Extension of Paid Parental Leave." Paper given at the Competing Responsibilities: The Ethics and Politics of Responsibilities in Contemporary Life conference, Wellington, New Zealand, August 15–17.

Martin, Emily. 1997. "Managing Americans: Policy and Changes in the Meanings of Work and the Self." In *Anthropology of Policy: Critical Perspective on Governance and Power*, edited by Cris Shore and Susan Wright, 239–260. London and New York: Routledge.

———. 2006. "The Pharmaceutical Person." *BioSocieties* 1(3): 273–288.

———. 2009. *Bipolar Expeditions: Mania and Depression in American Culture*. Princeton, NJ: Princeton University Press.

Mattingly, Cheryl. 2010. *The Paradox of Hope: Journeys through a Clinical Borderland*. Berkeley: University of California Press.

Mauss, Marcel. [1925] 1954. *The Gift: Forms and Functions for Exchange in Archaic Societies*. New York and London: Norton.

McNally, Andrew, Chris Frampton, John Garrett, and Philip Pattemore. 2004. "Application of Asthma Action Plans to Childhood Asthma: National Survey Repeated." *New Zealand Medical Journal* June 8, 117(1196).

Mertl, Jan. 2008. "Proč je důležitý standard zdravotní péče". *Britské Listy*. December 2. Retrieved on November 19, 2014, from http://blisty.cz/art/44031.html.

Miller, Peter, and Nikolas Rose. 2008. *Governing the Present: Administering Economic, Social and Personal Life*. Malden, MA: Polity Press.

Ministry of Health. 2013. *New Zealand Health Survey: Annual Update of Key Findings 2012/13*. Wellington: Ministry of Health.

Mol, Annemarie. 2008. *The Logic of Care: Health and the Problem of Patient Choice*. London: Routledge.

Mol, Annemarie, Ingunn Moser, and Jeanette Pols. 2010. "Care: Putting Practice into Theory." In *Care in Practice: On Tinkering in Clinics, Homes and Farms*, edited by Annemarie Mol, Ingunn Moser, and Jeanette Pols, 7–26. Bielefeld, Germany: Transcript Verlag.

Morton, Jamie. 2014. "17 NZ Centres Rank in New Global Air Quality Report." *The New Zealand Herald*. Online edition. May 8. Retrieved on October 24, 2014, from www .nzherald.co.nz/nz/news/article.cfm?c_id=1&objectid=11251714.

Murphy, Kevin R., Eli O. Meltzer, Michael S. Blaiss, Robert A. Nathan, Stuart W. Stoloff, and Dennis E. Doherty. 2012. "Asthma Management and Control in the United States: Results of the 2009 Asthma Insight and Management Survey." *Allergy and Asthma Proceedings* 33(1): 54–64.

OECD. 2011. *Health at a Glance 2011: OECD Indicators*. Figure 4.1.1 "Doctors Consultations Per Capita, 2009 and Change between 2000 and 2009." Retrieved on March 14, 2015, from www.oecd-ilibrary.org/sites/health_glance-2011-en/04/01/g4-01-01.html?content Type=&itemId=/content/chapter/health_glance-2011-56-en&containerItemId=/ content/serial/19991312&accessItemIds=/content/book/health_glance-2011-en& mimeType=text/html&_csp_=b4bf40bb1ec2d91d47c1a2dfdfc70aed.

Oldani, Michael J. 2010. "Assessing the 'Relative Value' of Diabetic Patients Treated through an Incentivized, Corporate Compliance Model." *Anthropology & Medicine* 17(2): 215–228.

"Ostrava." *Wikipedia*. Last modified March 9, 2014. Available at http://en.wikipedia.org/ wiki/Ostrava.

Ostrava Město Kultury. 2013. [Website promoting the city of Ostrava]. Retrieved on March 9, 2014, from www.ostrava2015.cz/web/structure/vitkovice-61.html?lang=en.

Park, Julie. 2000. "'The Worst Hassle Is You Can't Play Rugby': Haemophilia and Masculinity in New Zealand." *Current Anthropology* 41(3): 443–453.

———. 2013. "Painful Exclusion: Hepatitis C in the New Zealand Hemophilia Community." In *Senses and Citizenships: Embodying Political Life*, edited by Susanna Trnka, Christine Dureau, and Julie Park, 221–241. New York and London: Routledge.

Park, Julie, Kathryn Scott, Mike Carnahan, and Deon York. Forthcoming. *A Bleeding Nuisance: Living with Haemophilia in Aotearoa*.

Pearce, Neil. 2007 *Adverse Reactions: The Fenoterol Story*. Auckland: Auckland University Press.

———. 2011. "Non-allergic Asthma." Paper presented at the ISAAC 20 Year Anniversary Symposium, University of Auckland, Auckland, New Zealand, January 27.

Pearce, Neil, Richard Beasley, Julian Crane, Carl Burgess, and Rodney Jackson. 1995. "End of the New Zealand Asthma Mortality Epidemic." *Lancet* 345(8941): 41–44.

Peek, Bobby, Dana Sadykova, Darek Urbaniak, Jan Haverkamp, Jan Šrytr, Pippa Gallop, and Sunita Dubey. 2009. "ArcelorMittal: Going Nowhere Slowly: A review of the Global Steel Giant's Environmental and Social Impacts in 2008–2009." Published online.

Retrieved on March 9, 2014, from http://bankwatch.org/documents/ArcelorMittal_Going_Nowhere.pdf.

Peshkin, M. Murray. 1959. "Intractable Asthma of Childhood: Rehabilitation at the Institutional Level with a Follow-up of 150 Cases." *International Archives of Allergy*. 15(1–3): 91–112.

Petrášová, Lenka. 2013. "Nemocnice v Motole opráší "kulichy", připravuje protekční program." *iDnes* (newspaper), September 11. Retrieved on July 4, 2016, from http://praha.idnes.cz/nemocnice-v-motole-zavede-protekcni-program-kulich-fxj-/praha-zpravy.aspx?c=A130911_1975638_praha-zpravy_sfo.

Petryna, Adriana. 2009. *When Experiments Travel: Clinical Trials and the Global Search for Human Subjects*. Princeton, NJ: Princeton University Press.

———. 2011. "Pharmaceuticals and the Right to Health: Reclaiming Patients and the Evidence Base of New Drugs." *Anthropological Quarterly* 84(2): 305–330.

Pleva, Martin. 2008. "ArcelorMittal: Víme, že škodíme. Zlepšíme se." *Deník* (newspaper), October 19. Retrieved on March 9, 2014, from www.denik.cz/ekonomika/arcelormittal_skoda_zlepseni20081018.html.

Pohlman, Betsy, and Gay Becker. 2006. "'Stress Knocks Hard on Your Immune System': Asthma and the Discourse on Stress." *Medical Anthropology* 25(3): 265–295.

Polese, Abel. 2014. "Informal Payments in Ukrainian Hospitals: On the Boundary between Informal Payments, Gifts, and Bribes." *Anthropological Forum* 24(4): 381–395.

Pols, Jeanette. 2014. "Knowing Patients: Turning Patient Knowledge into Science." *Science, Technology, & Human Values* 39(1): 73–97.

Prior, Lindsay. 2003. "Belief, Knowledge and Expertise: The Emergence of the Lay Expert in Medical Sociology." *Sociology of Health & Illness* 25(3): 41–57.

Prout, Alan, Lesley Hayes, and Lesley Gelder. 1999. "Medicines and the Maintenance of Ordinariness in the Household Management of Childhood Asthma." *Sociology of Health & Illness* 21(2): 137–162.

Quintela, Maria Manuel. 2011. "'Seeking 'Energy' vs. Pain Relief in Spas in Brazil (Caldas da Imperatriz) and Portugal (Termas da Sulfúrea)." *Anthropology & Medicine* 18(1): 23–35.

Rabeharisoa, Vololona, and Michel Callon. 2004. "Patients and Scientists in French Muscular Dystrophy Research." In *States of Knowledge: The Co-Production of Science and Social Order*, edited by Shelia Jasanoff, 300–340. London and New York: Routledge.

Rabeharisoa, Vololona, Tiago Moreira, and Madeleine Akrich. 2014. "Evidence-Based Activism: Patients', Users' and Activists' Groups in Knowledge Society." *BioSocieties* 9(2): 111–128.

Raikhel, Eugene. 2010. "Post-Soviet Placebos: Epistemology and Authority in Russian Treatments for Alcoholism." *Culture, Medicine and Psychiatry* 34(1): 132–168.

RCP (Royal College of Physicians). 2014. *Why Asthma Still Kills: The National Review of Asthma Deaths (NRAD) Confidential Enquiry Report*. London: RCP.

Read, Rosie. 2007. "Labour and Love: Competing Constructions of 'Care' in a Czech Nursing Home." *Critique of Anthropology* 27(2): 203–222.

Rehak, Jana Kopelentova. 2012. *Czech Political Prisoners: Recovering Face*. Lanham, MD: Lexington Books.

Rich, Michael, Steven Lamola, and Elizabeth R. Woods. 2006. "Effects of Creating Visual Illness Narratives on Quality of Life with Asthma: A Pilot Intervention Study." *Journal of Adolescent Health* 38(6): 748–752.

Rich, Michael, Jennifer Patashnick, and Richard Chalfen. 2002. "Visual Illness Narratives of Asthma: Explanatory Models and Health-Related Behavior." *American Journal of Health Behavior* 26(6): 442–453.

Romieu, Isabelle, Fernando Meneses, Silvia Ruiz, Juan Jose Sienra, Jose Huerta, Mary C. White, and Ruth A. Etzel. 1996. "Effects of Air Pollution on the Respiratory Health of Asthmatic Children Living in Mexico City." *American Journal of Respiratory and Critical Care Medicine* 154(2): 300–307.

Rose, Gabrielle, and Lenore Manderson. 2000. "More Than a Breath of Difference: Competing Paradigms of Asthma." *Anthropology & Medicine* 7(3): 335–350.

Rose, Nikolas. 1996. "The Death of the Social? Re-figuring the Territory of Government." *Economy & Society* 25(3): 327–356.

———. 2003. "Neurochemical Selves." *Society* 41(1): 45–59.

———. 2006. *The Politics of Life Itself: Biomedicine, Power, and Subjectivity in the Twenty-First Century*. Princeton, NJ: Princeton University Press.

Rossi, Giovanni A., Franklin Cerasoli, and Mario Cazzola. 2007. "Safety of Inhaled Corticosteroids: Room for Improvement." *Pulmonary Pharmacology & Therapeutics* 20(1): 23–35.

Rouse, Carolyn. 2010. "Patient and Practitioner Noncompliance: Rationing, Therapeutic Uncertainty, and the Missing Conversation." *Anthropology & Medicine* 17(2): 187–200.

Saunders, Barry E. 2008. *CT Suite: The Work of Diagnosis in the Age of Noninvasive Cutting*. Durham, NC: Duke University Press.

Schwartz, Norah Anita. 2004. "Childhood Asthma on the Northern Mexico Border." *Medical Anthropology Quarterly*. 18(2): 214–229.

Schwartz, Norah Anita, Christine Alysse von Glascoe, Victor Torres, Lorena Ramos, and Claudia Soria-Delgado. 2015. "'Where They (Live, Work and) Spray': Pesticide Exposure, Childhood Asthma and Environmental Justice among Mexican-American Farmworkers." *Health & Place* 32: 83–92.

Shore, Cris, and Susanna Trnka, eds. 2013. *Up Close and Personal: On Peripheral Perspectives and the Production of Anthropological Knowledge*. Oxford, UK, and New York: Berghahn Books.

Shore, Cris, and Susan Wright. 2000. "Coercive Accountability: The Rise of Audit Culture in Education." In *Audit Cultures: Anthropological Studies in Accountability, Ethics and the Academy*, edited by Marilyn Strathern, 57–89. London and New York: Routledge.

———. 2011. "Conceptualizing Policy: Technologies of Governance and the Politics of Visibility." In *Policy Worlds: Anthropology and the Analysis of Contemporary Power*, edited by Cris Shore, Susan Wright, and Davide Però, 1–25. Oxford, UK, and New York: Berghahn Books.

Šiklová, Jiřina. 1997. "Feminism and the Roots of Apathy in the Czech Republic." *Social Research* 64(2): 258–280.

Skalník, Peter. 2010. "Political Anthropology of the Postcommunist Czech Republic: Local-National and Rural-Urban Scenes." In *Postsocialist Europe: Anthropological Perspectives from Home*, edited by László Kürti and Peter Skalník, 227–251. Oxford, UK, and New York: Berghahn Books.

Skýbová, Pavla. 2009. "Závěrečná zpráva o projektu. Nebe nad Ostravou" [Closing report on the project Air above Ostrava by the NGO Vzduch]. November 29. Made available by the author.

Šmídová, Iva. 1999. "Men in the Czech Republic: A Few Questions and Thoughts on Studying (Some) Men." *Czech Sociological Review* 7(2): 215–222.

Smith, Lorraine, Sinthia Z. Bosnic-Anticevich, Bernadette Mitchell, Bandana Saini, Ines Krass, and Carol Armour. 2007. "Treating Asthma with a Self-Management Model of Illness Behaviour in an Australian Community Pharmacy Setting." *Social Science & Medicine* 64(7):1501–1511.

Smith-Morris, Carolyn, ed. 2016. *Diagnostic Controversy: Cultural Perspectives on Competing Knowledge in Healthcare*. New York: Routledge.

Sokolová, Věra. 2005. "Planned Parenthood behind the Curtain: Population Policy and Sterilization of Romani Women in Communist Czechoslovakia, 1972–1989." *The Anthropology of East Europe Review* 23(1): 79–98.

Speier, Amy. 2008. "Czech Balneotherapy: Border Medicine and Health Tourism." *Anthropological Journal of European Cultures* 17(2): 145–159.

———. 2011. "Health Tourism in a Czech Health Spa." *Anthropology & Medicine* 18(1): 55–66.

———. 2016. *Fertility Holidays: IVF Tourism and the Reproduction of Whiteness*. New York: New York University Press.

Speier, Amy, Iva Šmídová, and Hubert Wierciński. 2014. "Health and Medicine: Postsocialist Perspectives." *Czech Sociological Review* 50(6): 815–820.

Šrám, Radim, Miroslav Dostál, Helena Libalová, Pavel Rossner Jr., Andrea Rossnerová, Vlasta Svecova, Jan Topinka, and Alena Bartoňová. 2013. "The European Hot Spot of B[a]P and PM2.5 Exposure: The Ostrava Region, Czech Republic: Health Research Results." *ISRN Public Health*: 1–12.

Stan, Sabina. 2012. "Neither Commodities nor Gifts: Post-Socialist Informal Exchanges in the Romanian Healthcare System" *Journal of the Royal Anthropological Institute* 18(1): 65–82.

Stark, Jennifer, and Russell Stark. 2002. *The Carbon Dioxide Syndrome*. Coorparoo, Australia: Buteyko Works.

Stoller, Paul. 1997. *Sensuous Scholarship*. Philadelphia: University of Pennsylvania Press.

Streuli, Jürg C., Margot Michel, and Effy Vayena. 2011. "Children's Rights in Pediatrics." *European Journal of Pediatrics* 170(1): 9–14.

Stuart, Richard B., ed. 1977. *Behavioral Self-Management: Strategies, Techniques and Outcomes*. New York: Brunner/Mazel Publishers.

Sudetic, Chuck. 2013. "Roma in Political Life: Czech Republic—Dependency and Political Development." *Open Society Foundations* (website). September 10. Retrieved on March 14, 2014, from www.opensocietyfoundations.org/voices/roma-political-life-czech-republic-dependency-and-political-development.

Sunder Rajan, Kaushik. 2012. "Pharmaceutical Crises and Questions of Value: Terrains and Logics of Global Therapeutic Politics." *South Atlantic Quarterly* 111(2): 321–346.

Tap, Relinde. 2007. "High-Wire Dancers: Middle-Class Pakeha and Dutch Childhoods in New Zealand." PhD thesis, Department of Anthropology, University of Auckland.

Taplin, Paul S., and Thomas L. Creer. 1978. "A Procedure for Using Peak Expiratory Flow Rate Data to Increase the Predictability of Asthma Episodes." *Journal of Asthma Research* 16(1): 15–19.

Tennant, Margaret. 1994. *Children's Health, the Nation's Wealth: A History of Children's Health Camps*. Wellington: Bridget Williams Books.

Tesar, Marek. 2012. "Governing Childhoods through Stories: A Havelian Analysis of Childhood Subjectivities." PhD thesis, Department of Education, University of Auckland.

"Test kontroly astmatu." n.d. Retrieved on April 2, 2015, from www.astmatest.cz.

Timmermans, Stefan, and Marc Berg. 2003. *The Gold Standard: The Challenge of Evidence-Based Medicine and Standardization in Health Care*. Philadelphia: Temple University Press.

Trnka, Susanna. 2012. "When the World Went Color: Emotions, Senses and Spaces in Contemporary Accounts of the Czechoslovak Velvet Revolution." *Emotion, Space and Society* 5(1): 45–51.

———. 2013. "Forgotten Pasts and Fearful Futures in Czechs' Remembrances of Communism." In *Focaal: Journal of Global and Historical Anthropology* 2013(66): 36–46.

———. 2015. "Playing Cowboys and Indians: The Therapeutics of Nostalgia." *Canadian Slavonic Papers/Revue canadienne des slavistes* 57(3–4): 284–298.

Trnka, Susanna, and Laura Busheikin, eds. 1993. *Bodies of Bread and Butter: Reconfiguring Women's Lives in the Post-Communist Czech Republic*. Prague: Gender Studies Centre.

Trnka, Susanna, Christine Dureau, and Julie Park, eds. 2013. *Senses and Citizenships: Embodying Political Life*. New York and London: Routledge.

Trnka, Susanna, and Laura McLaughlan. 2012. "Becoming 'Half a Doctor': Parent-Experts and the Normalisation of Childhood Asthma in Aotearoa/New Zealand." *Sites*. 9(2): 3–22.

Trnka Susanna, and Catherine Trundle. 2014. "Competing Responsibilities: Moving beyond Neoliberal Responsibilisation." *Anthropological Forum*. 24(2): 136–153.

———, eds. 2017a. *Competing Responsibilities: The Ethics and Politics of Contemporary Life*. Durham, NC: Duke University Press.

———. 2017b. "Competing Responsibilities: Reckoning Personal Responsibility, Care for the Other, and the Social Contract in Contemporary Life." In *Competing Responsibilities: The Ethics and Politics of Contemporary Life*, edited by Susanna Trnka and Catherine Trundle. Durham, NC: Duke University Press.

Trollvik, Anne, and Elisabeth Severinsson. 2004. "Parents' Experiences of Asthma: Process from Chaos to Coping." *Nursing & Health Sciences* 6(2): 93–99.

Trostle, James A. 1988. "Medical Compliance as an Ideology." *Social Science & Medicine* 27(12): 1299–1308.

Tuček, Milan. 2013. "Prestiž povolání—červen 2013" [Occupational prestige, June 2013]. Prague: Public Opinion Research Center, Institute of Sociology of the Czech Academy of Sciences.

Turner, Victor. 1964. "Betwixt and Between: The Liminal Period in *Rites de Passage*." In *Symposium on New Approaches to the Study of Religion: Proceedings of the 1964 Annual Spring Meeting of the American Ethnological Society*, edited by Judith Helm, 4–20. Seattle: University of Washington Press.

TV Nova. 2013. "Ostrava žaluje stát a ministerstva kvůli znečištění ovzduší! Soud žalobu smetl ze stolu" News report, October 18. Retrieved on March 9, 2014, from http://tn.nova .cz/zpravy/domaci/ostrava-zaluje-stat-a-ministerstva-kvuli-znecisteni-ovzdusi-soud-zalobu-smetl-ze-stolu.html.

Van der Geest, Sjaak, and Susan Reynolds Whyte. 1989. "The Charm of Medicines: Metaphors and Metonyms." *Medical Anthropology Quarterly* 3(4): 345–367.

Van Sickle, David. 2009. "Diagnosis and Management of Asthma in the Medical Marketplace of India: Implications for Efforts to Improve Global Respiratory Health." In *Anthropology and Public Health: Bridging Differences in Culture and Society*, edited by Robert A. Hahn and Marcia C. Inhorn, 65–93. Oxford, UK: Oxford University Press.

Vaněk, Miroslav. 1996. *Nedalo se tady dýchat: Ekologie v českých zemích v letech 1968 až 1989*. Prague: Maxdorf.

Večerník, Jiří. 2008. "Social Policy in the Czech 'Republic': The Past and the Future of Reforms." *East European Politics & Societies* 22(3): 496–517.

Velinger, Jan. 2015. "Health Reports Says that Air Pollution Leads to More Than 5,000 Deaths in Czech Republic Annually." *Český rozhlas*, October 3. Available from www .radio.cz/en/section/czech-life/health-reports-says-that-air-pollution-leads-to-more-than-5000-deaths-in-czech-republic-annually/.

Viviano, Frank. 1994. "Europe's Dark Center, Ostrava." *Mother Jones*. March/April issue. Retrieved on March 29, 2014, from www.motherjones.com/politics/1994/03/europes-dark-center-ostrava.

Vossler, Teri, Libor Cernikovsky, Jiri Novak, Helena Placha, Blanka Krejci, Irina Nikolova, Eva Chalupnickova, and Ronald Williams. 2015. "An Investigation of Local and Regional Sources of Fine Particulate Matter in Ostrava, the Czech Republic." *Atmospheric Pollution Research* 6 (3): 454–463.

Weismantel, Mary. 2001. *Cholas and Pishtacos: Stories of Race and Sex in the Andes*. Chicago: University of Chicago Press.

Wheaton, Bernard, and Zdeněk Kavan. 1992. *The Velvet Revolution: Czechoslovakia, 1988–1991*. Boulder, CO: Westview.

Whitmarsh, Ian. 2008a. *Biomedical Ambiguity: Race, Asthma, and the Contested Meaning of Genetic Research in the Caribbean*. Ithaca, NY: Cornell University Press.

————. 2008b. "Biomedical Ambivalence: Asthma Diagnosis, the Pharmaceutical, and Other Contradictions in Barbados." *American Ethnologist* 35(1): 49–63.

Willems, Dick. 2000. "Managing One's Body Using Self-Management Techniques: Practicing Autonomy." *Theoretical Medicine and Bioethics* 21(1): 23–38.

Williams, Clare. 2000. "Doing Health, Doing Gender: Teenagers, Diabetes and Asthma." *Social Science & Medicine* 50(3): 387–396.

Wilson, Patricia M., Sally Kendall, and Fiona Brooks. 2007. "The Expert Patients Programme: A Paradox of Patient Empowerment and Medical Dominance." *Health and Social Care in the Community* 15(5): 426–438.

Yonkers, Kimberly A., Steven E. Bruce, Ingrid R. Dyck, and Martin B. Keller. 2003. "Chronicity, Relapse, and Illness—Course of Panic Disorder, Social Phobia, and Generalized Anxiety Disorder: Findings in Men and Women from 8 Years of Follow-up." *Depression and Anxiety* 17(3): 173–179.

Yurchak, Alexei. 2005. *Everything Was Forever, until It Was No More: The Last Soviet Generation*. Princeton, NJ: Princeton University Press.

Index

Anthropology of Policy

Cris Shore and Susan Wright, editors

SERIES DESCRIPTION:

The Anthropology of Policy series promotes innovative methodological and theoretical approaches to the study of policy. The series challenges the assumption that policy is a top-down, linear and rational process, and a field of study primarily for policy professionals. Books in the series analyze the contradictory nature and effects of policy, including the intricate ways in which people engage with policy, the meanings it holds for different local, regional, national, and internationally-based actors and the complex relationships and social worlds that it produces.